Edgefield County, South Carolina Deed Books 34 and 35

❧

Abstracted by Carol Wells

❧

HERITAGE BOOKS
2006

HERITAGE BOOKS

AN IMPRINT OF HERITAGE BOOKS, INC.

Books, CDs, and more—Worldwide

For our listing of thousands of titles see our website
at
www.HeritageBooks.com

Published 2006 by
HERITAGE BOOKS, INC.
Publishing Division
65 East Main Street
Westminster, Maryland 21157-5026

International Standard Book Number: 978-0-7884-1668-5

CONTENTS

FOREWORD

In addition to dates of conveyances and names of grantors and grantees as listed in courthouse indexes, deeds name place of residence which may be in another district, state, or country. Deeds possibly give location of land, names of watercourses, names of adjoining landowners, original grantee, wives or mothers with dower interests to the land, and names of witnesses. Deeds concerning inheritances may list siblings and parents. Prenuptial agreements may include names of previous spouses and children. Deeds of Gift may explain kinship or friendship with grantees. Trust deeds name friends who are to care for dependent persons named within. Connections with other locations are shown in powers of attorney, while other deeds name parties to lawsuits or partition of inherited land. Depositions, often about an ear bit off in a fight, name combatants and witnesses.

Abstracted from microfilm, deed books 34 and 35 lack some names which have been lost in tight binding and cropped pages. Ink has faded so disastrously that some pages are nearly unreadable. As is common with handwritten records, some letters can look alike and thus lead to misinterpretation of names. For accuracy, the original books should always be consulted.

Some of the within deeds date back as early as the 1760s, and chains of title to the 1740s.   Carol Wells

ABBREVIATIONS

Note: All persons are of Edgefield District
unless otherwise noted. All places are of
South Carolina unless location is named.

adj	adjoining
afsd	aforesaid
atty	attorney
br	branch
co	county, company
cr	creek
decd	deceased
dist	district
D S	deputy surveyor
dist	district
exn	execution
exr	executor
extx	executrix
f.m.c.	free man of color
f.w.c.	free woman "
L&R	lease & release
P/A	power of atty
re	road
rec	recorded
/s/	signed
Scot	Scotland
sd	said
shff	sheriff
will	last will and testament
wit	witness

p.1 Macartan Campbell's Heirs, Division of Real Estate. Georgia, Chatham County, 29 January 1813, Mrs Maria Killoch wife of Doctor Lemuel Killoch late Maria Campbell, Mrs Sarah Jones wife of Noble W Jones Esqr late Sarah Campbell, Edward F Campbell Esqr, Martha G Campbell, and Harriet Campbell, heirs of estate of late Macartan Campbell Esqr, decd, entitled to plantation in South Carolina called Horse Creek, deed dated 18 March 1795 between Mrs Sarah Campbell widow of sd Macartan Campbell and mother to sd heirs; heirs agree to have estate appraised to make fair division, valued at Forty thousand Dollars making Eight thousand Dollars for each heir, with consent of George Jones and Ebenezer Jackson surviving trustees to marriage settlement of Mrs Maria Kolloch and also of George Jones, Lemuel Killoch and Edward F Campbell as trustees to marriage settlement of Mrs Sarah Jones have come to division of real estate. Tract of 750 acres in Edgefield County, adj Savannah River, Horse Creek, land of Thomas Lamar, valued at Sixteen thousand five hundred Dollars and was drawn and accepted as the share of sd Maria Kolloch and Edward F Campbell. Land called Cotton Patch of 100 acres adj lands of Delaig[lost in binding], Villers, estate of Beal, town common of Augusta, Creswells lott #22, of Verdrey, and estate of Beal being lots #31 and #40 in Augusta, Richmond County; also 232.5 acres adj Augusta, parts of lotts #78 and 9, whole of lotts #16, 17, 23 in Augusta, adj lands of Creswell, Forsyth, McKinne, lot #10, Broad Street, Furys road; also 100 acres near Augusta originally granted to Absalom Fears and conveyed by him to late Macartan Campbell adj lands of Jackson, Hemphill, Mead, Watson, Graves, Clay, valued at Nine thousand Dollars drawn and accepted as portion of Sarah Jones. Five hundred acres known by name Canoe Creek plantation in Richmond County adj lands of [blank] Bugg, Savannah River, estate of [blank] Turkenet, appraised at Fourteen thousand five hundred Dollars was drawn and accepted as share of Martha Campbell and Harriet Campbell. [Other arrangements here omitted]. Wit Job T Bolles JP, Chas Harris. /s/ M G Campbell, /s/ H Campbell, /s/ George Jones, /s/ E Jackson, /s/ Maria Kollock, /s/ Leml Kollock, /s/ Sarah Jones, /s/ N W Jones. Proven Edgefield District, 8 March 1817 by Edmund Bacon Esqr, well acquainted with handwriting of Job T Bolles and Charles Harris of Georgia, and believes the writing to be theirs; M Mims CCP. Rec 8 March 1817.

p.19 Charles Williams of Madison County, Mississippi Territory, to James Morris, Deed, 15 November 1816, Four hundred fifty Dollars, 150 acres on Rockey Creek of Stephens Creek adj lines of Robertson, Edward Collier, William Morris. Wit Elijah Lyon, Thos Chappell. /s/ Charles Williams. Proven 25 February 1817 by Thomas

Chappell; James Adams J P. Rec 11 March 1817.

p.20   William C Harden and Henry G Harden to George Parker, Deed, 17 January 1817, Five thousand Dollars, three tracts of land situate adj Cherokee Ponds; one of 200 acres originally granted to Henry Sizemore 26 September 1772; another of 100 acres originally granted to Jethro Roundtree 26 July 1774 of 80.5 acres, 19.5 acres having been sold out of sd hundred acre tract to Sarah ---ance[part of name lost in the binding] and which are hereby excepted; the other third of which three tracts is of 352 acres originally granted to Francis Settles on 5 February 1787, fifteen acres of which being in a tract lately held by Dionysius Oliver decd under an older grant is hereby excepted, which several tracts were conveyed by Christopher Shaw unto sd William C Harden and Henry G Harden on 26 February 1808, resurvey made by William Cloud. Wit Jacob Zinn, Edmund Bacon. /s/ William C Harden, /s/ Henry G Harden. Justice John Tarrance certifies relinquishment of dower rights by Martha Harden wife of William C Harden, 3 March 1817; /s/ Martha (x) Harden. Proven 20 May 1817 by Edmund Bacon; M Mims CCP.   Rec 20 May 1817.

p.23   Joseph Crafton and wife Lucinda G Crafton as heirs of estate of Daniel Barksdale decd and Susannah Barksdale decd wife of sd Daniel to Thomas Meriwether, Deed of Quit Claim, 7 January 1817, Eight hundred Dollars, claims against sd estates. Wit William Thomas. /s/ Joseph Crafton, /s/ Lucy Green Crafton. Proven 11 March 1817 by Wm Thomas; [name lost in binding] Edmunds J P. Rec 11th March 1817.

p.24   William Abney to March, Deed of Manumission, 11 February 1817, Four hundred dollars, slave March about 28 years old. Wit Urbane Nicholson, Zachariah Abney. /s/ William (x) Abney. Undersigned justices of the Quorum and freeholders of District certify March is not of bad character and is capable of gaining a livelihood by honest means, 11 February 1817. /s/ Thos Anderson, /s/ Urbane Nicholson, /s/ Zachariah Abney, /s/ Wm Moore, /s/ Jones Wills, /s/ Thos Spragens. Proven 11 February 1817 by Urbane Nicholson; Thomas Anderson J Q. Rec 14 March 1817.

p.26   Thomas Bishop to Abraham Rutland, Deed, 31 August 1816, Seventy five Dollars, 37 ½ acres being part of land formerly belonging to Buckner Blalock on Streets branch. Wit Jno P Bush, Ezekiel Bishop. /s/ Thomas (x) Bishop. Proven 14 October 1814[sic] by John P Bush Esqr; Charles Oneale QU. Rec 14 March 1817.

p.28   George Lamkin to Thomas W Morton, Deed, 2 December 1816, Four hundred seventy seven Dollars fifty cents, 95 ½ acres on Cuffeetown Creek of Stephens Creek. Wit Edward Settle, Joshua Harris. /s/George Lamkin. Plat by E Settle D S 28 November 1816 shows adj owners George Lamkin, Richard Quarles, Thomas Morton. Justice John Lyon certifies relinquishment of dower by Susannah Lamkin

2

wife of George Lamkin, 10 February 1817; /s/ Susannah (S) Lamkin. Proven 2 December 1816 by Edward Settle; John Lyon QU. Rec 14 March 1817.

p.30 Abraham Rutland to Thomas Bishop, Deed, 31 August 1816, Ten Dollars, [acreage lost in binding] part of land formerly belonging to John Blalock adj lands of Lewis Clarks old mill, South Edisto River and Brices Creek. Wit John P Bush, Ezekiel Bishop. /s/ Abraham Rutland. Proven 14 March 1817 by Jno P Bush; John Loveless J P. Rec 14 March 1817.

p.31 Thomas Bishop to Henry Spann, Deed, 7 September 1816, Five hundred Dollars, 270 acres whereon I now live, on South Edisto River adj Lewis Clarks old mill dam on Mill Creek, adj Abraham Rutland, Streets Branch, Cooks corner, including part of several tracts of land granted to Joseph Walker and Lewis Clark. Wit Michael Blow, William McClendon. /s/ Thomas (x) Bishop. Justice Peter Lamkin certifies relinquishment of dower rights by Elizabeth Bishop wife of Thomas Bishop 10 March 1817; /s/ Elizabeth (x) Bishop. Proven 20 January 1817 by Wm McClendon; Lewis Holmes J P. Rec 15 March 1817.

p.33 Hezekiah Harris to William Blackburn, Deed, 30 December 1816, Thirty Dollars, three acres on Beaverdam Creek of Turkey Creek of Savannah River adj N on land of John Hollingsworth, W on estate of Thomas Riddle, S on Wm Blackburn. Wit Elias Blackburn, Lee Blackburn. /s/ Hezekiah Harris. Proven 15 March 1817 by Lee Blackburn; Wm Hagens J P. Rec 15 March 1817.

p.35 William Brazier, physician, to William Blackburn, farmer, Deed, 1 January 1816, Twelve hundred Dollars, 322 acres I lately purchased from William Ellison Esqr; also 50 acres, part of tract originally granted to Angus McDaniel 15 May 1772, adj N on Beaverdam Creek, E on land of Joseph Eddins, S and W on land now Joseph Eddins and land lately mine. Wit Elias Blackburn, Lee Blackburn. /s/ William Brazier. Proven 15 March 1817 by Lee Blackburn; Wm Hagens J P. Rec 15 March 1817.

p.37 Barkley M Blocker to Nancey Bird, Deed, 27 January 1817, One hundred three Dollars, 103 acres on Dun[Deen?] Creek of Log Creek, Stephens Creek, it being part of land originally granted to John Blocker Senr, adj sd Nancy Birds line, estate of Thomas Bradberry. Wit Elijah Smith, Mary Bird. /s/ Barkley M Blocker. Proven 27 January 1817 by Elijah Smith; Jesse Blocker QU. Rec 15 March 1817.

p.39 Matthew Mims to Henry Shultz of Augusta, Georgia, Deed, 27 March 1817, Two hundred seventy Dollars, one half acre except twelve feet in village of Edgefield on the corner of Jefferson and Madison Streets known as #15 in a plan drawn by Robert Lang Esqr adj lot now owned by Stephen Pixley; also ½ acres except twelve feet directly back of above lot, on Madison Street, the lot whereon Augustus G Nagel

3

now lives. Wit J Hatcher, Richard H Tutt. /s/ M Mims. Justice Eldred Simkins certifies relinquishment of dower rights by Eliza Mims wife of Matthew Mims, 27 March 1817; /s/ Eliza Mims. Proved 27 March 1817 by Richard H Tutt; Eldred Simkins QU. Recorded 27 March 1817.

p.41 William A Gray to Nathan Trotter, Deed, 23 March 1817, Three hundred dollars, [number lost in binding] hundred acres adj Jas Cheney, granted 27 Feby 1773 on Big Creek of Saluda. Wit Thomas (T) Tirk, Joseph Taylor, Gideon Christian. /s/ William A Gray. Proven [no date] by Gideon Christian JQ. Rec 4 April 1817.

p.42 Samuel Berry to Nathan Trotter, Deed, 30 July 1804, One hundred Dollars, 183 acres on Big Creek of Little Saluda River, formerly the property of Matthew Wills decd, conveyed to Nancy Berry wife of sd Samuel Berry in part of her legacy of real estate of her father the sd Matthew Wills decd. Sd tract adj lands of W Abney, Richard Turner, W George, Willis Shores. Wit William White, Thomas (-) Turk. /s/ Samuel Berry. Proven [day lost in binding] August 1804 by Thomas Turk; Gideon Christian J P. Rec 4 April 1817.

p.43 William Ward of Abbeville District to Nathan Trotter, Deed, 19 February 1810, One hundred thirty Dollars, 100 acres on Baleys Branch of Big Creek adj NW on lands of sd Nathan Trotter, SW on Jeremiah Wilson, N on Thomas Turk, part of original grant to Joel Pardue and conveyed to Nathan Trotter 12 February 1794. Wit Sarah (x) Doggins, Joab Wilson. /s/ William (x) Ward. Justice William Nibbs certifies relinquishment of dower rights by Jane Ward wife of William Ward, 19 February 1810; /s/ Jane (-) Ward. Proven 19 February 1810 by Joab Wilson; Wm Nibbs J Q. Rec 4 April 1817.

p.45 James Cleveland, Daniel Mosely, John Cleveland, legal heirs of Rice Cleveland decd to William Hagens, Deed, One hundred sixty Dollars, 50 acres on head waters of Cedar Creek originally granted unto Nicholas Dillard 1772 and adj Sampson Butler, Tutt, William Hagens. Wit Edmund Keiling, Wm Robertson, Edwd Christian, Abner Youngblood. /s/ James Cleveland, /s/ Daniel Moseley, /s/ John Cleveland. Justice Matthew Mims certifies relinquishment of dower rights by Elizabeth Cleveland wife of James Cleveland, 4 April 1817; /s/ Elizabeth Cleveland. Proven 28 March 1817 by Wm Robertson; M Mims CCP. Proven 28 March 1817 by Abner Youngblood; M Mims CCP. Rec 4 April 1817.

p48 John Lewis to Lewis Ethridge, Deed, 4 October 1816, Five hundred forty five Dollars, 200 acres on Sleepy Creek, it being part of 200 acres, part of two tracts, one originally granted to Thomas Pinkett or William Robertson, the other to Isaac Ramsay, adj lines of Henry King, Falkner, Stibham, up Little Creek, dividing the

4

spring. Wit Jonathan Clegg, John Kirksey. /s/ John Lewis. Justice Lewis Miles certifies relinquishment of dower rights by Latisia Lewis wife of John Lewis, 8 March 1817; /s/ Lettina (x) Lewis. Proven 12 October 1816 by Jonathan Clegg; James Adams JP. Rec 7 April 1817.

p.50 Elizabeth Dicks of Savannah, Georgia, to David Bowers, Deed, 4 December 1816, Seventy five Dollars, 12 acres adj estate of Williams, land of Thomas Golphin; sd tract conveyed by Thomas Golphin to Mr Williams, sd Williams to Asa Hix, representatives of sd Hix to John Glover, from sd Glover to Thomas Brux, and from Brux to sd Elizabeth Dicks. Wit James B Collier, Jonathan Dicks. /s/ Eliza Dicks. Proven 11 March 1817 by Jonathan Dicks, Jno Sturzenegger J P. Rec 7 April 1817.

p.52 Jacob Guiton to John Sturzenegger, Deed, 5 April 1817, Thirty seven Dollars, on Horse Creek of Savannah River adj lands of George Walters, land formerly James Jones but now sd Sturzeneggers, George Wallace now J Dicks, and Peppers Branch; containing sixteen hundred acres, originally granted to Ariaus Gorley and since conveyed to Phillip Lamar and from sd Lamar to John Jones and from Clainey B[lost in binding] formerly Clainy Jones widow of sd John Jones to Jacob Guiton. Wit Sion Jones, John Rountree. /s/ Jacob Guiton. Proven 7 April 1817 by Sion Jones; M Mims CCP. Rec 7 April 1817.

p.54 Alexander Travis to Reeves Martin, Deed, 29 January 1817, Two thousand two hundred Dollars, 544 acres being two tracts; one of 262 acres conveyed by Archey Mayson and Toliver Levingston to sd Alexr Travis; the other containing 282 acres conveyed by John C Mayson and Washington Bostick to sd Alexr Travis, being the plantation on which the sd Travis lately resided, situate on waters of Ninety six Creek and adj lands of sd Reeves Martin, Ramsey, land formerly estate of Doctor James Moore, Charles Cooper, Phillip Burt. Wit Mackerness Goode, James Griffin, Eugene Brenan. /s/ Alexander Travis. Justice William Robinson certifies relinquishment of dower rights by Polly Travis wife of Alexander Travis, 4 April 1817; /s/ Mary Ann Travis. Proven 7 April 1817 by James Griffin; Jesse Blocker J Q. Rec 7 April 1817.

p.56 John Baugh to Daniel Bullock, Deed, 4 September 1815, Five hundred Dollars, 100 acres on Beaverdam Creek, in two tracts adj sd Daniel Bullocks spring branch to Stockleys old line to Joseph Curbos land, William Oliphant, to Long Cane Road, being first granted to James Harris. Wit Dennis Collins, John McCarry. /s/ John Baugh. Proven 21 December 1815 by Dennis Collins; John Cheatham J P. Rec 7th April 1817.

p.58 John Arledge and Ann Arledge to Mark Mathis during the life of our daughter Easter Weakes, Deed of Gift, 3 December 1816, for support of our Easther Weakes and children, Negro woman named Lucy and her children Amy and Claricy; sd

5

Negroes to be kept in possession of sd Mathis during life of Esther, at her death sd Negroes and increase to be equally divided amongst our daughters children [other provisions here omitted]. Wit James Forest, James Wright. /s/ John (I) Arledge; /s/ Ann (A) Arledge. Proven 22 March 1817 by James Forest; Thomas Dozier J Q. Rec 7th April 1817.

p.59 Mark Mathis and John Adams to John Aldridge, Bill of Sale, 3 December 1816, Eleven hundred Dollars, three Negroes: Lucy, Amey, Clarisy. Wit James Forest, James Wright. /s/ Mark Matthews, /s/ John (A) Adams. Proven 28 March 1817 by James Wright; Thomas Dozier J Q. Rec 7 April 1817.

p.60 Jane Andrews Senr, George R Brown, Saml L Andrews and Jane Andrews Junr of Jefferson County [probably Georgia] to Robert Gilliam of Abbeville County, SC, Deed, Georgia, 24 February 1816, Four hundred forty Dollars, 100 acres in Edgefield County on Cuffeetown Creek adj lands of James Walker, Benjamin Barton, Asa Holloway, originally granted Jane Spence. Wit Thos M Patterson, John (x) Wooten. /s/ Jane (x) Andrews, /s/ George R Brown, /s/ Saml L Andrews, /s/ Jane (x) Andrews Junr. Proven, Jefferson County, Georgia, 24 February 1817 by Thomas M Patterson; Jno Paulett J P. Rec 7th March 1817.

p.62 John Dolton to Edward Holmes, Deed, 25 September 1816, One hundred thirty Dollars, 30 acres on Beaverdam Creek, plat by Wm Coursey D S, being part of 100 acres granted unto Obediah Kilcrease in 1771. Wit W Coursey, Lewis Clark. /s/ John (x) Dolton. Proven 7 April 1817 by William Coursey; M Mims CCP. Rec 7 April 1817.

p.64 Samuel Wardleworth of Abbeville District to Jared E Groce, 7 April 1817, Negroes, Six thousand three hundred seventy four Dollars: Negro slaves Pompey, Worley, Stephen, John, Flora and two of her children Mary and Willis, and Sally and her child Rose; it is expressly understood that the Negroes are only mortgaged. Condition that Samuel Wardleworth is to sell two Negroes named Harry and Henry, and Groce holds a bond on sd Wardleworth executed 31 October 1816 for Six thousand three hundred seventy four Dollars due 1 December 1817 with interest from date. [Other provisions here omitted.] Wit Jno S Jeter, Isaac Randolph. /s/ Saml Wardleworth. Proven 8 April 1817 by John S Jeter; M Mims CCP. Rec 8th April 1817.

p.66 Elisha Asbell to Jarvis Asbell, Deed, 16 January 1815, Eighty Dollars, 50 acres, all that part of land that fell to me from my fathers estate the land whereon my father lived when he died. Wit Stephen Fedrick, Charles Williamson. /s/ Elisha (x) Asbell. Proven 21 January 1815 by Charles Williamson; Jno P Bush J P. Rec 14 April 1817.

DEED BOOK 34

p.67   Elisha Asbell to Jarvis Asbell, Deed, 25 January [1806?], Two hundred fifty Dollars, 48 acres being part of land granted to Thomas Adams 6 July 1795. Wit Willliam Raborn, Susanna (x) Raborn. /s/ Elisha (x) Asbell. Proven 2 January [year lost in binding] by William Raborn; Jno Loveless. Rec 14ᵗʰ April 1817.

p.68   Elisha Asbell to Jarvis Asbell, Deed, 25 January 1816, Four hundred fifty Dollars, 203 acres on Mackbees Creek of South Edisto adj Samuel Medlock, Martin Witt, Joseph Williams, William Loveless. Wit William Raborn, Susanna (x) Raborn. /s/ Elisha (x) Asbell. Proven 2 Jan 1817 by William Raborn; John Loveless J P. Rec 14 April 1817.

p.70   George S Turner to David Richardson, Deed, 6 March 1815, two Negroes, Juner a woman about forty years of age, and Willice a son of Juner about three years old, mortgaged to David Richardson; if George S Turner doth pay on or before 1 January next one note of hand due 9 December 1811 for Twenty four Dollars 72 cents; also one note due 15 January last for Two hundred seventy two Dollars 7 cents with lawful interests thereon, the mortgage to be void.   Negroes to remain in possession of David Richardson. Wit Hugh Neal, Jefferson Richardson. /s/ George S Turner. Proven 15 April 1817 by Jefferson Richardson; James Adams. Rec 15 April 1817.

p.72   Henry Parkman to Lark Abney, Deed, 7 January 1817, Five hundred sixty Dollars thirty nine cents. 143 acres on Mountain Creek adj lands of John Coursey, Jacob Harling, John Bolgar. Condition if Henry Parkman in twelve months pays Lark Abney Five hundred sixty Dollars thirty nine cents with lawful interest, this instrument to be void. Wit Martin Cook, William Forsyth. /s/ Henry (x) Parkman. Proven 9 January 1817 by Martin Cook; Robert Walker J P. Rec 15 April 1817.

p.73   Daniel Bullock, planter, to his wife Hannah Bullock, Deed of Gift, 5 May 1815, love, Negro man named Jim, woman named Nan, woman named Amy, [livestock, chattels not here itemized] not to be taken to pay any part of sd Daniel Bullocks debts.   Wit Dennis Collins, Charles Adams, David Bullock. /s/ Daniel Bullock. Proven 11 November 1815 by Dannis Collins; John Cheatham JP. Rec 19 April 1817.

p.75   Martha Odom to her daughter Charity Cotton, Deed of Gift, 6 October 1816, love for Charity and her children Patsey, Patience, Delana and Wrotha Cotton, Negro woman Sylvia and her two children Cu[lost in binding]nd and Goodwin; also four cows and calves, and furniture; after Charity Cotton's decease to descend to her four children and as many more children as Charity may leave at time of her death. Wit Alexander C Mackay, James W Cotton. /s/ Martha (x) Odom. Proven 6 October 1816 by Alexander C Mackay; Chas Neale J Q. Rec 26 April 1817.

7

DEED BOOK 34

p.76 Martha Odom to her granddaughter Mary Perry, Deed of Gift, 31 December 1816, love, Negro girl Dilly with her increase, bed and furniture, afsd to remain in my possession during my life. Wit Elizabeth R Hahnbaum, Mary C Oneale. /s/ Martha (x) Odom. Proven 2 January 1817 by Elizabeth R Hahnbaum; Chas Oneale J Q U. Rec 26 April 1817.

p.77 Martha Odom to daughter Keziah Willis of Barnwell District, Deed of Gift, 6 January 1817, love, at my decease Negro woman Fenar, Negro girl Phillis, their future increase, bed with furniture, to remain in my possession during my natural life. Wit Elizabeth R Hahnbaum, M C Oneale. /s/ Martha (x) Odom. Proven 6 January 1817 by Elizabeth R Hahnbaum; Chas Oneale. Rec 26 April 1817.

p.79 Martha Odom to granddaughter Martha Perry, Deed of Gift, 31 December 1816, love, Negro girl Muggy with her increase, bed and furniture, to remain in my possession during my natural life. Wit Elizabeth R Hahnbaum, M C Oneale. /s/ Martha (x) Odom. Proven 3 January 1817 by Elizabeth R Hahnbaum; Chas Oneale J Q U. Rec 26 April 1817.

p.80 Daniel McKie Junr to Thomas Meriweather, Deed, 26 April 1817, Thirty eight Dollars, 19 acres on Stephens Creek adj lands of estate of Daniel Barksdale, Elon Rees, Henry Ware, plat made 10 December 1816. Wit Moses Spivy, Benjamin Tutt. /s/ Daniel McKie. Proven 26 April 1817 by Benjamin Tutt; A Edmunds J P. Rec 26 April 1817.

p.81 Ezekiel McClendon to his son Joel McClendon, Deed of Gift, 2 May 1817, 160.5 acres which is part of my plantation where I now reside; also Negro girl Rainy about 4 or 5 years old, a dark mulatto child of Charitas. Wit John Farrow, Phillip Raiford, Allen McClendon. /s/ Ezekiel McClendon. Proven 5 May 1817 by John Farrow; M Mims CCP. Rec 5 May 1817.

p.82 Sheriff Jeremiah Hatcher to Levi Jester, Sheriffs Title, first Monday October 1809. At suit of Josiah Langley against Samuel Carter, sheriff to seize plantation and after notice of intended sale publicly to sell land to highest bidder for ready money at Edgefield courthouse. Struck off to Levi Jester for One hundred Dollars be being highest and last bidder for same; 300 acres Cuffeetown Creek adj lands of John Mosely, Daniel Rustons old plantation, and all property which sd Samuel Carter had. Wit R H Tutt, Jesse Frazier. /s/ J Hatcher SED. Proven 5 May 1817 by Richard H Tutt; M Mims CCP. Rec 5 May 1817.

p.84 James Wright to Jonathan Weaver, Deed, 20 December 1816, Twelve hundred Dollars, 450 acres on Rockey Creek of Stephens Creek being land conveyed by Benjamin Eddins to sd Wright adj W on Bartlet Blocker, N on Mrs Nicholson,

8

Benjamin Frazier, and James Coats, E on Charles Barronton and David Nicholson. Wit Theophilus Hill, Jonathan Dabbs, James Forrest. /s/ James Wright. Justice Thomas Dozier certifies relinquishment of dower rights by Elizabeth Wright wife of James Wright, 1 May 1817; /s/ Elizabeth (x) Wright. Proven 3 May 1817 by Jonathan Dabbs; Thomas Dozier JQ. Rec 5 May 1817.

p.87   Daniel Bird, Sanders Rareden admrs of estate of Daniel Bird Senr decd to George Johnson, Deed, 18 March 1816, Three hundred fifty Dollars, 200 acres being part of land granted to Boon and from Boon conveyed to Arvin Moore and from Moore to Morris and then to Daniel Bird Senr, on waters of Dun [Deen?] Creek of Turkey Creek adj Daniel Bullock, John M Kennedy, Elijah Bird, Daniel Bird Junr. Wit Benjamin Winn, John C Rareden. /s/ D Bird admr, /s/ S Rarden admr. Plat certified 13 July 1813 by Jesse Blocker D S. Proven 5 May 1817 by John C Rareden; Jordan Holloway J P. Rec 5 May 1817.

p.89   Buckner Blalock to William McClendon, Deed, 3 December 1813, One hundred sixty Dollars, 80 acres it being part of two tracts formerly held by Lewis Clark decd and John Blalock lying on Bushes Mill Creek of Edisto River adj mouth of Gainy Spring branch, Mrs Wimberly, Blalocks old line. Wit John Bell, David Campbell. /s/ Buckner (M) Blalock. Proven 25 January 1817 by David Campbell; John Loveless J P. Rec 5 May 1817.

p.90   Henry Spann to Alexander Jenkins of Lexington District, Deed, 19 March 1817, Eleven Hundred Dollars, 250 acres on South Edisto river adj Abraham Rutland, Thomas Bishop, Streets[Sheets?] Branch, Lewis Clark, Mill Creek, Benjamin Blow, Henry Spann, Ganys spring branch, it being part of several tracts granted to Joseph Walker and Lewis Clark. Wit Wm McClendon, Benjamin Blow. /s/ Henry Spann. Proven 22 March 1817 by William McClendon; John Loveless J P. Rec 5 May 1817.

p.92   Jemmima Hix relict of Joseph Hix, planter, decd, John Hicks only son, Elizabeth Hicks now Elizabeth Glover, John Glover her husband, Sarah Hicks the children and only heirs of afsd Joseph deceased all of lawful age to James Panton Esqr, Deed, 7 December 1812, Six hundred Dollars, 26 acres adj land of Abraham Ardis, Captain Jacob Zinn, Savannah River. Wit Henry C Pay, Thomas Broom. /s/ John Hicks, /s/ Jemmima (x) Hicks, /s/ Elizabeth (x) Glover, /s/ Sarah (x) Hicks. Proven 5 May 1817 by Thomas Broom; John Sturzenegger J P. Rec 9 May 1817.

p.94   James Panton, planter, to Jonathan Dicks, Deed, 15 February 1817, One thousand Dollars, 26 acres adj lands of Abraham Ardis, Capt Jacob Zinn, Savannah River. Wit E Williams, Andrew Butler. /s/ Jas Panton. Barnwell District, Justice John Heard certifies relinquishment of dower rights by Ann Panton wife of James Panton, 5 March 1817; /s/ Ann Panton. Proven 27 March 1817 by E Willliams; John

DEED BOOK 34

Sturzenegger J P. Rec 9 May 1817.

p.96   Ann Williams, Gabriel Williams and wife Sally, Reuben Pates and wife Margaret, David Walker and wife Milly, Elizabeth Williams, Catharine Williams and Ann J Williams of Woodford County, Kentucky, to John Williams, Woodford County, Kentucky, 23 November 1816, 150 pounds lawful money of Kentucky, 100 acres in Edgefield County on Hardlabour Creek of Stephens Creek adj S on Abner Perris, SW on George Sullivan, N on William Perrin, NE and E on Samuel Perrin, conveyed by Richard Tutt Esqr to Paul Williams. Wit Lewis Tutt, Milly Linch, George G Tutt. /s/ Elizabeth Williams, /s/ Catharine Williams, /s/ Ann J Williams, /s/ Ann Williams, /s/ Milley Walker, /s/ D Walker, /s/ G Williams, /s/ Sally Williams. Woodford County, Kentucky, proven 24 November 1816 by Lewis Tutt, George G Tutt; E H Blekburn J P. Rec 12 May 1817.

p.98   Ann Williams, Elizabeth Williams, Margaret Pates, Reuben Pates, and John Williams of Edgefield to David Williams, Deed, 28 October 1815, Four hundred fifty Dollars, 100 acres on Cuffeetown Creek of Stephens Creek, beingpart of 300 acres laid out for William Rowan, adj NW on Pleasant Thurmond, SE on heirs of Richard Tutt. Wit James Sanders, John R Morton. /s/ Reuben (x) Pates, /s/ John Williams, /s/ Ann Williams, /s/ Margaret Pates, /s/ Elizabeth Williams. Proven 5 May 1817 by James Sanders; John Lyon QU. Rec 12 May 1817.

p.100   David Walker, Milley Walker and Gabriel Williams of Scott County, Kentucky to David Williams of Edgefield, Deed, Scott County, Kentucky, 16 December 1815, Four hundred fifty Dollars, 100 acres on Cuffeetown Creek being part of 300 acres laid out for William Rowen and adj NW Pleasant Thurmond, SE by heirs of Richard Tutt. Wit Hansford Tutt, John Williams. /s/ G Williams, /s/ D Walker, /s/ Milley Walker. Proven Edgefield District, 11 January 1817 by John Williams; John Lyon QU. Rec 12 May 1817.

p.101   Ezekiel McClendon to William Hagens, Mortgage, 2 December 1816, Two hundred Dollars paid by William Hagens, Negro girl Hannah about twelve years old with her increase; provided if Ezekiel McClendon pays on or before 25 December 1817 sd sum Two hundred Dollars, this to be null and void. Wit Eugene Brenan. /s/ Ezekiel McClendon. Note it is understood sd Ezekiel McClendon is to clothe and pay the taxes of sd Hannah.-- E Brenan. Proven 6 May 1817 by Eugene Brenan; Charles Tell QU. Rec 12 May 1817. Note Satisfaction on this mortgage and cancelled same 7 July 1817 Wm Hagens.

p.103   George Parker to Isaac Parker, Trust Deed, Whereas Benjamin Mazyck of Parish of St Stephens Goose Creek by will 1 July 1797 bequeathed Six hundred Pounds to Peter Porcher and others in trust to be vested in Bank Stock for use of his

10

DEED BOOK 34

grand daughter Elizabeth wife of George Parker during her natural life and at her death to use of such issue of sd Elizabeth; [lost in binding] trustees declining to act Isaac Parker was substituted; by court order legacy vested in Negroes for separate use of sd Elizabeth Parker and her children, monies arising from labor of sd Negroes was appropriated to purchase of land called Elim in Edgefield District which was vested in sd Isaac Parker for use mentioned, George Parker appropriated money arising from Elim tract to purchase of three tracts from William C Harden and Henry G Harden which they conveyed to sd George Parker 17 January 1817. Now George Parker in consideration of premises and one hundred dollars to me paid by sd Isaac Parker have sold unto sd Isaac Parker following tracts of land: 200 acres originally granted to Henry Sizemore of 26 September 1772; 80.5 being part of 100 acres originally granted to Jethro Roundtree on 26 July 1774; third tract of 352 acres originally granted to Francis Settles 5 February 1787, 15 acres of which lie in land lately held by Dionysius Oliver decd under an older grant, all adj Cherokee Ponds which three tracts are now called Hopewell and contain by resurvey 771 ½ acres. To Isaac Parker in trust for sole use of sd Elizabeth Parker wife of George Parker afsd, 20 May 1817. Wit Eldred Simkins, George McDuffie. /s/ Geo Parker. Plat shows adj land said to have been surveyed for Cockram, land formerly belonging to Dionysius Oliver decd, Mrs Hightower's land, land formerly Wm Pond now Hightower Thorn, land crossed by Five Notched road to Augusta, adj road from Columbia to Augusta, crossed by old road to Campbellton, shows lower Cherokee Pond, Settles Pond and two unnamed ponds, also Tarrants house. Plat certified 28 January 1816 by Stephen Tillman D S. Proven 16 May 1817 by George McDuffie; M Mims CCP. Rec 21ˢᵗ May 1817.

p.107 Richard Covington to Henry Shultz of Augusta, Georgia, 29 April 1817, Five hundred Dollars, land in township of Cambeltown known as Corner Lot and originally owned by West Cook. Wit Wm W Olds, Daniel Frazer. /s/ Richard Covington. Justice John Tarrance certifies relinquishment of dower rights by Jane Covington wife of Richard Covington, 8 May 1817; /s/ Jane (x) Covington. Proven 8 May 1817 by William W Olds; John Tarrance JQ. Rec 26 May 1817.

p.109 Charles Williams of Madison County, Mississippi Territory, to William Morris of Edgefield, Deed, 11 November 1816, Six hundred seventy five Dollars, [acreage not stated] on Rockey Creek of Stephens Creek adj lands of Nancy Palmore. Wit Peter Robertson, Edward Settle. /s/ Charles Williams. Proven 3 April 1817 by Peter Robertson; Garrett Freeman JP. Rec 29 May 1817.

p.111 Abner McMillion to Enoch Breazeale, Deed, 29 February 1817, Thirty Dollars, 31 acres on Beaverdam Creek being part of land granted to Isaac Cowther and sold by him to Shade Henderson and from him to John McCoole and from him to Abner McMillion, beginning where the county line crosses the Half mile Branch, county line being the upper line, old road, first dreen below Breazeales mill on

11

Beaverdam Creek adj land belonging to Abner McMillion, Partin Hagood. Wit James Walker, John Walker. /s/ Abner McMillian. Proven 15 May 1817 by James Walker; Robert Walker J P. Rec 2 June 1817.

p.112 John Calliham of Lunenburgh County, Virginia, planter, to his granddaughter Jainusary Garrett, Deed of Gift, 1 April 1793, love, Negro woman Milley and her increase. Wit John (x) Usary, Ambrose Grisome. /s/ John (x) Calliham. Rec 3 June 1817.

p.113 John Pope to Hardy Fluker, Deed, 20 November 1816, Three hundred ten Dollars and fifty [cents], 225 acres on Beaverdam Creek of Clouds Creek being part of land originally granted to Robert Allen 1 April 1799 by Gov Edward Rutledge which contained 500 acres, adj lines of John Pope, Robert Allen, Cumbass, it being the dividing line between sd John Pope and Robert Allen, the afsd land was conveyed from Robert Allen to John Pope on 17 December 1810. Wit George Fluker, Solomon P Strother. /s/ John Pope. Proven 5 April 1817 by George Fluker; Valentine Corley J P. Rec 4 June 1817.

p.115 Thomas Butler to his daughter Fanny Butler, Deed of Gift, 26 March 1817, love, 100 acres on Stephens Creek at mouth of Upper Spring branch adj lines of Carpenter. Wit Charles Nix, Martin Nix. /s/ Thomas Butler. Proven 26 March 1817 by Charles Nix; Thomas Price J P. Rec 12 June 1817.

p.116 Thomas Butler to his daughter Fanny Butler, Deed of Gift, 25 August 1814, Four Dollars, all my household and kitchen furniture. Wit Thomas Price, Daniel Price, Thomas Barrett. /s/ Thomas Butler. Proven 3 June 1817 by Thomas Price; Ansel Talbert J P. Rec 12 June 1817.

p.117 Thomas Butler to his daughter Fanny Butler, Deed of Gift, 26 March 1817, love, young bay horse, heifer and calf. Wit Charles Nix, Martin Nix. /s/ Thomas Butler. Proven 3 June 1817 by Charles Nix; Thomas Price J P. Rec 12 June 1817.

p.118 James Whittle to Israel Martin, Deed, 20 July 1812, Sixteen Dollars fifty cents, eleven acres part of James Whittles land. Wit Martin Foutz, John Warren. /s/ James Whittle. Proven 16 January 1816 by Martin Foutz; Wm Hurtt J P. Rec 5 June 1817.

p.119 Dorcas Smith and Jordan Smith to William Deloach, Deed, 2 January 1815, Two hundred Dollars, 74 acres on Clouds Creek of Saluda River originally granted to Thomas Butler 7 January 1788 by Gov Thos Pinckney, adj W on Dennis McCartys land, SW on John Feaster, S and SE by Benjamin Sawyer and Jacob Reads old survey now held by J P Bond, on E and NE by Duke Harts land, N by Morgan Corder, and was conveyed by sd Thomas Butler to William McCarty 28 March 1789 and William McCarty conveyed same to sd Dorcas Smith 23 January 1806. Wit Morgan (x) Corder, Elizabeth (x) Smith. /s/ Dorcas (x) Smith, /s/ Jordan Smith. Proven 21 Jany 1815 by Morgan Corder; Chas Oneale J Q. Rec 5th June 1817.

p.121   Wright Jones to Israel Martin, Deed, 6 February 1817, One hundred thirty Dollars, 60 acres on Reedy Branch of Clouds Creek being part of land granted to Thomas Warren 24 June 1793. Wit Wm Dloach, Herod (x) Thompson. /s/ Wright (R) Jones. Proven 2 June 1817 by Wm Dloach; Peter Lamkin QU. Rec 5 June 1817.

p.122   Leonard Webb to Israel Martin, Deed, 18 January 1813, One hundred Dollars, 100 acres on a branch of Clouds Creek adj lands of James Whittle, Thomas Deen, Leonard Webb, Wilkin Smith. Wit James Whittle, Saml Deen. /s/ Leonard Webb, /s/Ann (x) Webb. Proven 13 February 1813 by Saml Deen; William Hurtt J P. Rec 5 June 1817.

p.124   William F Taylor legatee to exrs William Ross, Discharge, We Samuel Taylor residing at Lessendrum in parish of Drumblades and County of Aberdeen, North Britain brother german of deceased William Forbes Taylor of Edgefield District and Mrs Mary Taylor otherwise Rainy sister german of sd William Forbes Taylor and spouse of William Rainy schoolmaster of parish of Drumblade afsd and I sd William Rainy for myself and as taking burden on me for my sd spouse legatees of sd deceased William Forbes Taylor acknowledge to have received from Messrs John McAdam and company of Liverpool on behalf of Thomas Gardener of Savannah and Adam Hutchenson of Augusta, Georgia, exrs of William Ross late of Augusta, Georgia, decd, One thousand Four hundred eighty four Pounds 13(?) Shillings and eleven pence sterling in full of sd William Rosses intromissions with estate and effects of sd Wm Forbes Taylor and hereby discharge sd Thomas Gardener and Adam Hutchenson. /s/ Samuel Taylor, /s/ Mary Taylor, /s/ William Taylor. Wit John Sheirer, John Simpson. Notary Public Thomas George Massey of Liverpool, Lancaster, England certifies foregoing is true copy of original writing, 19 February 1817, /s/ Thos Geo Massey. Rec 23 June 1817.

p.126   Isaac Randolph, William Brazier, Hinchey Mitchell, Henry W Lowe, William Ellison, C F Breithaupt and Eldred Simkins with John S Jeter, atty in fact for Hon Richard Gantt, Covenant, 23 May 1817, $1200 for purchase of house & outhouses late property of Mrs Williamson near village of Edgefield & at least ten acres where houses stand [details here omitted]. /s/ H W Lowe; /s/ Eldred Simkins; /s/ W Ellison, /s/ John J Jeter agent in fact for R Gantt Esqr; /s/ Isaac Randolph; /s/ William Brazier; /s/ Hinchey Mitchell, C Breithaupt for myself and W W Fell. Rec 12 June 1817.

p.127   Isaac Randolph et al with Joshua Thurston, Agreement, 23 May 1817, whereas underwriters agree to purchase houses and ten acres late property of Mrs Eliza Williamson near Edgefield Village at price of Twelve hundred Dollars to be paid in two equal instalments, first on 1 January next, balance on 2 June thereafter; intention is to accommodate Joshua Thurston in sd place to establish a female academy thereon; sd Joshua agrees to establish sd academy 1 August next to be superintended by Misses Martha and Elizabeth Thurston his daughters who are to teach spelling, reading, writing, arithmetic, English grammar, geography, drawing and the French language [other arrangements here omitted]. /s/ Eldred Simkins, /s/ W Ellison, /s/ Joshua Thurston, /s/ Isaac Randolph, /s/ Wm Brazier, /s/ Hinchey Mitchell, /s/ H W Lowe. Rec 12 June 1817.

p.128   John S Glascock to Thomas Coleman, Deed, 30 May 1817, Four thousand Dollars, 887 ½ acres on Ninety Six and Handleys Creeks known by name of the Recess. Wit Robt Hamilton, James Payne. /s/ John S Glascock. Justice Matthew Mims certifies relinquishment of dower rights by Eliza Glascock wife of John S Glascock 16 June 1817; /s/ Eliza Glascock. Plat shows adjoining lands of Wm Burton decd, Jos Griffin, Thjos Coleman, C Cooper, Wilson, James Coleman, B Bunting, Bostick, Grigsby. Proven 3 June 1817 by James Payne; Thos Anderson JQ. Rec 16 June 1817.

p.131   John Smith to Temple Hargrove, Deed, 5 December 1814, Ninety Dollars, 100 acres on Ephraim Branch of Sleepy Creek of Turkey Creek of Savannah River adj Matthews road, adj lands of John Smith, Stephen Cotney, Miller, Carrom. Wit Daniel Wiseman, Briton Hargrove. /s/ John Smith. Proven 4 April 1817 by Briton Hargrove; James Adams J P. Rec 28th June 1817.

p.133   Abner Whatley to John S Jeter, Deed, 15 May 1817, Forty Dollars, one half acre of south side of Jefferson Street in Edgefield Village fronted by lot #13 at present owned by sd John S Jeter bounded by lot owned by sd Abner Whatley and lands of Arthur Simkins Senr. Wit Geo Butler, Whit Brooks. /s/ Abner Whatley. Justice Matthew Mims certifies relinquishment of dower rights by Mrs Eliza Whatley wife of Abner Whatley, 7 July 1817; /s/ Eliza L Whatley. Proven 7 June 1817 by George Butler Esqr; M Mims CCP. Rec 7 July 1817.

p.135   Abraham Riley to Michael Corley, Deed, 28 June 1817, Five hundred Dollars, 315 acres on Sleepy and Mountain Creeks of Turkey Creek adj John Gorman decd formerly William Clarks line; surveyed for John Bratcher 10 December 1795 and granted to Jesse Clark 7 November 1796. Wit Jacob P Abney, Esau Brooks. /s/ Abraham (x) Riley. Proven 7 July 1817 by Jacob P Abney; M Mims CCP. Rec 7 July 1817.

p.136   Abner Landrum to Richard Lewis, Deed, 15 August 1816, Sixty Dollars, one square acre on Cambridge road. Wit Thos (P) Presley, James W Meridith. /s/ Abner Landrum. Proven 7 July 1817 by Thomas Presley; M Mims CCP. Rec 7 July 1817.

p.138 Abner Landrum to Thomas Presley, Deed, 8 February 1817, One hundred eighty Dollars, one square acre on Cambridge road adj Richard Lewis. Wit Richard C Lewis, James W Meridith. Proven 7 July 1817 by R C Lewis; M Mims CCP. Rec 7 July 1817.

p.139 Whitfield Brooks, Commissioner of Court of Equity, to James Smiley, Deed, 4 June 1817, Smiley's bill of complaint 19 April against David Richardson, Charlote Strother and others, stating he made contract with George Strother for purchase of land, Strother executed bond to make title as soon as Twelve hundred Dollars be paid in part of purchase money; Brooks hath paid same but George J Strother died without having executed title; commissioner releases 436 acres on Little Stephens Creek to Smiley, adj land of William Ellison, Little Stephens [word lost in binding] meeting house, being land on which James Smiley now resides, adj David Allen, John McManus, Thomas McDaniel. Wit D Bird, James Woolf. /s/ Whitfield Brooks, Comr in Equity. Proven 7 July 1817 by Capt Daniel Bird; M Mims CCP. Rec 7 July 1817.

p.142 Joseph Eddins, planter, to David Gurganus, Deed, 13 March 1817, Three hundred thirty three Dollars, 70 acres near the Courthouse on Beaverdam Creek, being part of 150 acres originally granted to Anguish McDaniel 15 March 1772, adj land conveyed by sd Eddins to Charles Goodwin, James Beames, Charles Goodwin,. Wit Jeremiah Mitchell, Hinchey Mitchell. /s/ Joseph Eddins. Justice Eldred Simkins certifies relinquishment of dower rights by Elizabeth Eddins wife of Joseph Eddins, 14 March 1817; /s/ Elizabeth Eddins. Proven 7 July 18i17 by Hinchey Mitchell; Wm Hagens J P. Rec 7 July 1817.

p.144 Samuel Taylor, Family Record. 8 September 1768, Samuel Taylor in Loanhead had a son baptized named William; William Forbes and Nathaniel Forbes, witnesses. 15 June 1771 Samuel Taylor in Loanhead had a son baptized named Samuel; William Forbes and Robert Forbes, witnesses; 6 January 1778 Samuel Taylor in Loanhead had a daughter baptized named Mary; Nathaniel Forbes and John Allan, witnesses. Extracted from the register of baptisms of the parish of Drumblade 27 August 1815 by [no end to this sentence]. Within is faithful extract; Samuel and Mary Taylor therein mentioned are lawful brother and sister to the late William Forbes Taylor Esqr, merchant, South Carolina, is attested in presence of church session by Robert Gordan minister of parish of Drumblade, David Innes, and John Spence Elders of sd Parish 27 August 1815. By Robert Gordon minister, David Innes, Elder, John Spence, Elder. Andrew Jopp advocate in Aberdeen certifies within W Robert Gorden is minitser of the parish of Drumblade, and David Innes and John Spence are elders of sd Parish. Further certifies from his own knowledge thatSamuel and Mary Taylor are lawful brother & sister of William Forbes Taylor decd, and that he had no other brother or sister. Aberdeen 29 August 1815.

p.145   Benjamin Culpeper to Jonathan Weaver, Deed, 21 July 1817, Twelve hundred Dollars, 500 acres in three tracts; 150 acres granted to Robert Lang 26 January 1773, two tracts granted to Daniel Ravnal Junr, 150 acre and 200 acres, on waters of Mine Creek of Little Saluda adj lands William Herrin Senr, Reuben Kirkland, William Martin, Benjamin Loveless, Ogdell Cockroff, Andrew Gomillon. Wit Benjn Suddath, Lewis Suddath. /s/ Benjamin Culpeper. Justice Thomas Dozier certifies relinquish-ment of dower rights by Joice Culpeper wife of Benjamin Culpeper 21 July 1817; /s/ Joice (x) Culpeper. Proven 21 July 1817 by Benjamin Suddath; Thomas Dozier J Q. Rec 22 July 1817.

p.148   Edward Bozeman of Abbeville District to John Morgan, Deed, 3 February 1817, Eight hundred dollars, 23 acres on Martintown road adj lands formerly owned by James Martin, Lemuel Cantelow. Wit Henry Martin, Thos Murrah Jr. /s/ Edward Bozeman. Proven 26 July 1817 by Henry Martin; A Edmunds J P. Rec 28 July 1817.

p.149   John Morgan to Thomas Raney, Deed, 12 February 1817, One thousand Dollars, 23 acres on Martintown road whereon sd John Morgan now lives, adj land formerly owned by James Martin, E & S by land of Lemuel Cantelow. Wit James Maull, Saml Hammond. /s/ John Morgan. Proven 26 July 1817 by James Maull. Rec 25 July 1817.

p.151   Charles Nix to Sarah Scarborough, Receipt. Received of Sarah Scarborough Four hundred Dollars cash for Negro boy Mathew, 2 January 1817. Wit Thomas Price. /s/ Charles Nix. Proven 16 July 1817 by Thomas Price; A Edmunds J P. Rec 28 July 1817.

p.151   William Lane Wilson to William Kelly, Deed, 5 February 1813, Forty Dollars, 50 acres, being part of land where George Lane Wilson now lives on Boggy Branch of South Edisto River adj Widow Walker, Kelly's line. Wit George Wilson, Dildatha Odom.   /s/ William Lane Wilson. Proven 9 November 1816 by Dildatha Odom; Lewis Holmes J P. Rec 1 August 1817.

p.153   Ezekiel Walker to William Kelley, Deed, 25 November 1806, Ninety Dollars, 25 acres on South Edisto part of land originally granted to John Croner by Gov Wm Moultrie, adj Bog Branch. Wit Lewis Fedrick, Joseph Walker. /s/ Ezekiel (x) Walker. Proven 11 Decr 1816 by Joseph Walker; Lewis Holmes J P. Rec 1 Aug 1817.

p.155   William Carson to William Kelley, Deed, 16 October 1815, Two hundred Dollars, 200 acres being part of land originally granted to Richard Bush in 1797 on

South Edisto River adj land sold to John P Bush Esqr. Wit John Bettis, Hugh (x) Carson, Francis Bettis. /s/ William (x) Carson. Proven 3 November 1815 by John Bettis; Matthew Bettis J P. Rec 1 August 1817.

p.156 George L Wilson to William Carson, Deed, 10 November 1813, Fifty Dollars, 200 acres originally granted to Richard Bush 28 August 1797 on South Edisto adj land of John P Bush Esqr. Wit John Warren, Dennis Warren, William Kelley. /s/ George L (x) Wilson. Proven 10 November 1813 by William Kelley; Jno P Bush JP. Rec 1 Augst 1817.

p.157 Nathan Tally to Daniel Brunson, Deed, 27 May 1817, Five hundred Dollars, 618 acres being part of two tracts, one originally granted to Joshua Lockwood for 250 acres, the other originally granted to John Swillivan for 375 acres in 1786 June 5; the tract granted to Lockwood 16 September 1774, part being sold by sd Talley to Wm Terry; land bounded by Beaverdam Creek of Turkey Creek of Big Stevens Creek, Delaveign Cheatham and others. Wit Joseph Brunson, William Brunson. /s/ Nathan Talley. /s/ Nancey (x) Talley. Justice John Hollingsworth certifies relinquishment of dower rights by Nancey Tally wife of Nathan Talley, 17 July 1817; /s/ Nancey (x) Tally. Proven 15 July 1817 by William Brunson; John Hollingsworth JQ. Rec 31 July 1817.

p.160 Martha Odom to her daughter Mary Perry, Deed of Gift, 26 April 1817, love, Negro man Gerry, but Martha keeps Gerry untill her decease. Wit Ira Scott, Mary Perry. /s/ Martha (x) Odom. Proven 21 July 1817 by Ira Scott; John Loveless J P. Rec 4 August 1817.

p.161 Martha Odom to her daughter Mary Perry, Deed of Gift, 26 April 1817, love, bedsteads and furniture, Martha to keep same until her decease. Wit Ira Scott, Mary Perry. /s/ Martha (x) Odom. Proven 21 July 1817 by Ira Scott; John Loveless J P. Rec 4 August 1817.

p.162 Benjamin Ryan Jr to Doctor Reuben Reed, Power of Attorney, 9 July 1817, to recover Negroes, land, debts, legacies or other property, to sell what he thinks proper for my benefit and support. Wit John Hughes, David Gill. /s/ Benj Ryan. Proven 4 August 1817 by John Hughes; M Mims CCP. Rec 4 August 1817.

p.163 Zacheus Corley to his brother Valentine Corley Junr, Deed, 9 April 1803, Five hundred Dollars federal money, 150 acres on Indian Creek of Little Saluda River, being part of 300 acres originally granted to me 6 February 1786 by Gov Wm Moultrie, now adj land of Valentine Corley, James Blalock, Watery branch, sd Zacheus Corley, and Hugh Duffies land. Wit Jesse Samford, Hugh Duffey, Daniel (x) Goodman. /s/ Zacheus (x) Corley. Proven 21 December 1811 by Jesse Samford;

17

William Spragins J P. Rec 4 August 1817.

p.166   Valentine Corley to Stephen Bell, Deed, 16 December 1811, Four hundred fifty Dollars, 240 acres on Indian Creek of Little Saluda River and is part of two surveys, one of 300 acres granted to Zacheus Corley, the other of 181 acres granted to Asa Samford, which parts was by them conveyed to me, bounded by Watery branch, Zacheus Corley, Riley, Hendly Webb. Wit Sampson Pope, Hendley Webb. /s/ Valentine Corley. Justice Sampson Pope certifies relinquishment of dower rights by Sarah Corley wife of Valentine Corley, 3 December 1811; /s/ Sarah (x) Corley. Proven 11 May 1812 by Sampson Pope; Shepherd Spencer J P. Rec 4 August 1817.

p.169   Stephen Bell to John Riley and William Riley, 29 April 1815, Five hundred Dollars, 240 acres on Indian Creek of Little Saluda River and is part of two surveys one of 300 acres granted to Zacheus Corley, the other of 181 acres granted to Asa Samford, which parts was conveyed to Valentine Corley. The 240 acres adj Watery branch and lands of Samuel Davis, Riley, Levi Gentry, Hendly Webb. Wit Valentine Corley, Hendly Webb. /s/ Stephen (x) Bell.   Justice Sampson Pope certifies relinquishment of dower rights by Mary Bell wife of Stephen Bell 9 September 1815; /s/ Mary (x) Bell. Proven 12 April 1817 by Valentine Corley; John Abney J P. Rec 4 August 1817.

p.171   Sheriff James M Butler to William Mays, Sheriff Title, 1 July 1816, at suit of Stephen Whitley and wife Elizabeth against estate of Abney Mays for purpose of obtaining partition, land could not be fairly divided and to be openly and publicly sold after notice of sale. Struck off to William Mays for Five hundred fifty one Dollars he being highest and last bidder, 1197.5 acres on Halfway Swamp of Saluda River adj lands of Stark, John Troops, Weaver, and estate of Abney Mays decd. Wit A Blocker, Geo Butler. /s/ J M Butler SED. Proven 4 August 1817 by George Butler; M Mims CCP. Rec 4 August 1817.

p.174   Richard Walpole to John S Glascock, Deed, 26 November 1814, Five hundred sixty Dollars, 112 acres on Cedar Creek adj lines of Stephen Tillman, it being part of 1000 acres originally granted to James Parsons, conveyed to Peter Carns decd and conveyed by executors of Carnes to Abraham Boyd of Prince George County, Maryland, and Jonathan Wightt of Edgefield, and also conveyed by John Wightt of Abbeville District to John Woolfolk and by Woolfolk to Richard Walpole. Wit Stephen Mays, Gosper Gallman. /s/ R Walpole.   Justice William Jeter certifies relinquishment of dower rights by Agness Walpole wife of Richard Walpole, [blank] 1814; /s/ Agness Walpole. Proven 25 November 1814 by Stephen Mays; W Jeter Q U. Rec 4th August 1817.

p.177   John S Glascock to Jesse Bettis, Deed, 7 October 1816, Six hundred fifty

18

Dollars 112 acres on Cedar Creek adj lines of Stephen Tillman, it being part of 1000 acres originally granted to James Parsons, conveyed to Peter Carnes decd, conveyed by exors of sd Carns to Abraham Boyd of Prince George County, Maryland, and Jonathan Wightt of Edgefield District, conveyed by John Wightt of Abbeville District to John Woolfolk and by Woolfolk to Richard Walpole. Wit Wm Hill Senr, Drury Mims Jr. /s/ John S Glascock. Justice Matthew Mims certifies relinquishment of dower rights by Mrs Eliza Glascock wife of John S Glascock, 8 August 1817. Proven 4 August 1817 by William Hill Senr; M Mims CCP. Rec 8th August 1817.

p.179 Harman Colborn to William Colborn, Deed, 16 November 1816, Fifty Dollars, 50 acres being part of tract originally granted unto Lewis Ethridge. Wit Frederick Hartley, Separt (B) Bearley. /s/ Harman (H) Colborn. Justice William Hurtt certifies relinqishment of dower rights by Elizabeth Colborn wife of Harman Colborn, 10 May 1817; /s/ Elizabeth (x) Colborn. Proven 18 May 1817 by Separt Bearley; Wm Hurtt QU. Rec 11 August 1817.

p.181 Edmund Martin of Richmond County, Georgia, to Lemuel Cantelow, Deed, 12 August 1817, [number lost in binding] hundred thirty two Dollars, 58 acres on Rocky branch of Hornes Creek of Savannah River, it being part of 340 acres granted to Edmund Martin Esqr on 6 June 1785. Wit Henry Martin, Thos Murrah Jr. /s/ Edmund Martin. Plat shows 58 acres adj lands of Lemuel Cantelow, original survey, Suck Branch, George Martin, Giles or Rocky Branch of Hornes Creek, crossed by the road from Martintown to Edgefield Courthouse and path to Pantelow's plantation. Certified 14 May 1816 by Stephen Tillman D S. Justice Charles Hammond certifies the relinquishment of dower rights by Sally Martin wife of Edmund Martin, 12 August 1817; /s/ Sally Martin. Renunciation of claim by Benjamin Martin of Columbia County, Georgia, [no date]. /s/ Benj Martin. Proven 12 August 1817 by Henry Martin; Charles Hammond J Q. Rec 17 August 1817.

p.184 John Lowe of Barnwell District to Bud Davis, Deed, Barnwell District, 4 February 1815, One hundred Dollars, 400 acres in Barnwell and Edgefield Districts on [lost in binding]ises Creek adj lands of Richard Gantt, John Antony, Thomas Morris supposed to have been granted to John Blalock. Wit George Magness, Levi Red. /s/ John (x) Lowe. Proven 23 May 1815 by George Magness; Thos Morris J P. Rec Barnwell Dist, 2 February 1816, Orsamus D Allen Regt. Rec 25 Augt 1817.

p.186 Henry Martin to Ansel Talbert, Deed, 3 January 1817, Six hundred Dollars, land on Bird Creek of Stephens Creek. Wit John F Burriss, Thomas Martin. /s/ Henry Martin. Plat shows 160 acres adj lands of Moab Martin, , Thomas Martin, Absalom Martin, heirs of W R Mortan, Ansel Talbert. Survey shows 40 acres if Caldwell and 160 acres of Lofton. Resurveyed 2 January 1817; E Settle, D S. Proven 3 June 1817 by John F Burriss;Thomas Price J P. Rec 27 Aug 1817.

p.188 James Spann and wife Elizabeth late Eliza Anderson, John G Harris and wife Rachel late Rachel Anderson to Abram G Dozier and Charles Hammond, Deed, 4 May 1814, $841.87 ½, one thousand three hundred forty seven acres bounded by lands of Torrence and Butler, Char H Thorne, Col. LeRoy Hammond, land called Ralph Spence Phillips now claimed by Robert Stark Esqr, estate of Joseph Ashton decd, estate of John Easter decd. Wit Willis Bostick, William Bostick. Louis B Holloway, Henry C Barr. /s/ Jno G Harris, /s/ Rachel T Harris, /s/ James Spann, /s/ Elizabeth Spann. Proven Abbeville District, 26 August 1817 by Wm Bostick; B F Whitner J P. Proven Abbeville District 26 August 1817 by Henry C Barr; B F Whitner J P. Rec 28 August 1817.

p.190 John Ryan Senior, planter, to Stephen Medlock, Deed, 19 November 1816, Twenty two Dollars, 22 acres on head branches of Turkey Creek adj land of sd Medlock, land originally granted to Isaac Lessesne, land bought by sd Medlock from Elias Blackburn. Wit Wm Dobey, Andrew Gomillion. /s/ John Ryan. Proven 23 November 1816 by Andrew Gomillion; Charles Hammond J P. Rec 1 Sept 1817.

p.192 Abraham Holsonback to William Roberts, planter, Deed, 13 August 1816, Three hundred Dollars, 100 acres on a branch of Laweds Creek of Stephens Creek adj lands of Hezekiah Oden, Capt Hammons, old ridge road between Gunnels Creek and Laweds Creek, James Laser, Hezekiah Oden, being part of land originally granted unto John Login, surveyed for Thomas Oden 10 May 1773 and conveyed by sd John Login unto John Kilcrease. Wit Shearly Whatley, Jesse (x) Baley. /s/ Abraham (A) Holsonback. Justice Charles Hammond certifies relinquishment of dower rights by Jane Holsonback wife of Abraham Holsonback, 28 August 1817; /s/ Jane (x) Holsonback. Proven 28 August 1817 by Jesse (x) Bailey; Charles Hammond J Q. Rec 1 September 1817.

p.194 William Richardson to William Elliott, Deed, 6 December 1814, Five hundred Dollars, 180 acres on Log Creek, it being part of 964 acres originally surveyed for Andrew Broughton 24 August 1774 and conveyed from Thomas Broughton 7 October 1802 to Daniel Bird and from Daniel Bird to John Eddins 2 Feb 1809 and from John Eddins to James Long 5[15? 25?] December 1810, and from Long to sd William Richardson 22 Jany 1813. Present lines of 180 acres adj the waggon road, Thomas Winn. Wit Jeremiah Mobley Senr, William McDaniel, James (I) Bunanton. /s/ William Richardson. Fairfield District, 27 August 1816, Justice James Rogers certifies relinquishment of dower rights by Izette Richardson wife of William Richardson; /s/ Izeet Richardson. Proven 5 June 1815 by William McDaniel; Wm W Olds J P. Rec 1 September 1817.

p.197 John McDaniel to Jesse Bettis, Deed, 14 July 1817, One hundred sixty four Dollars forty cents six mills, 74 acres adjoining Stephen Tillman, John Woolfolk,

DEED BOOK 34

Edgefield Courthouse, Jesse Bettis, Ceder Creek, spring branch nearest the house, John S Glascock; it being part of land originally granted to James Parsons Esqr for 1000 acres. Wit Stephen Tillman, David Gill. /s/ John McDaniel. Justice Matthew Mims certifies the relinquishment of dower rights by Mary McDaniel wife of John McDaniel, 14 August 1817; /s/ Mary McDaniel. Proven 1 September 1817 by David Gill; M Mims CCP. Rec 1 September 1817.

p.199   John Miller to Roger M Williams, Deed, 18 July 1817, Five hundred thirty five Dollars, 100 acres, my undivided two thirds of land lying on both sides of the Martintown road on Horns Creek adj lands of Barksdale, Gardner, heirs of Drury Adams and land of sd Williams whereon he now lives. Wit William Pursell, Presley Sullivan. /s/ John Miller. Proven 18 July 1817 by William Pursell; Thomas Key JQ. Rec 1 September 1817.

p.201   Simeon Deming to Robert Gillam, Deed, 26 July 1817, Six hundred Dollars, 64 acres whereon Starling Kemp now lives on Beaverdam Creek of Cuffeetown Creek, it being lately property of Eli Thornton, adj lands of David Walker, James Walker. Wit Jared E Groce, Jno Harris. /s/ Simeon Deming. Justice Nathan Lipscomb certifies relinquishment of dower rights by Mary Deming wife of Simeon Deming, 21 July 1817; /s/ Mary Deming. Proven 21 July 1817 by John G Harris; Nathan Lipscomb J Q. Rec 1 September 1817.

p.203   John Wheeler to Owen Dailey, Deed, 26 November 1816, Five hundred Dollars, 130 acres adj lands of Owen Daily, Jesse Summers, Charles Oneall, Big Creek of Saluda River. Robt Gowan, Charles Oneall, David (x) Daily. /s/ John Wheeler. Justice Nathan Norris certifies relinquishment of dower rights by Susannah Wheeler wife of John Wheeler, 20 Augt 1817; /s/ Susannah Wheeler. Proven 20 August 1817 by David Daily; Nathan Norris JQ. Rec 1 September 1817.

p.205   Joseph Robertson to Stephen Medlock, Deed, 4 December 1810, Five hundred Dollars, 150 acres, five acres excepted supposed to be in an old survey if the old survey takes it, at SE corner, granted to Richard Johnson 7 April 1788 and conveyed from him to R Roberts and from sd Roberts to sd Joseph Robertson. Wit Francis Bettis, Robert Willis. /s/ Joseph Robertson. Justice Isaac Kirkland certifies relinquishment of dower rights by Elizabeth Robertson wife of Joseph Robertson, 29 December 1810; /s/ Elizabeth (x) Robertson. Proven 4 December 1810 by Francis Bettis; Isaac Kirkland J Q. Rec 3 September 1817.

p.207   John Woolfolk to Richard Walpole, Deed, 22 March 1811, One hundred Dollars, 25 acres on Cedar Creek where old ridge path crosseth old road, Stephen Tillman's land, being part of a thousand acres originally granted to James Parsons, conveyed by sd Parsons to Peter Carnes decd and by sd Carnes to Abraham Boyd of

21

Prince [George's] County, Maryland, and Jonathan Wightt of Edgefield District; also conveyed by John Wightt of Abbeville to John Woolfolk. Wit Stephen Mays, Matthew Mays. /s/ John Woolfolk. Justice Matthew Mims certifies relinquishment of dower rights by Margaret Woolfolk wife of John Woolfolk, 14 August 1817; /s/ Margaret T Woolfolk. Proven 5 September 1817 by Matthew Mays; M Mims CCP. Rec 5 September 1817.

p.209 Sheriff James M Butler to Charles Jones of Laurence District, Sheriffs Title, 3 January 1816, at suit of Livingston Mims against admrs of West Cook decd, sheriff to sell land after public notice; struck off to John Talbert for the use of Charles Jones for Five hundred five Dollars, he being highest and last bidder; paid by Charles Jones; 482 acres adj land of Catlett Corley, Hugh A Nixon. Wit Eugene Brenan, Richard H Tutt. /s/ J M Butler S.E.D. Plat at request of John Talbert admr estate of West Cook decd, John Blocker D S resurveyed 482 acres. Plat 2 May 1815 shows Savannah River, Spring branch, a mill house, and lands of Bodie, William Shannon. Proven 5 September 1817 by Richard H Tutt; M Mims CCP. Rec 5 September 1817.

p.212 Hannah Lesesne, widow and exr of Isaac Lesesne, planter, decd, to George Parker, Power of Attorney, Charleston, 27 February 1815, George Parker to sell land in Edgefield belonging to estate. Wit Eliza Conover. /s/ Hannah Lesesne. Proven 23 July 1817 by Eliza Conover; Gabriel Mangault Baunetheau QU. Rec 5 Sept 1817.

p.213 Joseph Nunn to William Nunn, Deed, 29 March 1817, Ten cents, 75 acres on Cedar branch of Mine Creek of Saluda River adj George Nunn, Perryman,, P Bland, Hart. Wit William Daniel, C Threewits. /s/ Joseph Nunn. Proven 6 September 1817 by William Daniel; M Mims CCP. Rec 6 September 1817.

p.215 Samuel Rowe to Thomas Youngblood, Certificate, 9 September 1817, Youngblood swears that 7 May last in fight between himself and Samuel Rowe he got his right ear cropped by Rowe. Samuel Rowe deposeth facts are true. /s/ Thomas Youngblood, /s/ Samuel (x) Rowe. Rec 9 September 1817.

p.215 Robert Lowery to Andrew Bittle, Deed, 7 December 1815, One hundred forty[?] Dollars, 10 acres Beech Island near old mills formerly belonging to David Colvin and conveyed by Colvin to sd Lowery, adj lands of estate of Thomas Galphin decd, estate of David Colvin decd. Wit Hezekiah Salmon, Benjn Bowers. /s/ Robert Lowry. Sarah Lowery relinquishes dower rights, 7 December 1815, in presence of Hezekiah Salmon, Benjamin Bowers. Proven 30 August 1817 by Benjamin Bowers; Jno Sturzenegger J P. Rec 10 September 1817.

p.218 Sarah Gunnels to her two children Stanmore Gunnels and Eliza Gunnels, Deed of Gift, 10 September 1817, love, [houehold goods] to be equally divided after my death. Wit Benj Frazier, John Kimbrell. /s/ Sarah (x) Gunnels. Proven 10 September 1817 by Benjamin Frazier; M Mims CCP. Rec 10 September 1817.

p.219   Josiah Nicholson to Shemuel Nicholson, Deed, 21 October 1816, Five hundred seventy five Dollars, 140 acres on Rockey Creek of Stephens Creek of Turkey Creek, Savannah River, bounded by lands of Thos Tant, sd Shemuel Nicholson, Amos Landrum, Josiah Nicholson, Josiah Horne.   Wit Theophilus Nicholson, J W Nicholson. /s/ Josiah Nicholson.   Proven 21 October 1816 by Theophilus Nicholson; Jesse Blocker JQ. Rec 11 Sept 1817.

p.221   Daniel Bird Senr to Conrod Lowery, Deed, 25 March 1806, Four hundred Dollars, the following tracts of land: 4/7 part of land granted to John Jacob Messersmith for 150 acres on Little Stephens Creek; also 4/7 parts of 200 acres on sd creek adj afsd tract granted to Marks and including the mills erected by John Jacob Messersmith; also 4/7 part of 100 acres adj above tracts granted to John George Shoemaker; also 4/7 part of 84 acres on Sleepy Creek adj above land granted to John Jacob Messersmith; also 82 acres in fork of Stephens Creek and Sleepy Creek granted to sd Daniel Bird Senr. Wit Danl Bird Jr, Moses Taylor; /s/ Daniel Bird. Proven 25 March 1806 by Daniel Bird Jr; John Blocker JQ. Rec 11 September 1817.

p.222   Cadwell Evans to Sarah Quarles, Deed, 10 September 1817, Six hundred Dollars, 127 acres on Cuffeetown Creek of Stephens Creek. Wit Edmd B Hibbler, John Quarles. /s/ Cadwell Evans. Proven 10 September 1817 by Edmund B Hibbler; E B Belcher J P. Rec 12 September 1817.

p.224   Elias Blackburn to Stephen Medlock, Deed, 5 February 1816, Two hundred four Dollars, 102 acres on branch of Turkey Creek of Stephens Creek of Savannah River adj lands of Stephn Medlock, John Ryan, Elias Blackburn, it being part of land originally granted to Isaac Lesesne. Wit Wm Blackburn, Matthew Melton. /s/ Elias Blackburn.   Justice Matthew Mims certifies relinquishment of dower rights by Margaret Blackburn wife of Elias Blackburn, 18 September 1817; /s/ Margaret (x) Blackburn. Proven 4 November 1817 by Matthew Melton; Lewis Holmes J P. Rec 18 September 1817.

p.226   Thomas Herrin to Thomas Cobb, Deed, 8 May 1816, Whereas Samuel Savage at time of decease was seized of 312 ½ acres on which he died, which land by will dated 27 January 1804 he bequeathed unto his wife Frances Savage for her life and after her decease to be equally divided between his two daughters Frances Heron and Elizabeth Lark, and as widow Frances Savage is late deceased by which Frances Heron and her husband Thomas Heron is entitled to one half the land mentioned; now Thomas and Frances Heron of Abbeville District for Twelve hundred Dollars, sell our undivided half of land above mentioned. Wit A Hunter, A Giles. /s/ Thos Heron, /s/

Frances Heron. Abbeville District, Justice Joseph Black certifies relinquishment of dower by Frances Heron wife of Thomas Heron, 1 January 1817; /s/ Frances Heron. Proven 17 May 1817 by Andrew Giles; A Hunter J P. Rec 29 September 1817.

p.228 Harden Blalock to Dalziel Randolph, Mortgage, 16 October 1817, Blalock by note dated 16 October 1817 for $1393.28 payable in six months; the other note 10 October 1817 for $1200 payable in twelve months, bound unto Dalziel Randolph for $2593.28. Secured by slaves: Abram age 50, Let age 40, Jack age 40, Young Abram age 25, Isaac about 23, Creasy about 20. If notes paid, deed void. Wit John S Jeter, Isaac Randolph. /s/ Harden Blalock. Proven 16 October 1817 by Isaac Randolph; A Edmunds J P. Rec 17 Octr 1817.

p.231 Isaac Hudson of Edgefield District to Zebulon Rudulph of Columbia, Richland District, merchant, Deed, 28 July 1817, 696 acres whereon I now reside on Little Saluda River, adj Arthur Simkins, Zebulon Rudulph, James Hudson, Samuel Norred, heirs of Jacob Smith, William Dozier. Wit Sampson Pope Junr, Charlotte Lewis. /s/ Isaac Hudson. Plat certified 28 July 1817 for 696 acres by Isaac Hudson; Sampson Pope Junr, Charlotte Lewis wits. Plat shows Great Canebreak Creek and Saluda River. Justice Thomas Dozier certifies relinquishment of dower rights by Ann Hudson wife of Isaac Hudson, 16 August 1817; /s/ Nancy Hudson. Proven 30 September 1817 by Sampson Pope Junr; M Mims CCP. Rec 30 Sept 1817.

p.234 John Pope to Zebulon Rudulph of Columbia, Richland District, Deed, 30 April 1817, Ten thousand Dollars, 2680 acres whereon Sampson Pope Junr now lives, being on Mine Creek, Red Bank Creek and Little Saluda River, adj land sold by Isaac Hudson to sd Zebulon Rudulph, James Hudson, heirs of James Ogilvie Senr decd, Abel Pearson, Millican Norred, John Weaver, James Hart, Mumford Perryman, [blank] Reaves, Abraham Furgurson, Sophia Bonham, heirs of James Oharra, Christopher Ward, Thomas Pitts, Stephen Johnson, heirs of George Strother, heirs of Robert Newport Senr decd, and [blank] Simkins Esqr. Wit Osmund Ross, John Courser. /s/ John Pope. P.S. The family graveyard is excepted; /s/ John Pope. Plat certified 30 April 1817; /s/ John Pope. Plat shows two roads, two bridges, above adj owners plus James Hart, Isaac Hudson. Proven 30 April 1817 by Osmond Ross; J J Faust J P. Rec 30 September 1817.

p.238 Thomas B Oden to Alexander Edmunds, Deed, 20 November 1813, Two hundred Dollars, 50 acres on Stephens Cr, adj lands of sd Edmunds, Demsey Bussey, Elisha Palmer, John Griffith, Edmund Lamar, sd Edmunds, being part of tract originally granted to Thomas Key Esqr. Wit B Reese, Benjn Davis. /s/ Thos B Oden. Proven 26 April 1817 by Burrell Reese; Thos Meriweather J P. Rec 6 Oct 1817.

p.240 John C Mayson and Washington Bostick, exrs estate of Doctor James Moore decd, both of Abbeville and Edgefield Districts to Alexander Travis, 17 May 1813, One hundred fifty Dollars, 282 acres on Ninety Six Creek adj lands of Charles Cooper, Phillip Burt. Wit James Shackelford, Ramsay Mayson. /s/ John C Mayson Exr, /s/ Washington Bostick, Exr. Proven Abbeville District, 9 April 1817, by Ramsay Mayson; B F Whitner J P. Rec 6th October 1817.

p.241   James Sanders Atty for Henry S Halley executor of William Halley decd to Robert Harrison, Deed, 27 February 1816, Eleven hundred Dollars, 500 acres on Cuffeetown and Hardlabor Creeks of Stephens Creek of Savannah River, original grant made to afsd Wm Halley decd, being part of sd premises. Wit Stephen Tomkins, Samuel Tomkins. /s/ James Sanders atty in fact for Henry S Halley. Proven 27 February 1816 by Stephen Tomkins; John Lyon QU. Rec 6 Oct 1817.

p.243   William Burnett to William Quarles, Deed, 1 July 1817, whereas Thomas Burnett late of sd District was possessed of 435 acres on Chaveses Creek, about 15 October 1796 died intestate leaving sd Wm Burnett one of his heirs at law, entitled to one seventh undivided share in sd land, Quarles hath purchased his interest in sd premises for Seven hundred seventy five Dollars. Wit Hugh Ballantine, Samuel Quarles, Thomas L Shaw. Proven 30 September 1817 by Samuel Quarles; William Samuel J P. Rec 6th October 1817.

p.245   Joseph Collier to William Roberts, Receipt. Received 29 January 1817 of William Roberts Two hundred fifty Dollars in full for land sold him adj lands of sd Roberts and Murtle[?] Sansum to which I promise to make title. /s/ Joseph Collier. Rec 6th October 1817.

p.246   Benjamin Blow to Henry Spann, Deed, 19 March 1817, One hundred Dollars, 20 acres, part of land called Clarks old Mill seat, on South Edisto River adj Lewis Clarks old mill dam on Horse Creek, Benjamin Blow, Henry Spann, Ganys Spring Branch.   Wit Wm McClendon, Alexander Jenkins. /s/ Benjamin Blow. Proven 27 September 1817 by William McClendon; John Loveless JP. Rec 6 October 1817.

p.247   Martha Odom to her son Elijah Watson, Deed of Gift, 26 April 1817, benefits of negro man Sam, Martha to keep Sam until her death. Wit Ira Scott, Mary Perry. /s/ Martha (x) Odum. Proven 4 Sept 1817 by Ira Scott; Peter Lamkin JQU. Rec 6th October 1817.

p.248   Martha Odum to Elijah Watson, Deed, 27 April 1817, Eight hundred Dollars, 125 acres on Charleston Road just below Jesse Simkins, adj [names lost in binding]. Wit Thomas Reynolds, Henry Fallow, Ira Scott. /s/ Martha (x) Odum. Proven 4th September 1817 by Ira Scott; Peter Lamkin JQU. Rec 6th October 1817.

p.250 George Kitson to Charles Findly, Deed, 4 February 1815, One hundred ten Dollars, 56 acres being part of 323 acres granted to Drury Pace on a branch of Savannah River, the 56 acres adj lands of John Kilcrease, Charles Findley, survey by John Boyd D S. Wit Nehemiah (x) Lindy, Joseph Mealing, Robt Lang. /s/ George Getzen. Justice Thomas Key certifies relinqu9shment of dower rights by Sally Kitson wife of George Kitson, 11 December 1816; /s/ Sally (x) Kitson. Proven 24 June 1815 by Nehemiah Lundy; A Edmunds J P. Rec 6th October 1817.

p.252 James Martin son of James Martin of Martintown formerly of Ninety Six now Edgefield District to William Flinn, Deed, 23 February 1813, Sixty one Dollars, 15 1/4 acres on Stephens Creek, adj southeast corner of land originally granted unto Hannah Flick for 19 acres, adj bounded by land originally granted unto Christian Buckhalter, Charles Waldrum, plat 7 January 1813 by Stephen Tillman D S. Wit Thos Green, Augustus G Nagel. /s/ James Martin. Justice Charles Hammond certifies relinquishment of dower rights by Elizabeth Martin wife of James Martin, 23 February 1813; /s/ Elizabeth Martin. Proven 23 February 1813 by Thomas Green; Charles Hammond JQ. Rec 6th October 1817.

p.254 Henry Horlbeck of Charleston to George Reiser, planter, Deed, 5 April 1816, Six hundred Dollars, 325 acres being the moiety of a tract laid out to William Stent in July 1773 containing 650 acres on Lick Creek of Clouds Creek in [then] Colleton County, adj N lands surveyed by John Fairchild, E by Silas Carter, S by John Kinslow, Jeremiah Strader, Nathaniel Powel and Peter Mazyck, west by Moses Prescot. Wit John Williams, Minor Wooley. /s/ Henry Horlbeck. Charleston District, Justice Charles Fell certifies relinquishment of dower rights by Margaret B Horlbeck wife of Henry Horlbeck 25 April 1816; /s/ Margaret B Horlbeck. Proven 7 October 1817 by John Williams; Nathan Norris JQ. Rec 7th October 1817.

p.256 John Asbell to Charles Shrirah, Deed, 24 January 1815, One hundred fifty Dollars, 100 acres on Double Branch of Clouds Creek of Saluday River, sd land part of 365 acres granted to Wheaton Pines 2 June 1794 by Gov Wm Moultrie, sd land adj lands of John Stone, Caunous, John Taylor, Elkanah Sawyer; was conveyed from Wheaton Pynes to Jeremiah Gist, from Gixzt to David Williams, from Williams to John Asbell. Wit Elkanah Sawyer, Ralph Sawyer. /s/ John Asbell. Proven 10 December 1815 by Ralph Sawyer; Elkanah Sawyer JQ. [Date recorded not given.]

p.258 Patrick Ardagh to John Pope, Deed, 10 May 1810, One hundred fifty Dollars, equal division of goods of copartnership of John Pope and Patrick Ardagh; John Pope 3 July 1807 received two tracts of land valued at $150 each, of which my part was $150 at close of partnership, now sells undivided 650 acres originally granted to Jesse Pitts on 4 June 1792 by Gov Charles Pinckney situate on Saluda River, one of afsd tracts 200 acres conveyed to Pope and Ardagh 3 January 1804 by Edward Lindsey,

140 acres conveyed to Pope & Ardagh 24 March 1807 by Absalom Rhodes. Wit David Richardson, Jesse Forest. /s/ Pat^k Ardagh. Proven 20 August 1817 by David Richardson; Mumford Perryman J P. Rec 8th October 1817.

p.261 James Ohara to John Pope, Deed, 10 April 1817, Twenty two Dollars fifty cents, 15 acres on Redbank Creek of Little Saluda River, it being part of 650 acres granted to Jesse Pitts 4 June 1792 by Charles Pinckney Esqr, divided from remainder of sd tract, bounded by lands of heirs of Robert Newport, James Oharrow, John Pope, Robert Newports heirs, and is part of land conveyed from William Burdel to James Vaughn and by lines of my father and left by him to me. Wit Abraham Furgurson, Frances Furgurson. /s/ James Ohara. Proven 16 August 1817 by Abram Furgurson; Mumford Perryman J P. Rec 8th October 1817.

p.262 Robert Allen to John Pope, Deed, 17 December 1810, Two hundred fifty Dollars, 225 acres on Beaverdam branch of Clouds Creek of Little Saluda River, it being part of land originally granted to Robert Allen 1 April 1799 by Gov Edward Rutledge which contained 500 acres, now adj land of J J Farchild, Cumbess, line run by Amos Sotcher DS. Wit Sampson Pope, Solomon P Strother. Proven 13 July 1807[?]; Sampson Pope Junr; Sampson Pope J Q. Rec 8th October 1817.

p.264 Solomon Douglas to John Pope, Deed, 15 February 1812, One hundred Dollars, land that my grandfather John Douglas willed me, 150 acres, being the tract whereon I now live on Dobeys branch of Dry Creek of Mine Creek of Little Saluda River, originally granted to my grandfather John Douglas by Gov Thos Pinckney 3 November 1788. Wit James C Douglas, Terry Davis, Caleb (x) Maulden. /s/ Solomon (x) Douglas. Justice Sampson Pope certifies relinquishment of dower rights by Sally Douglas wife of Solomon Douglas, 12 October 1812; /s/ Sally (x) Douglas. Proven 17 August 1817 by James Douglas; Mumford Perryman J P. Rec 8 Oct 1817.

p.267 Nathan Porter and wife Polly Porter of Barnwell District to John Pope, Deed, 8 August 1812, One hundred fifty Dollars, 100 acres originally granted to John Douglas 3 November 1788 by Gov Thos Pinckney, which is all the land that John Douglas willed to Polly Douglas now Porter. Wit Wm H Lewis, James C Douglas, Ch Partin. /s/ Nathan (x) Porter, /s/ Polly (x) Porter. Justice Elijah Watson certifies the relinquishment of dower rights by Polly Porter wife of Nathan Porter, 1 January 1814; /s/ Polly (x) Porter. Proven 17 August 1817 by James C Douglas; Mumford Perryman J P. Rec 8th October 1817.

p.269 Joseph Rhodes to Pope & Ardagh, Deed, 3 April 1807, Seven Dollars paid by John Pope and Patrick Ardagh in Company, 7 acres on Little Saluda adj lands of Brittain Osborn, land formerly Absalom Rhodes and conveyed by him to sd Pope & Ardagh being part of land conveyed to Jesse Pitts 4 June 1792. Wit Henry Pope,

Henry (x) Corley. /s/ Joseph Rhodes. Proven 18 August 1817 by Henry Corley; Mumford Perryman J P. Rec 8th October 1817.

p.271 David Osborne to Absalom Rhodes, Deed, 11 March 1800, One hundred forty five Dollars, 140 acres, being part of 650 acres granted to Jesse Pitts 4 June 1792, sd 140 acres on Little Saluda bounded by lands of Thomas Pitts, Joel Brown, William Burdet, Joseph Rhodes. Wit Henry King, Mary King, Avarilla King. /s/ David Osborne. Proven 16 August 1817 by Henry King; Mumford Perryman J P. Rec 8th October 1817.

p.272 Isaac Sadler to William Abney, Deed, 4 March 1816, Two hundred twenty five Dollars, 150 acres on Big Creek of Little Saluda, it being part of land originally granted to Joel Perdue on 12 October 1792, the same being whereon William Sadler and myself now live, adj lands of William Wilson, William Abney. Wit William H Sadler, Ransom Christian, Wm (x) Steel. /s/ Isaac (IS) Sadler. Plat surveyed 12 March 1793 pr Saml Mays D S, shows also adj and of Jack Perdue. Proven 29 September 1817 by William Steel; James Bell J P. Rec 8th October 1817.

p.274 Francis Walker to William Wimberly, Deed, 1 April 1816, Seventy one Dollars, 63 acres, part of tract granted to Wm Swift, conveyed by his heirs to Francis Walker, adj Bushes Mill Cr. Wit Stephen Fedrick, Joseph Walker. /s/ Francis Walker. Proven 7 October 1817 by Stephen Fredrick; John Loveless JP. Rec 8 Oct 1817.

p.276 Moses Haddocks of Mine Creek to Barratt Traverse, Deed, 13 February 1802, Twenty nine Dollars, 30 acres being part of 600 acres granted to John Mobley 7 October 1793 by Gov Wm Moultrie, near road from Purkins ford to Edgefield Courthouse on Barratt Traverse line. Wit Mumford Perryman, James Dozier. /s/ Moses (H) Haddocks. Proven 8 October 1817 by Mumford Perryman; Thomas Dozier JQ. Rec 9th October 1817.

p.277 Levi Jester to Heron Bush, Deed, 5 February 1816, Four hundred seventeen Dollars, 300 acres on Cuffeetown Creek adj lands of John Moseley, land known as Daniel Rustons old place. Also another tract on Cuffeetown Creek of 150 acres known as Nuetons old place adj 300 acres sold by the sheriff to Jeremiah Hatcher 1st Monday October 1809; so both of these tracts here described was sold by sd sheriff the same time and bought by sd Jester, now conveyed by Jester to Heron Bush. Wit Charles Barronton, William Couch. /s/ Levi Jester. Justice Eldred Simkins certifies relinquishment of dower rights by Rozannah Jester wife of Levi Jester, 6th October 1817; /s/ Rozannah (x) Jester. Proven 5th February 1816 by Charles Barronton; Lewis Holmes J P. Rec 9th October 1817.

p.279 Marshal Martin to Edmund Martin and Lemuel Cantelow, 5 September 1816,

My son Edmund Martin and my son-in-law Lemuel Cantelow has lent me money several times to amount of Two thousand twenty five Dollars, secured by the following property: three negroes, Harry, Jacob, and Winney, ten head cattle, 30 hogs, 4 horses, household and kitchen furnishings and utensils, and all present crop deducting the present overseers part. If Edmund and Lemuel shall be paid before 1 January 1819, the above deed to be of no effect. Wit Isaac (x) Vann, Reuben Newman, Robert Martin. /s/ Marshall Martin. Proven 10 October 1817 by Reuben Newman; M Mims CCP. Rec 10 October 1817.

p.281 Sherley Whatley Senr to his daughter Martha M Palmer, Deed of gift, 3 February 1816, love, Negro wench Lydia and her increase. Wit Wilson M Whatley, Wilson Palmer. /s/ Sherley Whatley Senr. Proven 14 August 1817 by Wilson Palmer; A Edmunds J P. Rec 11 October 1817.

p.282 James Allen to William Sheppard Thomas, Bill of Sale, 26 September 1817, Sixty Dollars, chesnut sorrel mare aged three years. Wit John L Thomas, Minarva Allen. /s/ James Allen. Proven 13 October 1817 by John L Thomas; M Mims CCP. Rec 13th October 1817.

p.280 George S Turner and wife Sarah Turner to Henry Councel Turner, Bill of Sale, 3 March 1817, Two hundred Dollars, goods and chattels. Wit Thos Winn, Allen Burton, Richard Burton. /s/ Sarah (x) Turner, /s/ George S Turner. Proven 6 October 1817 by Allen Burton; Wm Hagens J P. Rec 11 October 1817.

p.284 Elias Minor to John Killcrease, Deed, 10 February 1817, Two hundred Dollars, 28 1/3 acres on Stephens Creek granted to Nicholas Minor being my undivided distributive share of real estate of my father Nicholas Minor, that is to say one fourth part of land granted to sd Nicholas Minor containing 143 acres. Wit John Boyd, Arnold Johnson. /s/ Alias (x) Minor. Proven 22 February 1817 by Arnold Johnson; Thomas Price J P. Rec 13 October 1817.

p.285 Thomas Jennings to John Killcrease, Deed, 30 January 1817, Six hundred thirty three Dollars, 181 acres Stephens Creek, William Cox, Christopher Blair, John Killcrease, containing 183 acres by resurvey, 100 by original grant made to Nicholas Minor, whereon Jennings formerly resided. Wit John Boyd, Jeremiah Jennings. /s/ Thos Jennings. Justice John Lyon certifies relinquishment of dower rights by Elizabeth Jennings wife of Thomas Jennings, 10 May 1817; /s/ Elizabeth Jennings. Proven 7 October 1817 by Jeremiah Jennings; W Jeter QU. Rec 13 Oct 1817.

p.287 Jesse Johnston to Edward Johnson, Deed, 31 July 1812, Fifty Dollars, 40 acres being part of land granted to Levi Cannon on Clouds Creek adj Benjamin Adkins, John Stone. Wit Howell Johnston, Jacob (x) Johnston. /s/ Jesse Johnston.

29

Plat by Thos Cargill D S, Jesse Johnson & Edward Johnson chain carriers, shows adj lands of Jesse Johnson, Ned Johnson. Proven 14 November 1812 by Jacob Johnston; Elijah Watson Q U. Rec 15 October 1817.

p.289   Edward Johnston to Thomas Warren, Deed, 22 January 1817, Fifty Dollars, 40 acres being part of 100 acres that was granted to Levi Cannon on waters of Clouds Creek adj Benjamin Adkins and John Stone. Wit Daniel (AD) Shots, Thomas Warren Jr. /s/ Edward Johnston. Proven 2d July 1817 by Daniel Shots; Peter Lamkin JQU. Rec 15th October 1817.

p.290   Archey Mayson, Elihu Creswell, trustees for Elizabeth Swift late Elizabeth Ball decd and Jonathan Swift and William Swift to James Myers, 22 November 1816, Ninety Dollars, 276 acres on Big horse Creek at Toblers old ford, adj James Myers on all sides. Wit Austin Pollard, James L Mayson. /s/ Aʸ Mayson trustee, /s/ Elihu Creswell trustee, /s/ Jonathan Swift, /s/ William Swift. Justice Thomas Anderson certifies relinquishment of dower by Mary Swift wife of Jonathan Swift and also Mary Ann Swift wife of William Swift, 25 November 1816. /s/ Mary Swift, /s/ Mary Ann Swift. Proven 25 November 1816 by James L Mayson; Thomas Anderson JQ. Rec 16th October 1817.

p.292   Sarah Smith to Isaac Crouch, Deed, 11 October 1814, One hundred fifty Dollars, 150 acres, called Deloaches old place, bounded by Thomas Williams, Wm Butler, estate of Luke Smith. Wit J M Butler, Simpson Wilson. /s/ Sarah Smith. Proven 20 August 1817 by S Wilson; Nathan Norris JQ. Rec 16th October 1817.

p.294   Thomas Williams to Isaac Crouch, Deed, 10 July 1816, Forty two Dollars, 42 acres on Richland Creek adj lands of Henry Tate, afsd Crouch. Wit Henry Tate, Nathaniel Tate. /s/ Thomas Williams. Proven 20 August 1817 by Henry Tate; Nathan Norris JQU. Rec 16th October 1817.

p.298   Joel Hill to Sally Quarles, Deed, 14 October 1817, Two thousand five hundred Dollars, 217 acres on Hardlabor and Stevens Creeks of Savannah River adj lands of Anthony Lowe, afsd Sally Quarles, George Harris and whereon sd Joel Hill now resides. Wit E B Belcher, John Dover. /s/ Joel Hill. Justice John Lyon certifies the relinquishment of dower rights by Anna Hill wife of Joel Hill, 14 October 1817; /s/ Anna Hill. Proven 14 October 1817 by Edmund Belcher; John Lyon QU. Rec 18 October 1817.

p. 297   Nancy Rigel to Stephen Bettis, Bill of Sale, 9 September 1816, Five hundred fifty Dollars, Negro girl Rose. Wit Joshua Monk, Henry Drake, Elijah Bettis. /s/ Nancy (N) Ridgel. Proven 18th October 1817 by Harvey Drake; M Mims CCP. Rec 18th October 1817.

p.298 Lewis Whitley to Thomas Pitts, Deed, 21 October 1816, Two hundred fifty Dollars, 126 acres excepting my mothers life time on it, situated on Halfway Swamp Creek, adj Daniel Rogers, Elizabeth Whitley, Jeremiah Troter. Wit William Pitts, Thomas Pitts Junr. /s/ Lewis Whitley. Proven 20 October 1817 by Thomas Pitts; Mumford Perryman. Rec 20th October 1817.

p.300 John S Glascock to Edmund Bacon and Nicholas Fox, Mortgage, 10 October 1817, Glascock bound to Bacon and Fox in penal sum $2800; condition payment of One thousand two hundred Dollars on or before 5 November next; security: slaves Jack, Phillis, Louisa, Emily, Washington, Nancy, Peter and their future increase. If Glascock pays One thousand four hundred Dollars by 5 Nov, present deed to be of no effect. Wit Eugene Brenan. /s/ John S Glascock. Proven 15 October 1817 by Eugene Brenan; Jesse Blocker JQ. Rec 22d October 1817.

p.302 Daniel Bullock to his son David Bullock, Deed of Gift, 18 October 1817, love, [acreage not stated] on Beaverdam Creek being part of tract surveyed by John Purvis for Alexander Cormack 26 July 1773, now adj John Buckhalter, Smith. Wit John Frazier, J ohn McCarry, Robert Walker. /s/ Daniel Bullock. Proven 3 November 1817 by John Frazier; John Cheatham J P. Rec 3d Novr 1817.

p.304 Daniel Bullock to his son David Bullock, Deed of Gift, 18 October 1817, love, Negro boy Peter and 100 acres on Beaverdam Creek where Long Cain road crosses my spring branch, Beaverdam Creek, adj lines of Shockley, John Buckhalter, William Oliphant. Wit Robert Walker, John Frazier, John McCarry. /s/ Daniel Bullock. Proven 3 Nov 1817 by John Frazier; John Cheatham. Rec 3 Nov 1817.

p.305 Daniel Bullock to his daughter Mary Wootan, Deed of Gift, 18 October 1817, love, 150 acres on Beaverdam Creek, Turkey Creek, being part of tract surveyed by John Purves for Alexander Cormack 6 July 1773, now adj John McCarry and John Buckhalter, my spring branch, Edgefield road, William Welch, Long Cain Road. Not to have possession until after decease of myself and her mother Hannah Bullock; after death of Mary Wootan her children namely Mary Wootan, Martha J Wootan, John R Wootan after all arrive to age twenty one shall have above land. The husband of Mary is never to have any manner of possession nor none of the benefits arising from sd land. My two sons Thomas and David Bullock sd Marys agents. Wit John Frazier, John McCarry, Robert Walker. /s/ Daniel Bullock. Proven 3 November 1817 by John Frazier; John Cheatham J P. Rec 3d November 1817.

p.307 Benjamin W Richards to Ezekiel Morris, Deed of Trust, One Dollar, goods and chattels, land in village of Yorkville, York District, to be held for Wilmouth Richards wife of sd Benjamin W Richards for support of sd Wilmoth and the children which I have by her. Wit Wilson Crane, Adalied C Rackford. /s/ B W Richards.

31

Proven 7th Novr 1817 by Adalied C Rackford; M Mims CCP. Rec 7 Nov 1817.

p.309   William Conolly to Joseph Morris junior, Deed, 7 Agusut 1817, Three hundred Dollars, 100 acres on Halfway Swamp Creek of Saluda River being part of tract originally granted to Thomas Fair, on Charleston Road, adj lands of Jordan Holloway. Wit Joseph (I) Morris, James (x) Martin. /s/ William Conolly. Proven 4 November 1817 by Joseph Morris; Wm Robinson JQ. Rec 20 Nov 1817.

p.311   Absalom Napper and wife Elizabeth Napper to Richard Blalock junior of Barnwell District, Deed, 16 March 1816, One hundred fifty Dollars, 500 acres on Bridge Creek being part of two tracts, one granted to Absalom Napper 5 August 1793, the other granted to Henry Buckhalter 17 July 1793, originally adj Abraham Richardson, adj sd Buckhalter. Wit Richard Blalock Senr, William Ravencroft. /s/ Absalom Napper, /s/ Elizabeth (x) Napper. Proven [day lost in binding] July 1817 by Richard Blalock; John Blalock QU. Rec 21 Novr 1817.

p.313   William Holmes Senr to Anderson Holmes and Jesse Holmes, 21 November 1817, Three hundred Dollars, 227 acres on Cyper Creek of Turkey Creek of Savannah River, adj land surveyed by Godfrey Jones, Robert Stokes, William Morgan, Covington Searls, Thomas Ogilvie. Wit Reubin Homes, Rhydon G Hill. /s/ William Holmes. Justice John Hollingworth certifies relinquishment of dower by Anna Mariah Terry the widow of John Terry decd, 8th De, 1817; /s/ Anna Maria (x) Terry. Proven 21 Nov 1817 by Rhydon G Hill; John Lark JQU. Rec 22 Nov 1817.

p.315   James Permenter and John Permenter of Bork County, Georgia, to John Bush, Deed, 28 October 1817, Two hundred thirty Dollars, part of a tract containing 250 acres, being part granted Elventon Squires represented by his grant for 887 acres, adj lands of Absalom Landerm, Bush, except a mill seat thereon and three acres. Wit Prescot Bush, William Prescott, Bethuley (x) Minter. /s/ James Permenter, /s/ John (x) Permenter. Proven 8 November 1817 by Prescott Bush; Lewis Holmes J P. Rec 26 November 1817.

p.317   John Bush of Barnwell District to West Patterson, Deed, 10 November 1817, Deed, One hundred eighty Dollars, 170 acres being part of land granted to Elventon Squires, adj lands of John Bush, Lewis Holmes, Michael Frish, Rocky Creek, excepting a mill seat and three acres to the mouth of Dark(Duck?) Branch. Wit James Don, John B (x) Bush. /s/ John (B) Bush. Proven 22 November 1817 by James Don; Lewis Holmes JP. Rec 26th Novr 1817.

p.318   Henry Parkman to Lydia Parkman, Deed, 25 November 1817, Henry Parkman was bound unto Serana Parkman in his lifetime in obligation bearing date 7 January 1786 for One hundred pounds sterling, condition that sd Henry Parkman should make

DEED BOOK 34

lawful title to land when he should arrive to age twenty one years, but since that time Serana Parkman has departed his life without such title. Henry Parkman sells unto Lydia Parkman the wife of above Serana Parkman and his children John Parkman, Charles, Charlesey, Lucretia, Izebel, Henry, and Serana Parkman children & heirs of sd Serana Parkman decd 70 acres on Cedar Creek adj Anna McDaniel, John Mims, Daniel Parkman, Joshua Hammond. Wit Richd H Tutt, Danl Parkman. /s/ Henry (x) Parkman. Proven 26 Nov 1817 by Richd H Tutt; M Mims CCP. Rec 26 Nov 1817.

p.321 Elisha Stevens to John Adams, Deed, 4 February 1817, Four hundred Dollars, two plantations, one tract of 110 acres, the other of 60 acres, both originally granted to Ebenetus Stevens on Rockey Creek, former tract adj land claimed by William Partain, Ebenetus Stevens, Kenedas. The latter a grant, adj John Adams, Jacob Green. Wit R H Scott, John Murphey. /s/ Elisha Stevens. Proven 20 October 1817 by R H Scott; Jesse Blocker JQ. Rec 28 Nov 1817.

p.323 Solomon Adams to John Adams Senr, Deed, 13 August 1816, Six hundred Dollars, 220 acres, it being part of 437 acres granted to Elisha Stevens on Rockey Creek of Little Stevens Creek of Savannah River adj lands of Jacob Green, Solomon Adams, David Nicholson, John Aldredges, originally granted to Elisha Stevens. Wit Charles Barronton, John Bolger. /s/ Solomon (x) Adams. Justice Thomas Dozier certifies relinquishment of dower rights by Martha Adams wife of Solomon Adams, 9 September 1817; /s/ Martha (x) Adams. Proven 9 September 1817 by Charles Barronton; Thos Dozier J P. Rec 28 November 1817.

p.325 David Gurganus to Robert Carter, Deed, 14 October 1817, One hundred Dollars, 25 acres on Beaverdam Creek adj lands of Lewis Youngblood, John Hollingsworth, David Gurganus. Wit Jesse Blocker, John Lofton. /s/ David Gurganus. Plat shows adj owners, land originally granted to John Garrett, certified 10 October 1817 [signature lost in binding]. Justice Jesse Blocker certifies relinquishment of dower rights by Rebecca Gurganus wife of David Gurganus, 14 October 1817; /s/ Rebecca (x) Gurganus. Proven 14 October 1817 by John Lofton; Wm Hagens J P. Rec 1st Dec 1817.

p.327 Samuel Mitchell of Wilkinson County, Mississippi Territory, to Eli Morgan, Bill of Sale, 6 May 1817, Three hundred fifty Dollars, my interest in estate of William Glover decd. Wit David Glover, Lloyd Barnett. /s/ Saml Mitchell. Proven 1 December 1817 by David Glover; M Mims CCP. Rec 1 Decr 1817.

p.328 Temple Hargrove to John May, Deed, 29 November 1817, Three hundred Dollars, 100 acres being part of tract originally granted Wm Willison on Little Stevens Creek and Sleepy Creek of Savannah River adj Charles May, Matthews road, Gideon Christian, Stephen Cotney. Wit Ezekiel Crabtree, James (x) Huskey. /s/ Temple (x)

Hargrove. Justice Lewis Miles certifies relinquishment of dower rights by Elay Hargrove wife of Temple Hargrove, 29 November 1817; /s/ Ealy (x) Hargrove. Proven 29 November 1817 by James (H) Huskey. Rec 1 December 1817.

p.331   Conrod Lowery Senr to Shemuel Nicholson, Deed, 6 February 1817, One thousand Dollars, 286 acres by resurvey made by Jesse Blocker D.S. on Rockey and Stevens Creeks of Turkey Creek, Stevens Creek and Savannah River, being part of two bounty tracts originally granted to John Jacob Messersmith and Andrew Markes. Adj Wright Nicholson, Joseph W Nicholson. /s/ Conrod Lowery. Justice Jesse Blocker certifies relinquishment of dower by Elizabeth Lowery wife of Conrod Lowery Senr, 5 April 1817; /s/ Elizabeth (x) Lowery. Proven 20 October 1817 by Wright Nicholson; Jesse Blocker JQU. Rec 1 December 1817.

p.333   Hannah Lesesne of Charleston, widow, extx of will of Isaac Lesesne date 15 November 1792, decd, to Edmund Bacon, attorney, Deed, 20 May 1816,   Will appointed Thomas Winstanly and his son Isaac Lesesne on his arrival at age, executors; Hannah alone qualified, Four hundred Dollars, 500 acres originally granted to afsd Isaac Lesesne decd on 1 June 1775 situate in Granville County on branches of Beaverdam of Stevens Creek of Savannah River, now lying in Edgefield District, adj at time of grant on land of sd Isaac Lesesne, land surveyed by Richland, Daniel Rogers, Simkins, resurvey of Stephen Tillman Esqr 6 September last.Wit George Petre, Sarah Merchant, Mary Lesesne. /s/ H Lesesne. Proven 27 May 1816 by Isaac Lesesne[who said he had signed]; G M Bauetheau JQU. Rec 4 December 1817.

p. 336   Hannah Lesesne of Charleston, extx will of Isaac Lesesne, merchant, decd, to Edmund Bacon, Deed, Four hundred Dollars, land originally granted unto sd Isaac Lesesne 1775 500 acres on branches of Beaverdam Creek of Stevens Creek of Savannah River adj lands of sd Lesesne, Richland, Daniel Rogers, Simkins, [blank] survey by Stephen Tillman 6 September 1815. Wit Eliza Conover, George Petree, Ann Lesesne; G W Bounetheau J Q. /s/ H Lesesne. Plat shows 500 acres crosses by road from Edgefield to Columbia, lands of Eldred Simkins, Logan, John Simkins formerly Danl Rogers, Simkins formerly Youngblood, Edgefield courthouse, academy, certified 6 September 1815; StephenTillman D.S. Proven 15 October 1816 by George Petree; G W Bounetheau JQ. Rec 4 December 1817.

p.339   Christopher Ward to Daniel Ward, Deed, 24 November 1817, One hundred sixty four Dollars, 82 acres originally granted to Young Allen on Redbank and Barnetts Creeks of Saluda River adj lands of Christopher Ward, Mrs Garrett, Pitt. Wit Thomas Norton, Robert H Scott. /s/ Christopher (x) Ward. Proven 1 December 1817 by Thomas Norton; James Adams J P.   Rec 8 December 1817.

p.341   Abner Landrum to Thomas Nordan, Deed, 25 July 1813, Eighty three Dollars fifty cents, 83 ½ acres purchased by me from Saml Walker lying on Beaverdam and Shaws Creeks adj lands of Benjamin Frazier, Widow James, Widow Eddins, Benjamin Darby. Wit James Kerbee, William Close. /s/ Abner Landrum. Proven 29 November 1817 by William Close; Lewis Miles QU. Rec 8ᵗʰ December 1817.

p.342   Thomas Youngblood Senr to Moses Odom, planter, Deed, 29 December 1811, Fifty five Dollars, 25 acres on Ephraims branch of Sleepy Creek of Savannah River, adj lands of William Odom. Wit William Odom, James Odom. /s/ Thomas Youngblood Senr. Justice Dionysius Oliver certifies relinquishment of dower rights by Amy Youngblood wife of Thomas Youngblood Senr, 25 July 1813; /s/ Amy (x) Youngblood. Proven 17 July 1813 by William Odom; Dionysius Oliver JQ. Rec 8ᵗʰ December 1817.

p.344   Isaac Kirkland to Moody Bettis, Bill of Sale, 25 April 1812, Three hundred Dollars, Negro girl Dice and future increase. Wit Francis Bettis. /s/ Isaac Kirkland. Proven 25 April 1812 by Francis Bettis; Matthew Bettis. Rec 8ᵗʰ Decr 1817.

p.345   Zacheriah Smith Brooks to John Riley and Jeremiah Riley exrs of will of William Riley decd, 10 December 1817, Three hundred Dollars, sale not completed before Wm Riley's death, now completed, 100 acres on Big Creek of Saluda River, heirs of James Riley deceased to take only the part to which their father would have been entitled, taking equal share: John Riley, Jeremiah Riley, Enoch Riley, George Riley, Samuel Abney who married Mary Riley, William Marler who married Elizabeth Riley, all heirs in law of William Riley and children of James Riley decd; after death of Amelia King late widow of William Riley, deceased, reserving unto sd Amelia King a life estate in foregoing premises and after her death unto sd heirs.   Wit John Chapman, John Bolger Jr. /s/ Zah S Brooks. Proven 11 Decr 1817 by John Chapman, John Abney JP.   Rec 12ᵗʰ December 1817.

p.347   Buckner Blalock to Ezekiel Perry, Deed, 8 August 1817, Eight hundred fifty Dollars, 500 acres on Bech[Beech?] Creek of Edisto River, being part or all of four tracts conveyed to me, two of them by Benjamin McKinne, and by Joseph McKinne, and the other by Jeffcoat, and runs as follows, adj lands of Mrs Blaylock, Bruce, William Holston Senr, myself, Bell, William Holston Junr, James B[lost in binding], John Blaylock.   Wit Andrew T Perry, Matthias Jones. /s/ Buckner (M) Blalock. Justice Peter Lamkin certifies relinquishment of dower rights by Ann Blalock wife of Buckner Blalock, 18 August 1817; /s/ Ann (x) Blalock. Proven 18 Augt 1817 by Matthias Jones; Peter Lamkin QU. Rec 13ᵗʰ December 1817.

p.350   Henry Parkman to John Bolger, Deed, 2 December 1817, Seven hundred seventy Dollars, 140 acres on Big and Little Mountain Creeks, on the Long Cane Road, it being part of land originally granted to Jefferson Williams in 1768, adj lands of Lark Abney, John Bolger, Jacob Harling, John Coursey. Wit Jesse Blocker, Rhoda Gwyn. /s/ Henry (x) Parkman. Justice Jesse Blocker certifies relinquishment of dower rights by Massa Parkman wife of Henry Parkman, 2 Dec 1817; /s/ Massa (x) Parkman. Proven 18 Aug 1817 by Rhoda Gwyn; Jordan Holloway JP. Rec 15 Dec 1817.

p.352 Lot Smith to Henry Parkman, Deed, 30 July 1814, Three hundred Dollars, 100 acres on Mountain Creek of Turkey Creek of Stephens Creek on Long Cane Road, it being part of land granted to Stephen Smith 11 April 1803 adj lands of John Stedham, John Coursey, Jacob Harling, Little Mountain Creek. Wit Hamlin Freeman, Solomon (~) Ethridge. /s/ Lot Smith. Proven 10 December 1817 by Hamlin Freeman; Jordan Holloway J P. Rec 15 December 1817.

p.353 Jacob Harlen to Henry Parkman, Deed, 26 June 1815, Two hundred Dollars, 50 acres on Mountain Creek adj lands of John Coursey, Jacob Harlen; Henry Parkman to suffer Michael Harlen who at this time living on afsd land to continue on sd land four years from year 1813. Wit Dabney Palmer, John Bolger. /s/ Jacob Harlen. Proven 10 December 1817 by John Bolger; Jordan Holloway J P. Rec 15 Dec 1817.

p.354 Gosper Donaldson to Avory Gunnels, Deed, 15 December 1817, Three hundred ten Dollars, 144 acres, it being the plantation whereon my father David Donaldson now lives, adj lands of Sampson Butler, Augustus G Nagel, sd Avery Gunnels, [blank] Gaulman. Richd H Tutt, Jefferson Nichols. /s/ Gasper Donaldson. Plat shows resurvey 19 August 1817 by John Frazier D S, land granted to John Varnon, branch of Log Creek, Columbia Road. Proven 15 December 1817 by Jefferson Nichols; M Mims CCP. Rec 15 December 1817.

p.357 Robert Key to John McCain, Deed, 7 November 1813, Two hundred Dollars, 110 acres on Wine Creek of Turkey Creek of Stephens Creek of Savannah River, adj lands of Charles Nix, Samuel Stalnaker. Wit W D Cooper, John Terry Junr. /s/ Robert Key. Proven 24 November 1817 by William D Cooper; John Hollingsworth JQ. Rec 19th December 1817.

p.358 Gabriel Blair to William Cox, Deed, 29 November 1817, Three hundred fifty Dollars, 205 acres being part of tract granted to William Coursey on Stephens Creek adj lands of sd Wm Cox, William Holmes, Jonas Hom[lost in binding], Thomas Killcrease, plat by John Boyd DS. Wit Christopher Blair, Arnold Johnston, John (x) Harris. /s/ Gabriel (g) Blair. Justice Charles Hammond certifies relinquishment of dower rights by Barsheba Hill mother of Gabriel Blair, 4 December 1817; /s/ Barsheba Hill. Justice Charles Hammond certifies relinquishment of dower rights by Rebecca Blair, 4 December 1817; /s/ Rebecca (x) Blair. Proven 4 December 1817 by Christopher Blair; Charles Hammond JQ. Rec 19 December 1817.

DEED BOOK 34

p.361 Joseph Nunn to G Nunn, Deed, 12 February 1817, Five hundred Dollars, 150 acres being part of the land I now live on, Cedar Branch, adj lands of John Pow, James Hart, line by M Coats D S. Wit Allen Robinson, James Wolf, Phillip Nunn. /s/ Joseph Nunn. Proven 4 July 1817 by James Wolf; John Lark JQU. Rec 20 December 1817.

p.363 William Dicks of Springfield near Orangeburgh, Orangeburgh District, physician, to David Meyers of Barnwell District, planter, 24 November 1817, One hundred eighty five Dollars, undivided fifty acre lot being one third of 150 acres known by name of the Oak and Hickory lying above Hollow Creek in Edgefield District, formerly property of John Dicks Esqr from whom my father Thomas Dicks acquired right thereto. Wit Jonathan Meyer, Benjamin Cutter, L Griffis. /s/ Wm Dicks. Proven 25 November 1817 by Jonathan Meyer; A Patterson JP. Rec 23 December 1817.

p.364 Sterling Harrison to Richard Hardy, Deed, 23 January 1817, One thousand one hundred eighty Dollars, [acreage not stated] on Bird Branch of Stevens Creek.Wit Joseph Cunningham, Thos Hardy. /s/ Sterling Harrison. Justice John Lyon certifies relinquishment of dower rights by Louisa Harrison wife of Sterling Harrison, 7 October 1817; /s/ Louisa Harrison. Plat shows 236 acres on Straight and Troublesome Branches of Bird Creek adj lands of Charles Nix, Nicholas Griffin, Mrs Letcher, John Burress, resurveyed 16 January 1817 by E Settle D S. Justice John Lyon certifies relinquishment of dower rights by Agness Letcher, 7 October 1817; /s/ Agness (x) Letcher. Proven 8 October 1817 by Joseph Cunningham; Thomas Price J P. Rec 27th December 1817.

p.367 David Williams of Edgefield District and John Williams to George Coleman of Woodford County, Kentucky, heirs of Paul Williams deceased, Deed, Seven hundred twenty six Dollars, [acreage not stated] on Hardlabor Creek of Stephens Creek. Wit Daniel White, Harman P Cosper. /s/ John Williams, /s/ David Williams. Plat shows 121 acres adj lands of Buffington, Perrin, Sullivan, Martin, resurveyed 21 December 1816 by E Settle, D S. Proven 8 August 1817 by Harman P Cosper; John Lyon Q U. Rec 30th December 1817.

p.369 John Kilcrease to Basheba Hill, Deed, 10 December 1817, One hundred fifty Dollars, 150 acres, it being part of two tracts on Stevens Creek. Wit Charles Hammond, John Martin. /s/ John Kilcrease. Justice Charles Hammond certifies the relinquishment of dower rights by Mary Kilcrease wife of John Kilcrease, 10 December 1817; /s/ Mary (x) Kilcrease. Proven 31 December 1817 by Charles Hammond; M Mims CCP. Rec 31 December 1817.

p.372 John Randall Senr to Elijah T Summers of Newberry District, Deed, Barnwell

37

District, 10 November 1817, Three hundred Dollars, 263 acres being part of 630 acres originally granted to sd John Randall Senr, on the waters of Swams horse[?] and Savannah River adj lands of Abraham Richardson, Abraham Pond. Wit Sarah (x) Blalock. Wm W Williams. /s/ John Rongass(sic). Proven 20 December 1817 by Wm W Williams; John Blalock QU. Rec Jany 3d 1818.

p.373   Sarah Hagood to her son-in-law James Ambler, Deed, 25 December 1817, One Dollar and love of her daughter Susan, Negro man Jacob about forty years old, reserve to myself the service of sd slave during my natural life. Wit John M Moore, William Bostick. /s/ Sarah Hagood. Proven 3 January 1818 by William Bostick; M Mims CCP. Rec 3d January 1818.

p.374   Sarah Hagood to her son-in-law Matthew Ray, Deed, 25 December 1817, One Dollar & love of her daughter Halley, Negro wench named Tab about forty four years of age, one feather bed, one chest of drawers and six Windsor chairs, reserving possession during my natural life. Wit John M Moore, William Bostick. /s/ Sarah Hagood. Proven 3 January 1818 by William Bostick; M Mims CCP. Rec 3 Jan 1818.

p.376   Thomas Hunt Esqr, Commissioner of Court of Equity at Charleston, to Jonathan Glanton, Deed, 26 November 1817; George Peloquin Cosserat and Jane Graham Haworth his wife and John Dawson trustee of sd George Peloquin and Jane his wife, filed petition to sell trust property; decree--property to be sold at public auction; sold to Jonathan Glanton, One thousand fifty Dollars; 1000 acres on branches of Turkey Creek in Ninety Six District in Granville County; also 600 acres on Cyper Creek. Wit Sampson Butler, John S Jeter. /s/ Thomas Hunt. Plat A, precept from John Bremar Esqr D S Genl, laid out unto James Carson 1000 acres on Turkey Creek, adj land of James Gray, James Carson, James Simpson, surveyed 18 August 1772; Wm Goode D S. Plat B laid out unto James Carson 600 acres in Granville County adj land of John Rantowle; 15 July 1772; /s/ John Purves D S. Certification of plats, Columbia 26 November 1817 by Josiah Killgore Surv Genl. Proven 5 January 1818 by Sampson Butler; Jesse Blocker JQ. Rec 5th January 1818.

p.381   Thomas Hunt, Commissioner of Court of Equity, Charleston, to Shepherd Spencer, Deed, 26 November 1817, George Peloquin Cossserat and Jane Graham Howarth, and John Dawson trustee of George and Jane filed petition to sell; land sold to highest bidder for Four hundred fifty Dollars, 500 acres on Pike Creek of Turkey Creek in Ninety Six District, Granville County, adj land of John Purves, William Levingston, land granted to William Coursey. Wit Sampson Butler, John S Jeter. /s/ Thomas Hunt. Plat shows adj land of William Coursey, surveyed 31 October 1772 by John Purves D S; certified Columbia 26 Novr 1817 by Josiah Kilgore Surv genl. Proven 5 January 1818 by Sampson Butler; Jesse Blocker JQ. Rec 5 January 1818.

DEED BOOK 34

p.385 Moses Spivey to Mary Sharpton, Receipt, 24 November 1817, Fifty Dollars from Mary for land on Gunnels Creek, Cane patch Branch, adj land of Redocks Busey [acreage not stated]. Wit Hezekiah Lunday, Tapley B Spivy. /s/ Moses Spivy. Proven 26 November 1817 by Hezekiah Lunday; A Edmunds J P. Rec 5 Jan 1818.

p.386 Mary Sharpton to Zadock Bussey, 26 November 1817, One hundred eighty Dollars, 40 acres on Gunnels Creek of Stephens Creek adj sd Bussey, being part of land granted to John Briggs 1806. Wit Hezekiah Lunday, Sally (x) Edmunds. /s/ Mary (x) Sharpton. Proven 26 November 1817 by Hezekiah Lunday; A Edmunds J P. Rec 5th January 1818.

p.388 Susannah Burt, Aquila Miles, Lewis Miles, and Permelia Goode to John Moore, Deed, 18 October 1817, Two hundred fifty Dollars, undivided five sixths of land formerly belonging to Aquila Miles Senr, decd, 75 1/4 acres on Horns Creek adj lands of Robert Lang Senr, James Moseley, sd John Moore. Wit Daniel White. /s/ Susannah Burt, /s/ Permelia Goode, /s/ Aquila (x) Miles, /s/ Lewis Miles. Justice Thomas Dozier certifies relinquishment of dower right by Sally Miles wife of Lewis Miles, [blank] October 1817; /s/ Sally Miles. Proven 18 October 1817 by Daniel White; Lewis Miles JQ. Rec 5th January 1818.

p.390 Joshua Key and Edward Collier to John Moore, Deed, 25 June 1817, Fifty Dollars, undivided one sixth part of land formerly belonging to Aquila Miles Senr decd, 75 1/4 acres lying on Horns Creek adj lands of Robert Lang Sr, James Moseley, sd John Moore. Wit James M Scott, John Pursell. Justice Thomas Key certifies relinquishment of dower rights by Martha Key wife of Joshua Key and Lucy Collier wife of Edward Collier, 26 June 1817; /s/ Louisa Collier, /s/ Martha Key. Proven 8 December 1817 by John Pursell; Thomas Key JQ. Rec 5th January 1818.

p.392 Levi McDaniel, planter, to Jonas Jenkins, Deed, 16 February 1813, One hundred fifty Dollars, 100 acres being part of 761 acres originally granted unto John Thurmond deceased by Gov William Moultrie 2 December 1793; by Phillip Thurmond exr of John Thurmond conveyed to Edward Homes and from Edward conveyed to sd Levi McDaniel, on Big Branch adj lands of Riddelle, John Dorlton, widow Wetherford, Lewis Clark. Wit Edward Homes, Chs Coursey. /s/ Levi McDaniel. Proven 27 March 1814 by Edward Homes; D Crawford JP. Rec 5 Jan 1818.

p.394 Edward Homes, planter, to Levi McDaniel, Deed, 16 January 1813, One hundred Dollars, 100 acres being part of 761 acres originally granted to John Thurmond decd by Gov Wm Moultrie 2 December 1793; by Phillip Thurmond exr estate of John Thurmond decd conveyed to sd Edward Homes, sd 100 acres on Big Branch, adj Riddle, John Dorton, widow Weatherford, Lewis Clark.Wit Wm Coursey, and Lewis Clark. /s/ Edward Homes. Proven 3d February 1814 by Lewis Clark;

39

David Crawford J P. Rec 5th January 1818.

p.396   Polly Doolittle, extx of Samuel Doolittle Junr decd, to Benjamin Tutt, Deed, 10 November 1817, Six hundred twenty one Dollars, 100 acres on Lick Fork of Hornes Creek adj lands of Benjamin Martin, John Jones, Joshua Key, sd Benjamin Tutt, and estate of Samuel Doolittle; it being part of 299 ½ acres. Wit Thos Murrah Senr, John (x) Jones, Roger M Williams. /s/ Polly (x) Doolittle extx.   Plat certified 11 September 1817 by Stephen Tillman D S, 100 acres being part of two surveys each originally granted to William Morgan, first for 198 acres, second for 7[lost in binding], former on 1 May 1786, latter on 5 February 1787, in neighbourhood of Martintown; shows adj lands of Beckham formerly Russell, Benj Martin formerly Dahl Marquis, Joshua Key formerly Augustus Miles, John Jones formerly Beckhams. Proven 22 November 1817 by John Jones; Chs Hammond JQ. Rec 5 Jan 1818.

p.399   Jeremiah Roberts of Abbeville District to Benjamin Tutt, Deed, 7 January 1817, Five hundred Dollars, 100 acres on Lick fork branch of Horns Creek being part of land originally granted to William Moore adj lands of Benjamin Martin, Samuel Doolittle, heirs of James Thomas, John Jones. Wit John Sullivan, Samuel Quarels. /s/ Jeremiah Roberts.   Justice Charles Hammond certifies relinquishment of dower rights by Nancy Roberts wife of Jeremiah Roberts, 7 January 1817; /s/ Nancy (x) Roberts. Proven 7 January 1817 by John Sullivan; Charles Hammond JQU. Rec 5 Jan 1818.

p.401   Daniel Hardy to John Hardy, Deed, 9 December 1817, One thousand nine hundred eighty Dollars, 132 acres, it being part of land granted to Evan Morgan and John Hardy decd, on Stevens Creek.   Wit Robert Hardy, Henry Briggs. /s/ Daniel Hardy. Justice Charles Bussey certifies relinquishment of dower rights by Mary Hardy wife of Daniel Hardy, 16 December 1817; /s/ Mary Hardy.   Proven 16 December 1817 by Robert Hardy; Charles Bussey J P. Rec 5th January 1818.

p.403   Tandy M Key to Lewis Martin, Deed, 24 June 1816, Four hundred Dollars, 282 acres, it being part of land originally granted to William Key, on Wine Creek of Turkey Creek of Stevens Creek near the long pond, adj lands of Lewis Martin, John Canfield, sd Tandy M Key. Wit William Martin, Stephen Thomas. /s/ Tandy M Key. Proven 2 May 1817 by Stephen Thomas; Thomas Price JP. Rec 5th January 1818.

p.406   John Canfield to Lewis Martin, Deed, 24 June 1806, One hundred Dollars, 118 ½ acres, being part of land originally granted to John Canfield Senr on Wine Creek of Turkey Creek of Stevens Creek, the 118 ½ acres adj Seigh[lost in binding], Tandy M Key, Lewis Martin. Wit Stephen Thomas, Tandy M Key. /s/ John Canfield. Proven 2 May 1817 by Stephen Thomas; Thomas Price JP. Rec 5th January 1818.

p.407   Samuel White of Pennsylvania to Thomas Green, Deed, 2 January 1818, Four hundred fifty Dollars, 150 acres being part of 250 acres granted to John Rutledge esqr 6 December 1784, on Crooked Run adj land James Coursey, the 150 acres was conveyed to me by James White 5 February 1810; also 42 acres it being part of 148 acres granted to John Morris 5 September 1791 adj Age Garner, crossing the Augusta road, crossing Charleston road. Wit Clement Green, John Ingram, Henry W Barns. /s/ Samuel (x) White. Proven 2 January 1818 by John Ingram; John R Bartee JP. Rec 5th January 1818.

p.410   David Still of Mississippi Territory to Shemuel Nicholson, Deed, 28 February 1817, Mississippi Territory, Madison County, Six hundred Dollars, 134 acres on Stevens and Sleepy Creeks of Savannah River, being part of tract originally granted to Valentine Kunn, adj Martin Outs, Timmerman, estate of Bartlett Bledsoe, spring branch. Wit John Eddins, Joseph Adams, Benjamin Still. /s/ David Still, /s/ Cakthran (x) Still. Mississippi Territory, acknowledged by David Still, Cakthran Still wife of David Still relinquishes dower rights, 4 March 1817; Obadiah Jones, Judge of county afsd. Mississippi Territory, Madison County, William H Winston clark of county court certifies that Obadiah Jones is a judge of the superior court, 4 March 1817; W H Winston, Clerk. Proven Edgefield District, 5 January 1818 by Benjamin Still; Mumford Perryman J P. Rec 7th January 1818.

p.412   Lewis Whatley to Wm Johnston, George Warren Cross, James Jervey, trustees of Eliza Wigfall relict of Levi Durand Wigfall for term of her natural life and after her death in trust for benefit of Eliza Wigfall, James Hampden Wigfall, Arthur Wigfall, and Lewis Tresvant Wigfall children of Eliza Wigfall by her late husband Levi D Wigfall, Deed, 5 December 1817, Six hundred Dollars, 53 1/4 acres on Chavers Creek adj lands of William Glover Junr, Wm Boswell, Wm Glover Senr. Wit George Getzen, Eliza Wigfall Junr. /s/ Lewis Whatley. Justice Thomas Key certifies relinquishment of dower rights by Nancey Whatley wife of Lewis Whatley, 5 Decr 1817, /s/ Nancy Whatley. Proven 5 December 1817 by George Getzen; Thomas Key JQ. Rec 6th January 1818.

p.415   Mary Abney to John Inlow, Mortgage, 26 December 1817, three young Negroes: Sarah, Sulta, Susan, in consideration of making lawful title to 100 acres; Condition if Mary Abney make title to John Inlow of sd land, mortgage will be null & void. Wit Jno G Peterson, Zachariah Abney, James Carson. /s/ Mary (x) Abney. Proven 13 January 1818 by John G Peterson; John Abney J P. Rec 13 Jan 1818.

p.416   Mary Abney to William Coleman, Mortgage, 31 December 1817, three young Negroes: Charlotte, Benjamin, Charles, Mary to make legal title to Wm Coleman to 169 acres; when title be delivered by widow Mary Abney by whom the deed is conveyed and her legal heirs, Thos, Elizabeth, Maria, and Emily Abney, the above mortgage to be null and void. Wit John G Peterson, Mark Black, William Abney. /s/

41

Mary (x) Abney. Proven 10 January 1818 by John G Peterson; John Abney J P. Recorded 13th Jany 1818.

p.417   Richard Andrew Rapley, Commissioner Court of Equity for Ninety Six District, to Charles Nix, Deed, 7 January 1811; Joseph Hackney and wife Polly, John Downey and wife Sally, John Cook by his guardian Joseph Hackney, Caroline Cook by her guardian John Downey, Martha and Amanda by their guardian Charles Martin, and Charles Martin and wife Prudence, which Prudence was widow of West Cook decd, and which Polly Hackney, Sally Downey, John Cook, Caroline Cook, Martha Cook, Amanda Cook are the children of sd West Cook decd, 12 June last petitioned for partition; issued; and return as follows: 913 acres on Savannah River whereon Paces Ferry is established, two tracts making 560 acres, one tract of 170 acres below Lamars ferry known as the Keddingfield tract, 390 acres known as Hatchers tract, 200 acres on Savannah River, 620 acres on Stevens Creek known as Scotts big survey; also 638 acres of pine land; land to be sold at public auction; sold 621 acres to Charles Nix for Three hundred Dollars. Wit Edmund Bacon, John A Hoffer. /s/ R A Rapley comr. Proven 13 January 1818 by Edmund Bacon; M Mims CCP. Rec 15 Jany 1818.

p.421   Sheriff Jeremiah Hatcher to Shemuel Nicholson, Sheriffs Titles, 5 January 1818, at writ of Partition on application of Wiley K Goodwin and others representatives of Bartlett Bledsoe decd for purpose of dividing real estate of sd Bledsoe, 111 acres in fork of Stevens and Sleepy Creeks adj Jacob Timmerman and sd Shemuel Nicholson sold at public auction to high bidder Shemuel Nicholson for Seven hundred Dollars;   Wit Richard H Tutt, James Gray. /s/ Jer Hatcher SED. Proven 15th January 1818 by Richd H Tutt; M Mims CCP. Rec 15 Jan 1818.

p.423   Joseph Roberson to Sandford Roberson, Deed, 8 September 1816, One thousand Dollars, on Catfish Creek of Savannah River being part of two tracts, one originally granted to Elisha Roberson, the other to Colonel Scott and thence to William Robertson Senr decd, willed to Joseph Roberson son of sd deceased, adj lands of John Searles, Nathan Falkner, Joseph Cunningham, William Roberson, crossing Long Cane Road at pond between this conveyance and Thomas Price's field. Wit William Robinson, Samuel Cartledge. /s/ Joseph (x) Robinson. Justice John Lyon certifies relinquishment of dower rights by Betsy Roberson wife of Joseph Roberson, 17 October 1816; /s/ Betsy (x) Robertson. Proven 28 September 1816 by William Roberson; Thomas Price. Rec 16 January 1818.

p.426   Willis Odom to William Ellison, Mortgage, [blank] January 1817, One hundred Dollars, 102 acres on Little Stevens Creek adj Stevens Creek Meeting House with the mill thereon; Provided If Willis Odom shall pay William Ellison Two thousand Dollars [details here omitted] this deed to be utterly void or else to remain in full force. Wit Jacob Adams, William Moore. /s/ Willis (x) Odom. Proven 16 Jan

1818 by Jacob Adams; James Adams J P. Rec 19 Jany 1818.

p.428   Martha Jenkins to John Jenkins of Columbia County, Georgia, 20 January 1818, Forty Dollars, my distributive share of land belonging to estate of my Father, Samuel Jenkins, decd, also my distributive share of the real estate of my brother James Jenkins deceased, all of which remains undivided at this time, situate in fork of Big and Little Turkey Creeks of Stevens Creek and Savannah River adj lands of Young Allen, Col Benjamin Frazier, Arthur Simkins Esqr, John Arledge Junr. Wit William A Turner, Fred White. /s/ Martha (x) Jenkins. Proven 20 January 1818 by Fred White; Jesse Blocker JQ. Rec 21 January 1818.

p.429   Sarah Jenkins to John Jenkins of Columbia County, Georgia, Deed, 20 January 1818, Forty Dollars my share of lands of the estate of my father Samuel Jenkins decd; also my share of real estate of my brother James Jenkins decd, in forks of Big and Little Turkey Creeks, adj lands of Young Allen, Col Benjn Frazier, Arthur Simkins Esqr, John Arledge Junr. Wit Fred White, Wm A Turner. /s/ Sarah Jenkins. Proven by Frederick White, 20 Jan 1818; Jesse Blocker JQ. Rec 21st January 1818.

p.431   Esther Jenkins & Ann Jenkins to John Jenkins, Deed, 20 January 1818, Whereas Samuel Jenkins was seized of two tracts of 100 acres each; also of part of 100 acres bought by sd Samuel Jenkins of Robert Burton, quantity not known, one of which tracts of 100 acres each was sold by John Arledge to sd Samuel and is situate on Turkey Creek adj lands of Young Allen, the other was originally granted to Margaret Breunan and was sold by John Harlen and Jacob Harlen to Samuel Jenkins adj tract of John Arledge the part of 100 acres by Robert Burton to sd Samuel was granted to sd Robert; sd Samuel departed this life on 7 March 1804 intestate leaving his widow Esther Jenkins and ten children, whereof Ann Jenkins is one, entitled to share of sd land, Whereas James Jenkins one of the children of sd Samuel afterward departed this life intestate, unmarried and without issue whereby sd Esther and surviving brothers and sisters of sd James became entitled to their distributive shares of his estate, Now for Eighty Dollars paid by John Jenkins, one of the children of sd Samuel, all their several shares of same: one third of undivided distributive share of sd Esther and one tenth of two thirds of share of sd Ann, also two ninths of one tenth of share of sd Esther and Ann of the share of sd James deceased. Wit William A Turner, Fred White. /s/ Esther (x) Jenkins, /s/ Ann (x) Jenkins. Proven 20 January 1818 by Frederick White; Jesse Blocker JQ. Rec 21 January 1818.

p.433 Caleb Maulden to James Rustin, Deed, 9 February 1815, Three hundred fifty Dollars, 150 acres, part of tract originally granted to John Douglass and part of land originally granted to Aaron Weaver, on Mine Creek of Little Saluda River adj lands of James Douglass, Abel Pearson, Benjamin Watson, Luke Smith, John Weaver. Wit Sampson Pope Jnr, Alsey Hudson. /s/ Caleb (x) Maulden. Justice John Lark certifies relinquishment of dower rights by Judith Maulden, 20 April 1816; /s/ Judith (x) Maulden. Proven 25 May 1816 by Alsey Hudson; Spear Price J P. Rec 22 Jan 1818.

p.435 Edward Christian to Matthew Mims, Deed, 15 January 1818, Eleven hundred Dollars, 123 acres whereon I now live on Cedar Creek, being land purchased of Willis Burt, adj lands of Benjamin Harrison, Jesse Bettis, John Blackburn. Wit James Gray, Theophilus Johnson. /s/ Edward (x) Christian. Justice John Hollingworth certifies relinquishment of dower rights by Martha Christian wife of Edward Christian, 17 January 1818; /s/ Martha Christian. Proven 23 January 1818 by James Gray; Wm Hagens J P. Rec 23rd Jan 1818.

p.438 Benjamin Lindsey to Jonas Holmes, Deed, 5 January 1818, Twelve hundred Dollars, 100 and 250 adj acres Stevens Creek originally granted to Arther Gilchrist, conveyed by Gilchrist and wife by L&R 17 & 18 April 1791 to James Scott, by Scott & wife conveyed to Samuel Scott, from him to Charles Franklin, from Franklin to Sheriff Samson Butler to Benjn Lindsey 17 June 1804. Wit Mark McHan, W Coursey. Justice Matthew Mims certifies relinquishment of dower by Elizabeth Lindsey wife of Benjamin Lindsey, 23 January 1818; /s/ Elizabeth (x) Lindsey. Proven 23 January 1818 by William Coursey Esqr; M Mims CCP. Rec 23rd January 1818.

p.440 Jesse Taylor to Abram Carmichal of Newberry District, Deed, 26 January 1814, Three hundred fifty Dollars, part of 400 acres on Waistcoat Creek of Savannah River being part of 434 acres originally granted to Zephanah Nobles, conveyed to Jesse Taylor 5 October 1793 by Gov Wm Moultrie. Wit Moses Jacobs, Abram Young. /s/ Jesse (X) Taylor. Proven 12 September 1814 by Abram Young; Wm Sumers JQ. Rec 26th January 1818.

p.441 Jared E Groce to James Coleman, Deed, 1 January 1818, Two thousand five hundred Dollars, 425 acres on Henleys and Ninety six Creeks of Saluda River being SW part of tract late property of Tolaver Bostick decd adj lands of Thomas Chiles, Lyttelton Myrick, heirs of A G Dozier, Jonathan Moore, Isaac Bunting, and land laid off by Thomas Chiles, Jonathan Moore, William P Brooks commissioners for that purpose. Wit Willis Bostick, Talº Levingston, B F Whitner. /s/ Jared E Groce. Proven 24 January 1818 by Willis Bostick; Nathan Lipscomb JQ. Rec 26 Jan 1818.

p.443 Lark Abney to John Bolger, Relinquishment of Claim, 3 December 1817, Five hundred sixty Dollars thirty nine Cents paid by John Bolger, relinquish my title to 143 acres conveyed conditionally to me by Henry Parkman on Big and Little Mountain Creeks 7 Jany 1817. Wit Joseph Rareden, Nancey Rareden. /s/ Lark Abney. Proven 26 December 1817 by Joseph Rareden; Jordan Holloway JP. Rec 26 January 1818.

p.444 Sheriff Jeremiah Hatcher to Jared E Groce, 7 October 1817, at suits of John

Campbell, James Coleman and Franklin Scott against executors of Tolaver Bostick, land to be sold at public auction; struck off to Jared E Groce, Three thousand nine hundred two Dollars, 600 acres on Ninety six Creek adj lands of Thomas Chiles Esqr, Jonathan Moore, James Coleman. Wit Wm Lomax, Lyttleton Myrick, Jas Coleman. /s/ J Hatcher S E D. Proven 1 Jany 1818 by Lyttleton Myrick; Catlett Conner JP. Rec 26 January 1818.

p.445 Davis Williams to Jacob Harlin, Deed, 2 July 1808, Forty one Dollars, 41 acres on Mountain Creek of Stevens Creek of Savannah River it being part of land granted to Asbel Taylor by Davis Williams adj Michael Harlin, John Coursey, Jacob Harlin. Wit Jesse Blocker, John Mitchell, James Maulden. /s/ Daˢ Williams. Proven 26ᵗʰ December 1817 by John Mitchell; Jordan Holloway JP. Rec 26 January 1818.

p.447 Charles Jones to William Shannon, 9 December 1817, Two hundred fifty Dollars, 50 acres on small branch of Savannah River being part of land originally granted to James Clark and conveyed to Charles Jones. Wit W H Nixon, James Tomkins. /s/ Charles Jones. Plat surveyed 9 December 1817 by James Tomkins D S shows adj lands of Daniel Colvin, Charles Jones, and William Shannon. Justice Wm Burnside certifies relinquishment of dower rights by Nancey Jones wife of Charles Jones, 1 January 1818; /s/ Nancey Jones. Proven 10 December 1817 by James Tomkins; Thomas Price JP. Rec 29ᵗʰ January 1818.

p.450 James C Dozier to Aaron Weeks, 21 September 1816, Three hundred Dollars, 165 acres on branch of Rockey Creek of Stevens Creek adj lands of James Wright, Charles Barronton, James Coats. Wit John Arledge Junr, Samuel W Lockhart. /s/ James C Dozier. Proven 20ᵗʰ October 1817 by John (I) Arledge Junr; Jesse Blocker JP. Rec 29ᵗʰ January 1818.

p.451 Samuel Devall to John Coughorn, Quit Claim, 14 March 1816, I relinquish my right to Range Shoals land, all but the land in dispute between myself and Samuel Tomkins. Wit John Harris, Coleman Squires. /s/ Samuel Devall. Proven 21 January 1818 by Coleman Squires; Garrett Freeman JP. Rec 29ᵗʰ January 1818.

p.452 Samuel Wardleworth of Edisto, millwright, to James Nicholson of Charleston, Mortgage, condition for payment Wardleworth to pay Eight thousand six hundred Dollars with interest to Nicholson according to Bond; security, Negroes Limerick, Cipis, Bristol, Sandy, Mick (carpenters), London (blacksmith) Gower (bracklayer), Belfast, Pompy, Tony, and Farmer (fieldhands), provided if full sum be paid, these presents to be utterly void. Wit Simon Maris, B Marston. /s/ Samuel Wardleworth. Proven 11 Sept 1815 by B Marston; Saml Burger DS. Rec Charleston by Sam Burger Rec 29ᵗʰ January 1818.

p.455 Daniel Baugh of Putnam County, Georgia, to Joseph Hogh of Edgefield Dist,
Deed, 13 September 1811, Nine hundred fifty Dollars, 611 acres on Rockey Creek
of Turkey Creek of Stevens Creek, being part of 1000 acres granted to James Simson
15 May 1772. Wit Stewart Minor, William (x) Mann. /s/ Daniel Baugh. Proven 26
December 1818 by Stewart Minor; John Lyon JQ. Rec 2 February 1818.

p.456 John Mims to Drury Mims Junr, Deed, 19 January 1818, One hundred thirty
seven Dollars seventy Cents, 15 3/4 acres near Ray[lost in binding]meck, line near
present dwelling of Drury Mims Senr and John Mims and adj lands of Lee Blackburn.
Wit Daniel Parkman, Briton Mims. /s/ John Mims. Proven 2 February 1818 by Daniel
Parkman; M Mims C C P. Rec 2 February 1818.

p.458 Charles C Mayson of Abbeville District to Mark Travers, Deed, 2 June 1817,
Three hundred Dollars, 334 acres on waters of Penn Creek of Little Saluda being part
of two tracts granted originally to Revd Samuel Ha[lost in binding] in 1773 and 1775,
adj lands of [blank] Cockroft, Young Allen, Samuel Hart, Mobly. Wit John Sale, A
Allen. /s/ Chs C Mayson. Plat surveyed 27 February 1817 by Willis Mayson D S
shows adj land of Smallwood Travers. Proven 2 February 1818 by Aron Allen;
Mumford Perryman J P. Rec 2 February 1818.

p.460 Benjamin Medlock to Samuel Medlock, Deed, 12 November 1817, Four
hundred Fifty Dollars, 200 acres where sd Benjamin Medlock now lives adj sd Samuel
Medlock known as Suttons old Line, Hallbacks line. Wit Phinehas Sutton, Nancy (x)
Sutton. /s/ Benjamin Medlock. Proven 12 November 1817 by Phinehas Sutton; Lewis
Holmes J P. Rec 2 February 1818.

p.462 Hezekiah Palmer & Elizabeth Palmer formerly Elizabeth Roberts both of
Green County, Georgia, to Jonathan Limbecker, 30 December 1817, Six hundred
Dollars, one third part of plantation of 137 acres on Dry Creek of Horns Creek adj
lands of Mrs Sullivan, John Moore, Frederick Whatley, lands of sd Jonathan
Limbecker and known as Absalom Roberts land whereon sd Roberts died. Wit
William Pursell, Wilson M Whatley, Charles B Limbecker. /s/ Hezekiah Palmer. /s/
Elizabeth (x) Palmer. Justice Charles Hammond certifies relinquishment of dower
rights by Elizabeth Palmer wife of Hezekiah Palmer; /s/ Elizabeth (x) Palmer. Proven
2 Jany 1818 by William Pursell; Charles Hammond J Q. Rec 2d February 1818.

p.465 Shurley Whatley Senr to Charles Limbecker, Deed, 14 November 1817, One
hundred twenty five Dollars, 100 acres on branches of Stevens Creek adj lands of
Jonathan Limbecker, Holloway, Frederick Whatley, dividing line betwixt Sherly
Whatley Senr and Frederick Whatley. Wit William Pursell, Thos L Swillivan, Joseph
Mealing. /s/ Shurley Whatley Senr. Proven 2 January 1818 by William Pursell;
Charles Hammond JQ. Rec 2 February 1818.

p.466   William W Fell to James Bilbo, Deed, 1 January 1818, Three thousand five hundred Dollars, 450 acres on Buckhalters and Dry Creeks, adj lands of Mary Johnson, John Johnson road to Augusta called Reeds Road, Richard Gantt, Willliam Samuel, Lewis Nobles, Christian Breithaupt. Wit Christian Breithaupt, Reason Barnes. /s/ W W Fell. Justice Christian Breithaupt certifies relinquishment of dower rights by Elizabeth M Fell wife of William W Fell, 1 January 1818; /s/ Elizabeth Fell.
   Plat by Stephen Tillman D S, Reason Barnes and Paschal Tillman chain carriers, shows 495 acres, dated 2 and 3 January 1818. Proven 1 January 1818 by Reason Barnes; Christian Breithaupt QU. Rec 2 February 1818.

p.469   William C Bates to Phileman Bowers, Affadavit, 2 March 1818, Bates swears that on 25 December 1816 in vicinity of Beach Island he fought with Bowers and bit the lower end of his right ear off. /s/ W C Bates. A Edmunds J P. Rec 2 March 1818.

p.470   Sarah Smith to Nicholas Lowe, Deed, 25 April 1811, Two hundred Dollars, 100 acres adj sd Lowe, Watsons line, land originally granted to Jacob Smith 18 March 1793. Wit John Blocker Jr, James Allen. /s/ Sarah Smith. Proven 2 February 1818 by John Blocker; M Mims CCP. Rec 2 February 1818.

p.471   Charles Jones to John Buckhalter, Deed, 8 January 1818, Three thousand eight hundred eight Dollars, 1088 acres being part of several tracts originally granted unto sd Charles Jones and others lying on branches of Beaverdam Creek of Horns Creek, adj lands of Daniel Bird, John Cheatham, sd Charles Jones, Perrin Jones and Mims. Wit Stephen Terry Junr, James Buckhalter. /s/ Charles Jones. Justice William Burnside certifies relinquishment of dower rights by Nancey Jones wife of Charles Jones, 17 January 1818; /s/ Nancey Jones. Proven 8 Jany 1818 by Stephen Terry Junr; John Hollingsworth JQ. Rec 2 Fedruary 1818.

p.473   Susannah Boyd to her son Walter Boyd, Deed of Gift, 20 January 1818, love, Negro boy named Joe about age six years. Wit Jesse M Cogburn, Elizan Cogburn. /s/ Susannah (x) Boyd. Proven 2 February 1818 by Jesse M Cogburn; M Mims C C P. Rec 2 February 1818.

p.474   William Holsten to Hardyman Holmes, Deed, 25 February 1913, One hundred Dollars, 100 acres on branch of Beaverdam of Turkey Creek of Stevens Creek adj lands of John Elam, James White. Wit Wyatt Holmes, Levi McDaniel. /s/ William Holsten. Proven 10 January 1818 by Levi McDaniel; John Cheatham J P. Rec 3 February 1818.

p.476   Josiah Taylor to William Holsten Junr, Deed, 2 August 1812, One hundred Dollars, 100 acres on branches of Beaverdam Creek of Turkey Creek of Stevens Creek adjoining lands of John Elam, James White. Wit Phillip Ikner, John Couch. /s/

Josiah Taylor. Proven 2 August 1813 by Phillip Ikner; Wm Hagens J P. Rec 3 Feb 1818.

p.477 Hardaman Holmes to Levi McDaniel, Deed, 13 October 1817, Four hundred Dollars, 100 acres on branch of Beaverdam Creek of Turkey Cr of Stevens Cr adj lands of John Elam 2^d, Creek Br. Wit D M Loveless, Edward McDaniel. /s/ Hardaman (x) Holmes. Proven 22 January 1818 by Edward McDaniel who saw Hardyman Holmes sign, likewise David M Loveless; Lewis Holmes JQ. Rec 3 Feb 1818.

p.479 William Zachery of Columbia County, Georgia, to Thomas Freeman, Deed, 2 March 1808, Two hundred Dollars, 200 acres, part of tract granted to William Talbert on head of Swift Creek, Augusta [road], adj lands of Tomkins, sd Freeman. Wit Chas Simkins, Wade Bussy, John Boyd. /s/ W Zachery. Quit Claim of John Boyd, 23 March 1810; part of land mentioned lies within lines of land held by John Boyd for which Wm Zachery has not got titles from John Boyd, therefore I sd John Boyd relinquish claim, confirm unto Thomas Freeman terms of within deed. Wit Samuel Freeman, Wiley Freeman. /s/ John Boyd. Proven 23 June 1808 by John Boyd; Garrett Freeman J P. Rec 4 February 1818.

p.481 John Taylor and William Taylor to William Norris, Deed, 15 November 1816, Forty five Dollars, their parts of land Stephen Williams sold to John Taylor 24 October 1798 containing 400 acres; also their parts of tract granted to our father John Taylor containing 62 acres where our mother Mary Taylor now lives, all joining lands claimed by Phillip Rowls, Anel Sawyer, and sd William Norris. John Taylor and William Taylor being sons and heirs of sd John Taylor convey our parts of above land to William Norris, 50 acres; also house and buildings where Francis now lives. Wit Francis Taylor, Robert (x) Autry. /s/ John Taylor, /s/ William (x) Taylor. Proven 2 Feb 1818 by Francis Taylor; Nathan Norris JQ. Rec 3 February 1818.

p.483 Benjamin Darby to Thomas Christian, Deed, 5 August 1816, Five hundred Dollars, 502 acres on head branches of Hornes Creek and Shaws Creek of Savannah and Edisto Rivers, being part of three tracts originally granted to Dennis now land of Ezekiel McClendon and Benjamin Darby 1774, 1786, and 1795. Wit Henry W Lowe, James Coates. /s/ Benjamin Darby. Justice Eldred Simkins certifies relinquish-ment of dower rights by Olive Darby wife of Benjamin Darby, [blot] November 1816; /s/ Olive (x) Darby. Proven 5 August 1816 by Henry W Lowe; Jesse Blocker JQ. Rec 4 February 1818.

p.485 Benjamin Grumbles to Jeremiah Bussey, Deed, 28 January 1818, Eight hundred Dollars, 248 acres adj lands of D McWhorter, Joshua Thorn, sd Bussey, lying on Brewers Branch of Savannah River. Wit George H Traylor, T Traylor. /s/ B Grumbles. Justice Charles Bussey certifies the relinquishment of dower rights by

48

Kesiah Grumbles wife of Benjamin Grumbles, 3 February 1818; /s/ Keziah (x) Grumbles. Proven 3 [month omitted] 1818 by T Traylor; Charles Bussey. Rec 5 February 1818.

p.487 Sheriff James M Butler to John Blocker, Sheriffs Title, 2 December 1816; at suit John Blocker plf, John Spann and James Spann dfts, for partition of land, sd land to be publicly and openly sold; struck off to John Blocker for Three hundred Dollars, he being highest and last bidder; 940 acres on Rockey Creek and Hurricane branch adj lands of Obediah Henderson Junr, Peter Roberts, land formerly owned by Charles Williams, land formerly Simkins, land of Sarah Martin, John Rixey originally granted to William [torn]gan in 1772. Wit John S Jeter, George Butler. /s/ J M Butler S E D. Proven 5 February 1818 by John S Jeter; Charles Hammond JQ. Rec 5 Feb 1818.

p.490 James Delaughter to Richard Covington, Deed, 26 November 1817, One hundred seventy two Dollars, 86 acres in two tracts on Stevens Creek and Savannah River, one for 57 acres adj Busseys land, widow Fletcher, Widow Bussey; the other for 29 acres adj Widow Fletcher, lands of heirs of Charles Bussey. Wit Wm W Olds, E Covington. /s/ James Delaughter. Justice John Tarrance certifies relinquishment of dower rights by Frances Delaughter wife of James Delaughter, 9 December 1817; /s/ Frances (x) Delaughter. Proven 4 December 1817 by William W Olds Esqr; John Tarrance JQ. Rec 5 February 1818.

p.492 Benjamin Ryan to Mrs Eunice Reid, 24 March 1817, Bill of Sale, Fifteen hundred [Dollars] Negro woman named Silvy with her three children Atterman, David, and Harry with future increase; sd Negroes were lately in possession of Samuel Marsh but are my property in suit in Equity now pending concerning them. Wit Sally Gallman. /s/ Benjn Ryan. Proven 5 February 1818 by Sarah Gallman; /s/ Sally Gallman. M Mims C CP. Rec 5 February 1818.

p.493 Dudley Stewart to James Carson, Bill of Sale, 30 January 1818; received of James Carson One hundred thirty five Dollars for sorrel mare, bridle, saddle. Wit Urbane Nicholson, Thomas Bladon, Whitfield Brown. /s/ Dudley Stewart. Proven 5 February 1818 by U. Nicholson; James Bell JP. Rec 6th February 1818.

p.494 John Bolger to Joseph Taylor, Deed, 19 May 1817, Three hundred Dollars, 146 acres, it being part of 250 acres originally granted to John Abney decd, adj William Abney, John Taylor, and lying on Panther branch of Big Creek of Saluda River. Wit James Carson, Nancy Carson, Elizabeth (x) Walton. /s/ John Bolger. Proven 5 February 1818 by James Carson; James Bell JP. Rec 6th February 1818.

p.495 Sarah Carson to her son James Carson, Deed, 19 May 1817, One hundred Dollars, 153 acres on Panther Branch of Big Creek, being part of 250 acres conveyed by John Abney decd jointly to John Bolger and sd Sarah Carson on 22 June 1812, plat of sd 153 acres made by Thomas Anderson Esqr 23 September 1814, land adj lands of Joseph Taylor, Isaac Saddler, and Nathan Trotter. Wit John Bolger, Joseph Taylor, Nancy Carson. /s/ Sarah (x) Carson. Proven [blank] February 1818 by Joseph Taylor; James Bell J P. Rec 6 Feby 1818.

p.597 Thomas Spragins to Richard Coleman, Deed, 28 January 1818, Five hundred Fifty Dollars, [acres lost in binding] part of 1190 acres originally granted to John Abney decd situate on Water-mellon Branch of Big Creek and Little Saluda River, adj lands of William Abney, Runnels Gentry, Morgan Mills, May, and Charleston road. Wit Urbane Nicholson, Simpson Carson. /s/ Thomas Spragins. Proven 30 January 1818 by Urbane Nicholson; John Abney JP. Rec 6th February 1818.

p.498 William Abney to Richard Coleman, Deed, 27 January 1818, Two hundred Dollars, Twenty five acres on Watermillion Branch of Big Creek and Little Saluda River bounded by lands of sd Richard Coleman, William Abney. Wit Urbane Nicholson, James Carson. /s/ Wm (x) Abney. Proven 30 January 1818 by Urbane Nicholson; John Abney JP. Rec 6th February 1818.

p.500 John Bolger to Sarah Carson, Relinquishment of Claim, 21 April 1817, Whereas John Abney Esqr decd, by deed 22 June 1812 conveyed to John Bolger and Sarah Carson 299 acres on Big Creek which has since been resurveyed by Thomas Anderson D S, within plat of 153 acres laid off by him as Sarah Carsons part of sd land, which division I acknowledge myself satisfied with. Wit James Carson, Joseph Taylor, Nancy Carson. /s/ J Bolger. Plat 23 September 1814 shows adj lands of N Trotter, Taylor, and Saddler. Rec 6 February 1818.

p.501 Benjamin Ryan to Mrs Eunice Reid, Bill of Sale, 24 February 1817, Eight hundred fifty Dollars, Negro girl Hannah aged 15, Negro girl named Milly aged thirteen which were lately in possession of Samuel Marsh but are now claimed by me as my right in Equity suit now pending concerning them. Wit John Martin, C Vauner. /s/ Benjn Ryan. Proven 6 February 1818 by C Vauner; M Mims CCP. Rec 6 Feb 1818. [dates are as written in original]

p. 502 William Mann of Green County, Georgia, to Cadwell Evans, Deed, 14 January 1818, Fifty five Dollars, 67 1/3 acres where sd Cadwell Evans now liveth, it being part of 202 acres originally granted to Barbara Laraman, on waters of Rockey Creek of Turkey Creek of Stephens Creek, adj lands of John Gentry, Joseph Hogh, Stuard Miner, Joel Mann. Wit Joseph Hogh, John (x) Hogh. /s/ William (x) Mann. Proven 2 February 1818 by Joseph Hogh; Jordan Holloway JP. Rec 9th Feb 1818.

p.503 John Gentry to Cadwell Evans, Deed, 27 December 1817, Five hundred seventy five Dollars, 116 acres whereon sd John Gentry now liveth originally granted to Samuel Stalnaker Senr 24 August 1793 on Rockey Creek of Turkey Creek of Stephens Creek, adj Joseph Hogh, William Evans, Shepherd Spencer, John Terry. Wit H Freeman, George Longmire. /s/ John (x) Gentry. Justice Jesse Blocker certifies relinquishment of dower rights by Elizabeth Gentry wife of John Gentry, 27 December 1817; /s/ Elizabeth (x) Gentry. Proven 27 December 1817 by H Freeman; Jesse Blocker J P. Rec 9ᵗʰ February 1818.

p.506   Mack Lamar and Lydia Lamar to William Sceibles, 24 July 1817, Eight hundred Dollars, 129 acres near Fortmoore Bluff, ---okes Gulley branch of Savannah River, adj lands of Major Jacob Zinn, John Sturzenegger, Melines C Levenworth Esqr, survey by Stephen Tillman D S. Wit Phillip Lamar, George Keadle, Abram Mathis. /s/ Mack Lamar. /s/ Lydia (x) Lamar. Justice John Heard certifies relinquishment of dower by Rebecah Lamar wife of Mack Lamar, 20 November 1817; /s/ Rebecah (x) Lamar. Proven 12 Jany 1818 by Phillip Lamar; James Hunter JQ. Rec 10ᵗʰ February 1818.

p.508   Thomas Adams to Jonathan Dawson, 11 February 1804, Two hundred sixty Dollars, 260 acres on waters of Rockey Creek of Stephens Creek adj lands of James Darby, Thomas Adams. Wit Wright Nicholson, William McDowel, William (x) Nicholson. /s/ Thomas Adams. Proven 27 August 1805 by Wright Nicholson; Alexr Bean J P. Rec 12ᵗʰ February 1818.

p.509   Enoch Singleton to Betcy Hardy, Jenney[Jermey?] Hardy, Julian Hardy and Jesse J Hardy children of Kit Hardy and my present wife Polly then Polly Hardy, Deed of Gift, 12 February 1818, [household goods and livestock]. Wit Richard H Tutt. /s/ Enoch (x) Singleton. Proven 12 February 1818 by Richd H Tutt; M Mims CCP. Rec 12ᵗʰ February 1818.

p.510   William Johnson Jr of Charleston to William W Fell, 18 January 1812, Six thousand Dollars, between 750 and 800 acres on waters of Buckhalters and Dry Creeks, adj lands of Ephraim Ferrell, Richardson, Bartlett, Augusta road called Reids Road, a tract sold by me to Charles Stone, Christian Breithaupt, several tracts purchased by me of Richard Gantt, William Longstreet, and Wilson Woodroff, which lines includes all the land owned by me in sd District except tract sold to Mr Charles Stone. Wit John Cart, William L Smith. /s/ William Johnson Junr. Plat shows adj lands of Ferrell, Parker, Noble, Breithaupt, Stone, and course of the road. Justice William S Smith certifies relinquishment of dower rights by Sarah Johnson Junr wife of William Johnson, 15 January 18[blank]; /s/ Sarah Johnson Junr. Proven 31 January 1818 by John Cart; Charles Fell Q U. Rec 13ᵗʰ February 1818.

p.513   Moses Smith to Thomas Reynolds, Deed, 4 April 1814, Two hundred and [blank] Dollars, Negro girl named Winney about eleven years old. Wit Elisha (x) Smith. /s/ Moses (M) Smith, /s/ Sarry (S) Smith. Proven 31 May 1814 by Elisha Smith; Elijah Watson JQ. Rec 17th February 1818.

p.515 Stephen Christian to Elizabeth Christian, Marriage Settlement, [date blank] 1818, Marriage has been solemnized between Stephen Christian of village of Edgefield and Elizabeth Pardue of same place, articles hereafter mentioned belonged to Elizabeth Pardue now Elizabeth Christian at time of marriage, settle upon Elizabeth in trust for children of marriage, Thomas Christian and Sarah Pardue of the third part [inventory here omitted]. Thomas Christian and Sarah Pardue agree to permit Elizabeth to sell and dispose of articles afsd on application to them. Wit William Gurganus, Abner Whatley. /s/ Thos Christian, /s/ Stephen Christian, /s/ Sarah (x) Pardue. Proven 17th February 1818 by Abner Whatley. Rec 17th February 1818.

p.517 Thomas Christian to John Christian of Lunenbergh County, Virginia, Deed, 4 February 1818, Fifteen hundred Dollars, 502 acres on branches of Hornes Creek and Shaws Creek of Savannah and Edisto Rivers, being part of 300 acres originally granted to Dennis Nowland, Ezekiel McClendon, and Benjamin Darby in 1774, 1786, and 1795, down Poseys Branch. Wit P Laborde, John Allen. /s/ Thos Christian. Proven 17 February 1818 by John Allen; M Mims CCP. Rec 17th February 1818.

End of Deed Book 34

p.1   Simon Smith to William Smith, Deed, 13 August 1813, Two hundred Dollars, 150 acres, being land granted to Thomas Butler 7 January 1788 on waters of Moores Creek of Clouds Creek of Saluda River bounding NW on land of Solomon Edwards. Wit Anthony (x)Funderburgh, Morgan (x) Corder. /s/ Simon (SS) Smith. Proven 20 November 1813 by Anthony Funderburgh; Elijah Watson JQ. Rec 17 Feb 1818.

p.2   Thomas Jones, planter, to William Wash, Deed, 18 May 1804, Three hundred Dollars, 335 acres on both sides of Goffs Branch of Turkey Creek of Stephens Creek of Savannah River adj Cockran, Moss, being part of 1000 acres originally granted to Thomas Linch by Lt Gov Wm Bull. Wit Matt Scruggs, William Kilcrease. /s/ Thos Jones. Proven 21 May 1804 by William Kilcrease; Matt Martin JP. Rec 17 Feb 1818.

p.3   Francis Lowe to John Wash, Deed, 27 December 1816, Four hundred twenty five Dollars, 200 acres it being part of 200 acres originally granted to John Goff and part of 300 acres orginally granted to Henry Key on Turkey Creek of Stevens Creek adj lands of Robert Cockran, Wm Wash, Goffs branch, Richard Wilbern. Wit William Jones, Richard Wash. /s/ Francis Lowe.   Justice John Hollingworth certifies relinquishment of dower rights by Elizabeth Lowe wife of Francis Lowe, 22 January 1818; /s/ Elizabeth Lowe.   Proven 22 January 1818 by Richard Wash; John Hollingworth J P.   Rec 17th February 1818.

p.5   James Glenn of Newberry District to Gilbert Smith of Edgefield District, Deed, Newberry District, 10 December 1817, Two hundred Dollars, 200 acres on Saluda River adj lands of John Watson, Moseley, Persimon lick Creek, Thomas Brown, John Abney, William Abney, William Dun, it being part of two tracts granted to John Abney and conveyed by sd Abney unto William Brown and by Brown to Thomas Brown by L&R 12 May 1792, conveyed by Thomas Brown to James Glenn 30 September 1805. Wit John Glen, Henry Coate. /s/ James Glen.   Justice Henry Coate certifies relinquishment of dower by Margaret Glenn wife of James Glenn, 10 December 1817; /s/ Margaret (x) Glenn. Proven 10 December 1817 by John Glenn; Henry Coates JQ. Rec 20th February 1818.

p.7   Thomas Brown of Barnwell District to James Glenn of Newberry District, Deed, 30 September 1805, One hundred eighty Dollars, 200 acres on Saluda River adj lands of John Watson, Moseley, Watson, Persimon Lick Creek, sd Thomas Brown, John Abney, William Abney, William Dun, being part of two parcels of land granted to

John Abney and conveyed by sd John unto William Brown and from sd William to Thomas Brown by L&R 12 May 1792. Wit William Speer, Robert Speer Jr, Robert Speer Senr. /s/ Thomas Brown. Proven 21 January 1808 by William Speer; Henry Coate JQ. Rec 20 February 1818.

p.8 Isaac Bush to Catharine Logan, Mortgage, 1 January [year lost in binding], Catharine Logan executrix of John Logan Junr who was executor of John Logan Senr, Isaac Bush bound unto Catharine Logan; condition repayment of Three hundred eighty five Dollars; secured by 385 acres being whole of land granted to Isaac Lesesne for 500 acres excepting 130 acres now in possession of Benjamin Murrell adj lands of Isaac Lesesne, Powell, the whole tract granted to Isaac Lesesne 1 June 1775 on head branches of Turkey Creek. Wit Edwin Chipman, Robert C Cockran; /s/ Isaac Bush. [Written across p.9 is "Satisfied 1st May 1820."] Proven 9th February 1818 by Edwin Chipman; Henry Chipman JP. Rec 23rd February 1818.

p.9 Abner Landrum to Thomas Winn, Deed, 15 October 1817, Four hundred fifty Dollars, 225 acres on waters of Log Creek on each side of the road from Point Lookout to Log Creek, being part of land originally granted to Isaac Lesesne adj land of Wilson Barronton, Edmund Bacon, Coleman, sd Winn. Wit John Gray Junr, Richard H Tutt. /s/ Abner Landrum. Proven 24 February 1818 by Richard H Tutt; M Mims CCP. Rec 24th February 1818.

p.10 Wiley Stokes and Batt Stokes to Shepherd Spencer, Deed, 12 December 1817, Eleven hundred Dollars, 370 acres on Pike Creek of Turkey Creek adj on lands of Homes, Morgan or Geter, Smith and afsd Shepherd Spencer, [name lost in binding], originally granted to E Stokes 6 February 1804 by Gov James B Richards, conveyed by R E Stokes to Willey Stokes. Wit Robert E Stokes, Spencer Bell, Wiley Spencer. /s/ Wiley (x) Stokes, /s/ Batt Stokes. Proven 3 February 1818 by Spencer Bell; John Lyon JQ. Rec 26th February 1818.

p.11 James Jones, William Jones, Mary Jones to Alexander Hunter, Deed, 22 September 1817, One hundred Dollars, 44 ½ acres on waters of Savannah River, being part of land sold by Phillip Lamar decd to above James Jones, adj lands then belonging to Jacob Guiton, formerly marked off by James Jones to his brother John Jones decd on which sd John Jones resided. Wit William Wise, Jonathan Dicks. /s/ James Jones senr, /s/ William Jones, /s/ Mary (x) Jones. Justice James Hunter certifies relinquishment of dower rights by Susannah Jones wife of James Jones, 28th February 1818; /s/ Susannah (x) Jones. Proven 28 February 1818 by William T Wise; James Hunter J Q. Rec 2nd March 1818.

p.13 Abraham Mitchell to Daniel Banknight[Bauknight?], Deed, 5 January 1818, Five hundred Dollars, 150 acres on Saluda River it being part of land formerly granted

54

to Isum Langley 5 May 1773 for one hundred acres; the 50 acres dated by grant 1 October 1789 unto Isum Langley and then conveyed unto Michael 1790, sd Michael conveyed same unto David Megehe 1796, sd Megehe conveyed same unto Abraham Mitchell 5 August 1803, adj lands of Daniel Bauknight, Fon[lost in binding] Mitchell, John Johnston. Wit William C Mitchell, Richard Yarborough. /s/ Abraham (x) Mitchell. Justice William Hurt certifies relinquishment of dower rights by Polly Mitchell wife of Abraham Mitchell, 12 January 1818; /s/ Polly (x) Mitchell. Proven 12 January 1818 by Richard Yarbrough; Wm Hurtt J P. Rec 2nd March 1818.

p.15 Benjamin Gibson and John Gibson of Lexington District to Daniel Bauknight, Deed, 11 November 1816, Three hundred Dollars, 150 acres on Clouds Creek of Saluda Rier, being part of 250 acres originally granted to John Johnston 5 May 1773, conveyed by sd John to Isum Langley 10 December 1774, sd Isum conveyed unto John Beals 15 February 1791, and Beals unto John Gibson 1792, then willed by John Gibson to his three sons Benjamin Gibson, John Gibson and Samuel Gibson, which Samuel conveyed his part unto sd Benjamin; the land adj SW on land of [name lost in binding] Mackey, other sides vacant when granted. Wit Thomas K Poindexter, Rosey[Prosey?] Strum. /s/ Benjamin (x) Gibson, /s/ John Gibson. Lexington District: Justice West Caughman certifies relinquishment of dower by Amey Gibson and Catharine Gibson wifes of Benjamin and John Gibson, 25 November 1816; /s/ Amey (x) Gibson, /s/ Catharine (x) Gibson. Proven 26 November 1816 by Thomas K Poindexter; West Caughman. Rec 2nd March 1818.

p.16 Henry W Griffith to Joseph Rutherford, Deed, [day lost in binding] January 1817, Four hundred twenty eight Dollars, 110 acres, it being land left to me by my father Joseph Griffith decd, adj lands of James and Joseph Griffith, William Marlow, James Wiggons, Joseph Rutherford, William Griffith. Wit Charles Abney, Crawford (x) Perry, James B Griffith. /s/ Henry W Griffith. Proven 29 December 1817 by Charles Abney; [name lost in binding] Abney J P. Rec 2nd March 1818.

p.18 Uriah Lambard of Ninety Six District, planter, to David Bowers, planter, Deed, 6 April 1787, Ten Pounds lawful money of SC, 60 acres adj lands of George Galphin, George[?] Bender, John Isakin Zubly; granted to sd Uriah Lambard by Gov Wm Moultrie 21 February 178[lost in binding]. Wit David Bowers, John Yeaten, Thomas (x) Brunett. /s/ Uriah (x) Lambard. Proven [day lost in binding] December 1792 by David Bowers Junr; ---nes Jackson JQ. Rec 2d March 1818.

p.19 William Jackson to John Fox of Richmond County, Georgia, Quit claim Deed, Augusta, 28 February 1818, Sixty Dollars, relinquishes right to 150 acres on Cheves Creek of Savannah River adj lands of Thomas Marbary, James Booth, Henry Barnes and afsd John Fox, which land was originally owned by George & Jacob Stroup of Charleston and by them sold to Adam & Richard Booth as per agreement between sd

Booths and Richard Johnston agent of sd Stroups 5 December 1814 which transferred
to me 30 November 1817. Wit John Sturzenegger, William Bowie. /s/ Wm Jackson.
Proven 2 March1818 by William Bowie; M Mims CCP. Rec 2nd March 1818.

p.20   William Jackson junr of Richmond County, Georgia, to John Fox, Richmond
County, Georgia, 28 February 1818, Sixty Dollars, 40 acres on waters of Cheves Cr
of Savannah River, originally granted to John Herndon and by him conveyed to Lucy
Reach, adj lands of Thomas Marbary, James B[lost in binding] and afsd John Fox.
Wit John Sturzenegger, William Bowie. /s/ Wm Jackson. Proven 2nd March 1818 by
Wm Bowie; M Mims CCP. Rec 2nd March 1818.

p.21   William Jackson junr to Thomas H Penn, Richmond County, Georgia, Deed,
Richmond County, Georgia, 28 February 1818, Two hundred fifty Dollars, ---nty four
acres on waters of Cheves Creek of Savannah River adj lands of ---ert Samuel decd,
John R Bartee, Mary Lyon. Wit John Sturzenegger, Wm Bowie. /s/ Wm Jackson.
Proven 2 March 1818 by William Bowie; M Mims CCP. Rec 2nd March 1818.

p.21 Lucy Reach and Elizabeth Carter to David Monday, Deed, 9 November 1814,
Eighty Dollars, 40 acres originally granted to John Herrondon, by him conveyed to
Lucy Reach on Cheves Creek adj lands of Thomas Marbary, John Fox, James Booth.
Wit James Booth, Christian Breithaupt. /s/ Lucy (x) Reach, /s/ Elizabeth (x) Carter.
Proven 23rd March 1815 by James Booth; Isaac Kirkland JQ. Rec 2nd March 1818.

p.22   Isaac Hudson to James Hudson, Deed, [day and month left blank] 1817, Eight
hundred Dollars, 302 acres on Canebreak Branch. Wit Samuel Norred, Moses
Prescott. /s/ Isaac Hudson. Proven 2 March 1818 by Moses Prescott; ---n Corley J
P. Rec 2nd March 1818.

p.23   Benjamin Wofford to John Burkhalter, Deed, 24 September 1812, Six hundred
Dollars, 282 acres formerly belonging to Thomas Tod but now [dec]eased, on
Beaverdam Creek, warranted against myself, my heirs Ann Tod and her heirs. Wit
Andrew Gramling, Lacy Bobo. /s/ Benjamin Wofford. Spartanburgh district, Justice
Burrell Bobo certifies relinquishment of dower rights by Anna Wofford wife of
Benjamin Wofford, 24 September 1812; /s/ Anna Wofford. Proven 24 September
1812 by Lacy Bobo; Burrell Bobo QU. Rec 2nd March 1818.

p.24   William Lariman to Benjamin Melton and Willey, Deed, 5 August 1816, Four
hundred fifty Dollars, on head branches of Mill Creek of Savannah River adj lands of
Young Allen, Joseph Howell, John Buckelew, Christopher Ward. Wit Joseph Bolton,
Wm Forrest. /s/ William Larimon. Justice Lewis Miles certifies relinquishment of
dower rights by Hixey Larimon wife of William Larimon, 29 Nov 1816; Hixey (x)
Larimon. Proven 2 Mar 1818 by William Forrest;   James Bell J P. Rec 2 Mar 1818.

p.26 Jonathan Fox to Jonathan Glanton, Mortgage, 25 September 1817, Fox received from Glanton Three hundred Dollars, mortgages two Negroes, Nancy and her child Anna. Wit William Thurmond. /s/ Jonathan Fox. Proven 28 February 1818 by Wm Thurmond; E B Belcher J P. Rec 2nd March 1818.

p.26 Mary Johnson to Hugh Ballentine, Deed, 23 February 1818, Two hundred seventy five Dollars, 25 acres adj lands of sd Hugh Ballentine, James Jones, Reuben Cooper and others. Wit James Miller, John Butler, Ambrose Mills. /s/ Mary (x) Johnson. Proven 2 March 1818 by James Miller; John Loveless JP. Rec 2 Mar 1818.

p.27 Barbara Holmes of Barnwell District to her daughter Mary Bowers wife of Benjamin Bowers and also children of Benjamin and Mary: George Bowers, Aurelia Bowers, Julia Anna Bowers, Deed of Gift, 9 February 1818, One hundred Dollars, [number lost in the binding] hundred 92 acres known as Grays Point Tract situated in Barnwell District, also six Negroes: Patty, Tom, Mar--et, Jenny, Fenah, and Jim the son of Patty; also third of my cattle. Wit W C Bates, H C Pay. /s/ Barbª Holmes. Proven 2 March 1818 by William C Bates; John Sturzenegger JP. Rec 3 March 1818.

p.28 Buckner Blalock to Abraham Rutland, Deed, 7 October 1816, Four hundred fifty Dollars, 116 acres it being part of 420 acres granted to Arthur Watson 3 September 1784 on branch of Mud Creek of Little Saluda river, adj lands of James Clark. Wit Andrew T Perry, Stephen Fedrick. /s/ Buck (x) Blalock. Proven 2 January 1818 by Stephen Fredrick; Lewis Holmes JP. Rec 3 March 1818.

p.29 Thomas Deloach to Elizabeth Kirkland, Deed, 25 March 1809, Fifty Dollars, 50 acres being part of 420 acres granted to Arthur Watson 3 September 1787, adj lands of Keziah Fortner, Dry Creek, Shadrack Bailey. Wit Prescott Bush, Francis Walker. /s/ Thomas Deloach. Proven 12 April 1809 by Francis Walker; Isaac Foreman J P. Rec 3 March 1818.

p.30 Amos McCartey to John Moning[Morring? Merring?], Deed, 5 January 1818, One hundred ninety three Dollars, land of heirs of John Walker decd, purchased by A McCartey, shown in deed from heirs, viz Joseph, John, Samuel, & Francis Walker heirs to sd land, 76 acres on Bog Branch of South Edisto adj lands of Francis Walker Senr, William Kelly. Wit Matthias Jones, Henry Spann. /s/ Amos McCartey. Proven 2 March 1818 by Henry Spann; John Loveless JP. Rec 3 March 1818.

p.31 Joseph Walker, John Walker, Samuel Walker, and Francis Walker Junr to Amos McCartey, Deed, 5 October 1816, Two hundred Dollars, 76 acres on Bog Branch of South Edisto adj lands of Francis Walker Sr, Wm Kelly, being part of land which fell to us by heirship from estate of our father John Walker, decd, the place whereon he lived when he died. Wit James Murray, Andrew (x) Murray. /s/ Joseph

Walker Junr, /s/ John Walker, /s/ Samuel Walker Junr, /s/ Francis Walker Junr. Proven 22 March 1817 by James Murray; John Loveless JP. Rec 3 March 1818.

p.32 Matthias Jones to James Smith, Deed, 16 February 1816, One hundred forty Dollars, 32 3/4 acres adj sd Smiths land, it being part of tract I purchased of Thomas Lakey adj Spanns Spring Branch, Peters Creek. Wit Henry Spann, James Murray. /s/ Matthias Jones. Proven 12 July 1816 by Henry Spann; Charles Oneale QU. Rec 3 March 1818.

p.33 William Kelley to John Moring, Deed, 22 August 1817, Three hundred Dollars, being part of three tracts on Bog Branch and Bushes mill Creek, one part granted to John Croney, one part granted to Swift, and one granted to Richard Bush Senr on 4 September 1797, all adjoining; also 290 acres granted to sd William Kelley 7 July 1817 adj above land and sd Swift. Wit Henry Spann, Andrew T Perry. /s/ William Kelley. Justice Lewis Holmes certifies relinquishment of dower rights by Sally Kelly wife of William Kelley, 19 January 1818; /s/ Salley Kelley. Proven 30 September 1817 by Henry Spann; John Loveless J P. Rec 3 March 1818.

p.34 Hugh Carson to Henry Spann, Deed, 10 September 1817, Three hundred Dollars, 180 acres originally granted to James Tomlin in 1786 by Gov Wm Moultrie, on Beech Creek of Edisto River adj lands of Arthur Middleton, the above land was conveyed from Tomlin to Daniel Hern and from John Hearn, son of Daniel, to Hugh Carson. Wit Matthias Jones, Andrew T Perry. /s/ Hugh (H) Carson. Justice Peter Lamkin certifies relinquishment of dower rights by Nancy Carson wife of Hugh Carson 15 October 1817; /s/ Nancy (x) Carson. Proven 15 September 1817 by Matthias Jones; John Loveless J P. Rec 3 March 1818.

p.35 James Griffin to Richard Bullock, Deed, 15 March 1816, [number lost in binding] and seventy Dollars, one hundred and [number lost in binding] acres adj lands of Richard Bullock, Richard Hagood, estate of Col John Hamilton, estate of Joseph Williams decd, plat dated 27 December 1813 by Thomas Chiles D S. Wit James Matthews, Samuel Bell. /s/ James Griffin. Proven 15 March 1816 by James Matthews; Nathan Lipscomb JQ. Rec 3 March 1818.

p.36 Lark Abney to John Chapman of Newberry District, Deed, 5 April 1817, Fifteen hundred Dollars, three[?] hundred four acres on Tossetys Creek of Saluda River adj lands of Sarah Carson, estate of --ney decd, Paul Abney, estate of Samuel Abney decd, estate of John Abney, Azariah Abney. Wit Lewellen Patrick, Hugh Duffey. /s/ Lark Abney. Proven 13 August 1817 by Hugh Duffie; John Abney J P. Rec 3 March 1818.

p.38 Jesse Holloway to Jordan Holloway, Deed, 3 February 1816, Four hundred

Dollars, 100 acres on Mountain Creek of Savannah River, it being part of land granted to John Hill Senr 5 September 1796 adj lands of James Golman, Jordan Holloway. Wit Rebeccah Moore, Elizabeth Nobles. /s/ Jesse Holloway. Proven 20 November 1817 by Rebeckah Moore; J Holloway JP. Rec 3 March 1818.

p.39   Aaron Weeks to Barkley M Blocker, 23 October 1816, Thirteen hundred Dollars, [number lost in binding] hundred sixty acres on Rockey Creek of Turkey Creek, Stephens Creek originally granted to William Blackley and part of sd tract to James Miller, adj James Wargut, estate of Right Nicholson, estate of Thomas Adams, Daniel Mazyck, James Wright. Wit Jesse Blocker, William Sorgee. /s/ Aaron Weeks. Justice Jesse Blocker certifies relinquishment of dower rights by Nancey Weeks wife of Aaron Weeks, 23 October 1816; /s/ Nancy (x) Weeks. Proven 3 March [year lost in the binding]; M Mims CCP. Rec 3 March 1818.

p.40   John Holsonback Senr to John Holsonback Junr, Deed, 14 February 1818, valuable consideration, 48 acres on Middle Creek of Savannah River, being part of land granted to John Holsonback Senr. Wit Joseph Cook, Saml Tomkins. /s/ John Holsonback Senr. Plat surveyed 5 February 1818 by James Tomkins D S shows 48 acres adj lands of John Holsonback, Anthony White. Proven 24 February 1818 by Samuel Tomkins; Thomas Price JP. Rec 3 March 1818.

p.42   John Holsonback to Anthony White, Deed, 14 February 1818, valuable consideration, 83 acres on Middle Creek of Savannah River, being part of land granted to John Holsonback. Wit Joseph Cook, Samuel Tomkins. /s/ John Holsonback. Plat surveyed 5 February 1818 by James Tomkins D S shows adj lands of John Holsonback, Jacob Holsonback. Proven 3 March 1818 by Joseph Cook; Thomas Price J P. Rec 3 March 1818.

p.43   Thomas Jester to Daniel Hardy, Deed, 12 December 1817, Five hundred Dollars, 100 acres on Rockey Creek of Turkey Creek of Stevens Creek, being part of 1000 acres originally granted to James Simson 15 May 1772. Wit Jonathan Devore, Covington Hardy. /s/ Thomas (x) Jester. Justice John Lyon certifies relinquishment of dower rights by Polly Jester wife of Thomas Jester, 13 December 1817; /s/ Polly (x) Jester. Proven 16 December 1817 by Covington Hardy; Charles Bussey J Q. Rec 3rd March 1818.

p.44   Abram Kilcrease to Wyatt Holmes, Deed, 13 September 1817, Four hundred Dollars, sixty two acres, being part of 100 acres granted to Obediah Kilcrease decd. 20 October [year lost in binding], lying on Beaverdam creek of Turkey Creek of Savannah River. Wit W Coursey, Edward Holmes. /s/ Abraham Kilcrease. Proven 3 March 1818 by William Coursey; Lewis Holmes JP. Rec 3 March 1818.

p.45   John Clagg and Elizabeth Clagg to John Hamilton, Deed, 1 July 1817, Five hundred Dollars, 237 acres on Mountain Creek of Big Turkey Creek adj lands of Jacob Huffman, Jefferson Williams when surveyed, original grant to Archibald Gray 1 March 1785 by Lt Gov Wm Bull. Wit Loyd Skannel, Abel Skannel. /s/ John Clagg, /s/ Elizabeth Clagg. Proven 9 January 1818 by Abel Skannel; Robert Walker J P. Rec 3 March 1818.

p.46   Stephen Smith to Lott Smith, Deed, 28 March 1810, Deed, Four hundred Dollars, 116 acres on Mountain Creek. Wit James Thornton, Russell Falkner. /s/ Stephen (x) Smith. Proven 3 March 1818 by Russel Folkner; Davis Williams JP. Rec 3 March 1818.

p.47   Whitfield Brooks, Commissioner of the Court of Equity, to Richard Bullock, Deed, [day lost in binding] March 1817, Whereas D E Deavenport, guardian of Rebecca Williams and others, minors, 5 June last, petitioned for partition, stating that Marcus Williams lately deceased possessed 180 acres and that Rebecca Williams, Eliza Williams, James Williams, and John Williams are the only heirs of sd Marcus Williams; court recommended sale at public auction, land duly advertised and at public outcry on 4 March sold unto Richard Bullock for Two thousand four hundred sixty three cents 75 cents he being highest bidder, land on Ninety Six Creek adj lands of Richard Bullock, Jesse Paine, William Hagood, D E Deavenport. Wit George Butler, Phillip Dillard. /s/ Whit Brooks Comr in Equity E D. Proven 3 March 1818 by Major George Butler; M Mims C CP. Rec 3 March 1818.

p.49   Mary Muirhead to Hezekiah Almon of Orangeburgh District, Deed, [blank] January 1817, Fifty Dollars, 100 acres, part of a tract where Joel Dees senr now lives, on South Edisto River adj land formerly of James Whitehead. Wit George S D Smith, Holstun Almon. /s/ Mary (x) Muirhead. Proven 24 November 1817 by Holston Almon; John Loveless JP. Rec 4th March 1818.

p.50   George Roden and wife Sarah Roden to Hezekiah Almon, Deed, [day lost in binding] January 1817, Fifty Dollars, one third of land being part of tract where Joel Dees senior now lives containing 100 acres on South Edisto river, adj lands of Jones, land formerly of James Whitehead. Wit Catey Dozier, John M Dozier. /s/ George (x) Roden. /s/ Sarah (x) Roden. Proven 15 January 1817 by John M Dozier; Thomas Dozier JQ. Rec 4th March 1818.

p.51   Joel Dees junior to James Muirhead, Deed, 28 March 1815, Two hundred Dollars, 100 acres being part of land where Joel Dees junior now lives, on South Edisto River adj Jones, land formerly of James Whitehead. Wit James Sandy, Daniel (x) Dees. /s/ Joel (x) Dees. Proven 1 July 1815 by James Sanders; 1 July 1815. Rec 4th March 1818.

p.52   Solomon Collum and wife Margaret Collum to Hezekiah Almon, Deed, 5 December 1817, Fifty Dollars, third part of land whereon Joel Dees senior now lives containing 100 acres on South Edisto river, adj lands of Jones, James Whitehead. Wit Peter Lamkin, Holston Almon. /s/ Solomon (x) Collum, /s/ Margret (x) Collum. Proven 5 December 1817 by Holston Almon; Peter Lamkin JQ. Rec 4 March 1818.

p.53   John Monk to Harphrey Holland, Deed, 1 October 1810, Ten Pounds, 100 acres on South Edisto river, Ivy Island, granted to John Wootan 3 April 1786 by Hon Wm Moultrie, John Wootan granted to Aaron Kirkland junr 12 December 1797, sd Aaron Kirland jr granted to John Monk on 24 December 1800. Wit Joshua Monk, Sary (x) Monk. /s/ John Monk. Proven 30 July 1812 by Joshua Monk; Jno P Bush JP. Rec 4th March 1818.

p.55   Harphrey Holland to Hezekiah Almon of Orangeburgh District, Deed, 16 November 1814, One hundred Fifty Dollars, 100 acres on South Edisto River at Ivy Island, adj old coaling field, land granted to John Wootan on 3 April 1786 by Gov Wm Moultrie which John Wootan granted to Aaron Kirkland junr 12 December 1797 and Aaron Kirkland junr granted to John Monk 24 December 1800 and John Monk granted to sd Harphrey Holland 1 October 1810. Wit James Muirhead, William Burgess. /s/ Harfrey Holland. Proven 2 December 1817 by William Burgess; William Jones JP. Rec 4th March 1818.

p.56   Jesse Simkins to Dr Ira Scott, Deed, 16 June 1817, Fifty Dollars, two acre lot on Charleston Road being part of 250 acres granted to William Lemar 27 August 1764, two acres bounded by lines of Edward Couch. Wit Francis Walker, Pierce M Butler. /s/ Jesse Simkins. Proven 14 August 1817 by Francis Walker; John Loveless J P. Rec 4th March 1818.

p.57   Samuel Taylor to Adams Hutchison and Peter Bennock, Letter of Attorney, Augusta, Georgia, 2 April 1816, Samuel Taylor of Scotland in Great Britain but at present in Augusta, appoints for his sister Mary Raney and her husband William Raney also of Scotland, Adam Hutchison and Peter Bennock or either attorney to recover money owing to estate of William F Taylor in Kentucky belonging to me and my sister and her husband Wm Raney. Wit Nicholas Ware. /s/ Samuel Taylor. Proven 20 April 1818 by Nicholas Ware; W Jeter QU. Rec 22 Apr 1818.

p57   Adino Griffin of Abbeville District to Jacob Earnest, Deed, 7 January 1818, Two hundred Dollars, 200 acres on Halfway Swamp, part of 739 acres originally granted to Thomas Wilson, bounded North by that part of the original that was alotted to estate of Henry Wilson and land belonging to James Wilson, East by William Mays Junr, South by part of that half of the original that was alotted LittleBerry Wilson and West by James Wilson's land. Wit L Griffin, David Griffin.

/s/ Adino Griffin. Proven [day lost in binding] January 1818 by Larkin Griffin; Thos Anderson JQ. Rec 4ᵗʰ March 1818.

p.59   Phillip McCarty to Benjamin Corley, Deed, 5ᵗʰ January 1807, Two hundred twenty five Dollars, 50 acres, part of 750 acres on Clouds Creek, bounded North on Burkes old line, path that leads from Wests foard on Saluda to Davises on Clouds Creek, Slait Branch. Wit Robert Corley, Nathan Lipscomb. /s/ Phillip McCarty. Proven 13 January 1817 by Robert Corley; Spear Price JP. Rec 5th March 1818.

p.60   Gilfird Etheredge to Benjamin Corley, Deed, [blank] January 1816, Two hundred Dollars, [number lost in binding] hundred eighteen 3/4 acres on Little Saluda, being part of land formerly belonging to William Etheridge decd. Wit Joel Spencer, William Roe. /s/ Gilford Etheredge. Proven 13 January 1817 by Joel Spencer; Spear Price J P. Rec 5ᵗʰ March 1818.

p.61   Adam Hutchinson to Samuel Savage executor of estate of William F Taylor decd, Receipt, 2 April 1818, Ten thousand thirty seven Dollars thirty six and one quarter cents, in full of his doings on the estate up to this date. Wit John S Jeter, M Mims. /s/ Samuel Taylor, /s/ Willliam Raney & his wife per /s/ A Hutchinson their attorney. Rec 24ᵗʰ April 1818.

p.61   Jonas Jenkins to Benjamin Corley, Deed, 28 March 1815, Four hundred Dollars, 97 1/2 acres resurveyed 15 March 1815 by John Pope D S, lying on Clouds Creek and Beaverdam Creek of Little Saluda River, originally surveyed 14 September 1765 for Charles Banks, the above being only part of sd survey, adj Ethridge, Fluker, estate of Luke Smith, Joseph Pearson, afsd land conveyed to me by Jeremiah Hatcher Esqr, Sheriff, it being struck off to my friend Adkin Corley for my use 5 March 1810. Wit Joseph West, Nathaniel Corley, Thomas (x) West. /s/ Jonas (8) Jenkins. Proven 13 January 1817 by Joseph West; Spear Price, J P. Rec 5 March 1818.

p.62   Jonathan White to Blumer White junr, Deed, ---enth February 181--, Twelve hundred Dollars, 136 acres Cuffeetown Creek of Stephens Creek. Wit Henry Capehart, Stephen White Jr. /s/ Jonathan White. Justice Jno Lyon certifies relinquishment of dower rights by Elizabeth White wife of Jonathan White 7 February 1818; /s/ Elizabeth White. Proven 9 February 1818 by Henry Capehart; John Lyon JQ. Rec 7ᵗʰ March 1818.

p.64   Thomas Christian to Benjamin Frazier, Mortgage, 26 September 1817, Christian bound unto Frazier, two notes, both payable to Augustus G Nagel. Two notes, both payable to Benjamin Frazier. For securing notes, mortgages 502 acres on Shaws Creek and Hornes Creek on road from Edgefield Courthouse to Pine house, and formerly owned by Benjamin Darby Senr. If notes be paid at specified times, this sale to be void. Wit John S Jeter, Augustus G Nagel. /s/ Thomas Christian. Proven 7 March 1818 by Aug G Nagel; M Mims CCP. Rec 7ᵗʰ March 1818.

p.66   Morgan Corder to Arthur Padget, Deed, 18 January 1818, Two hundred Dollars, 60 acres on Moores Creek of Clouds Creek of Saluda River adj lines of sd Corder. Wit Micajah Whittle, Mark Padget. /s/ Morgan (x) Corder. Justice Nathan Norris certifies relinquishment of dower rights by Jenny Corder wife of Morgan Corder, 7 March 1818/ /s/ Jenny (x) Corder. Proven 20ᵗʰ January 1818 by Micajah Whittle; John Loveless J P.

p.67   William Coleman to Azariah Abney, Deed, 31 December 1817, One hundred Dollars, 25 ½ acres on Big Saluda adj lands of sd Abney, sd Coleman, Augusta road. Wit Thomas Harris, James Carson, Edwd (x) Coleman. /s/ William Coleman. Proven 26 February 1818 by Thomas Harris; John Abney JP. Rec 9ᵗʰ March 1818.

p.68   Jesse M Cogburn and Eliza Ann Cogburn to James Day, Deed, 30 August 1817, Five hundred forty Dollars, undivided part of 287[286?] acres on Foxes Creek of Savannah River originally granted unto Charles[?] Banks, sold by Sarah Banks unto Leroy Hammond Senr. sold by sd Hammond unto William Hall decd. Also undivided 49 ½ acres on Foxes Creek, part of two tracts, one granted to LeRoy Hammond Senr, the other to James Martin, by sd Martin to William Mathews and Mathews to LeRoy Hammond, and bounded on William Hall decd, Thomas Hall. Also their undivided part of 7 ½ acres bounded by land of William Hall decd and Alexander Stewart, adj land of William Forbes Taylor, being the land now held by Dr. McWhorter. Also all undivided part of 190 acres on Big Stephens Creek it being land that ---sdell Guardner sold unto William F Taylor, then sold unto William Hall decd by exrs of estate of sd Wm F Taylor decd, adj Levington Gardner, Sarah Gardner, Polly Grubbs formerly Polly Day, Stevens Creek, Nobles land, Levington Gardner. Wit Joseph R Addison, John Pierce Junr, David Ross, Daniel (x) Day. /s/ Jesse M Cogburn, /s/ Eliza Ann (x) Cogburn. Justice Charles Bussey certifies relinquishment of dower rights by Eliza Ann Cogburn wife of Jesse Cogburn, 4 March 1818; /s/ Eliza Ann Cogburn. Proven 12ᵗʰ Decr 1817 by Daniel (D) Day: John R Bartee J P. Rec 9ᵗʰ March 1818.

p.70   John Rushton, William Harrison, Nathan Rushton, William Rushton, Joseph Rushton and Thomas Ross, heirs of estate of James and Hannah Rushton, Articles of Agreement, 16 December 1817, agree to sell unto above named Nathan Rushton and Thomas Ross two of legatees of afsd property, the 286 acres whereon above named Hannah Rushton now lives, for Two thousand Dollars; afsd Nathan Rushton and Thomas Ross is to support afsd Hannah Rushton on sd plantation for her natural life. John Rushton, William Harrison, William Rushton and Joseph Rushton not to claim any part of afsd tract as the thirds or dower of sd Hannah Rushton after her decease. Wit Richard Henderson, Thomas Henderson. /s/ John Rushton, /s/ William Harrison,

DEED BOOK 35

/s/ Nathan Rushton, /s/ William Rushton, /s/ Joseph Rushton, /s/ Thomas Ross. Proven 23 Feby 1818 by Thomas Henderson; Catlett Conner JP. Rec 9 Mar 1818.

p.73   John Ricksey to George Rester, Deed, 4 February 1818, Sixty three Dollars, 31 ½ acres being part of land originally surveyed for Thomas Beckum and relapsed by James Millwee, on Middle Creek of Savannah River. Wit W H Nixon, James Tomkins. /s/ John (x) Ricksey. Plat by James Tomkins 4 February 1818 shows adjoining land of George Rester, J Ricksey, W Oenbey, John Ricksey. Justice John Lyon certifies relinquishment of dower rights by Rachel Ricksey wife of John Ricksey, 10 February 1818; /s/ Rachel (x) Ricksey. Proven 14 February 1818 by James Tomkins; Thomas Price J P. Rec 9ᵗʰ March 1818.

p.75   Lewis Curry, Benajah Curry and wife Susannah, Luke Devore and wife Caty, David Dobey and wife Patsey, Cader Curry, John Curry junior, to John Curry Senr, Bond, 11 February 1818, $2845.25 each; condition John Curry senior distributed among his children part of his estate on 25 September 1817. If foregoing legatees separately acknowledge agreement a just distribution and that they have received their separate parts, then above obligation to be of none effect. Wit John R Barett, Charles McKinze. /s/ David Dobey, /s/ Cader Curry, /s/ John Curry junr, /s/ Lewis Curry, /s/ Benajah (x) Curry, /s/ Luke L Devore.   Proven 11 February 1818 by Charles McKinze; John R Barett J P. Rec 9ᵗʰ March 1818.

p.76   John Curry senior to his daughter Susannah Curry, Deed of Gift, 1 August [year lost in binding], love, Negroes Jude and her child Robert with their future issue during her natural life and after death of my daughter to grandchildren, viz Robert Linear, Silas Linear, Keziah Hardy wife of Freeman Hardy junior, Betsy Linear, Lewis Linear, and Patsey Linear children of my sd daughter Susannah Curry share and share alike. Wit T Taylor, John Butler, John R Bartee. /s/ John (x) Curry Senr. Proven 24 January 1818 by John Butler; John R Bartee JP. Rec 9ᵗʰ March 1818.

p.77   Matthew Barrett to John Turpin, Quit Claim, 9 March 1818, Ten Dollars, 5 acres adj lands of late John Longmire decd with the exception of [number lost in the binding] feet square where the graveyard is; on road from Edgefield Courthouse to Abbeville Courthouse, and also liberty to move the store house from the west to east side of the road. Wit Matilda Longmire, Jincey Lyon. /s/ Matthew (x) Barrett. Justice John Lyon certifies the relinquishment of dower by Elizabeth Barrett wife of Matthew Barrett, 9 March 1818; /s/ Eliz Barrett. Proven 9 March 1818 by Charlotte Matilda Longmire; John Lyon QU. Rec 10ᵗʰ March 1818.

p.78   Catharine Logan exr to Isaac Bush, Deed of Conveyance, 1 January 1818, whereas John Logan late of St Bartholomews Parish was possessed of lands in Granville County now Edgefield District; sd John Logan on 31 January 1785 made

64

his will granting authority to exrs to sell lands 5187 acres, and apptd his sons John Logan Junr sole exr and after his death Dr George Logan to be exr of his will. John Logan junr proved sd will and undertook the execution on 19 Feb 1803; after death of Dr George Logan his wife Catharine Logan and others were extx and extrs of sd will; sd Catharine Logan undertook sole burden. Therefore Catharine Logan sole extx of John Logan Junr of St Bartholomew Parish, Three hundred eighty five Dollars paid by Isaac Bush of Edgefield granted 385 acres being the whole of land granted to Isaac Lesesne for100 acres except 130 acres in possession of Benjamin Murrell, adj lands of Singleton, estate of John Logan, Wm Sturges, Ezekiel McClendon, Benjamin Jurrell. Wit Robert E Cochran, Edwin Chipman. /s/ Catharine Logan extx. Proven 9 February 1818 by Edwin Chipman; Henry Chipman JP. Rec 10th March 1818.

p.80　George Lamkin to William Quarles, Deed,　10 November 1817, Seventeen hundred Dollars, 340 acres formerly granted to Abram Martin on Bird Creek of Stephens Creek bounded by lands of Thomas Morton, William Thurmond, John George, Spencer, James Lamkin. Wit Robert Brooks, Aaron Tullis, Newel Tullis. /s/ George Lamkin. Justice John Lyon certifies relinquishment of dower rights by Susannah Lamkin wife of George Lamkin 18 November 1817; /s/ Susannah (x) Lamkin. Plat by Patrick Gibson D S 27 October 1817 shows 340 acres shows Ellis' road. Proven 23 January 1818 by Aaron Tullis; John Lyon QU. Rec 10 March 1818.

p.82　John Pierce Senr to John Pierce Junr. Deed, 11 November 1817, Five Dollars, 75 acres Stephens Creek being part of land originally granted to John Hammond decd adj Brewers Spring Branch, Hancock and Howerton, John Pierce Senr, Benjamin Grumble. Wit Abram Pierce, Richard Covington, John Traylor. /s/ John (x) Pierce. Proven 7th March 1818 by John Traylor; Charles Bussey JQ. Rec 10th March 1818.

p.82　Sarah Q Hammond to John Hammond, Dower, Justice John Tarrance certifies relinquishment of dower rights by Sarah Hammond wife of LeRoy Hammond, 13 January 1817; /s/ Sarah Q Hammond. NB See Deed in Book GG pp 123 & 144. Rec 11th March 1818.

p.83　Stephen Terry Junr to John Hollingworth, Deed, 23 December 1817, One hundred forty four Dollars, 24 acres being part of land originally granted to William Todd, on waters of Beaverdam Creek of Stephens Creek, adj lands of sd Terry, Joel Roper, sd Hollingworth. Wit William Forguson, William (x) Williams. /s/ Stephen Terry junr. Justice Jesse Blocker certifies relinquishment of dower rights by Jincy Terry, 23 December 1817; /s/ Jincy (x)Terry. Proven 23 December 1817 by William Farguson; Jesse Blocker JQ. Rec 11th March 1818.

p.84　William Samuel to Isaac Parker, Bond, 11 March 1818, Wm Samuel bound unto Isaac Parker trustee for George Parker and Elizabeth Parker in penal sum One

DEED BOOK 35

Parker for George Parker & Elizabeth Parker afsd Eight hundred Dollars on or before 1 January next ensuing with interest on same from 8 October 1816. Wit William W Dunn, William C Harden. /s/ William Samuel. I assign within bond which is secured by mortgage to Henry G Harden but do not warranty performance of the contract, 11 March 1818. Wit William W Dunn, William C Hardin. /s/ Geo Parker agt. Proven 11 March 1818 by William C Harden; M Mims CCP. Rec 11th March 1818.

p.85 William Samuel to Isaac Parker trustee for George Parker and Elizabeth Parker, Wm Samuel is bound unto Isaac Parker trustee with condition that if Wm Samuel pay full sum of Eight hundred Dollars on or before first January 1819 with full interest sd obligation to be void; to secure payment, Wm Samuel grants 295 3/4 acres known as the Elim tract, bounded by lands of Charles Randolph, Francis Johnson, Lewis Nobles, Ephraim Ferrell. Wit William W Dunn, William C Harden. /s/ William Samuel. Proven 11 March 1818 by Wm C Harden; M Mims CCP. Rec 11 Mar 1818.

p.87 Isaac Parker Trustee of Elizabeth Parker and George Parker the husband of sd Elizabeth Parker and sd Elizabeth Parker to William Samuel, Deed, Court of Equity in June Term 1817 authorized Isaac Parker to make titles to William Samuel to 295 3/4 acres named Elim adj lands of Charles Randolph, Francis Johnson, Ephraim Ferrell, David Dobey, Nobles, plat by John Blocker and Robert Lang 8 July 1813. Therefore Isaac Parker, George Parker and Elizabeth Parker for Two thousand eight hundred Dollars paid by William Samuel have sold Elim unto William Samuel. Wit Susan P Snead, Edwin C Holland, Jos McCall. /s/ Isaac Parker trustee. /s/ Geo Parker. /s/ Elizabeth Parker. Commission from Gov A Pickens Junr, appointing Samuel Abbott a Justice of the Quorum to keep the peace and Notary Public, Charleston 6 February 1818. /s/ John G Brown Secy State. Deed proven 6 February 1818 by Edwin C Holland; Samuel Abbott QU. Deed proven 1st December 1817 by Susan P Snead; John Tarrance J P. Rec 11 March 1818.

p.89 Harman P Cosper to Henry Martin, Deed, 11 January 1817, Eight hundred fifty Dollars, 411 ½ acres granted to me 5 January 1801 on small branch of Bird Creek of Stevens Creek. Wit Robt Harrison, Thomas Mitchell. /s/ Harman P Cosper. Proven 11 January 1817 by Robt Harrison; John Lyon QU. Rec 13th March 1818.

p.90 Thomas Christian to Benjamin Hatcher, Deed, [day left blank] January 1818, Twenty two Dollars, 11 acres it being part of land sold to sd Thomas Christian by Benjamin Darby Senr adj lands of sd Benjamin Hatcher. Wit Mary Hatcher, Francis Bettis. /s/ Thomas Christian. Proven 14 March 1818 by Francis Bettis; Wm Hagens J P. Rec 14th March 1818.

p.91 Sampson Jenkins of Georgia to John Jenkins, Deed, 12 February 1818, Columbia County, Georgia, Forty Dollars, my distributive share of land of estate of

66

my father Samuel Jenkins decd, also my distributiove share of real estate of my brother James Jenkins decd, in Edgefield District on Little and Big Turkey Creeks, adj lands of Young Allen, Benjamin Frazier, Arthur Simkins, John Arledge Junr. Wit Elias Baggett, Thomas Fuller. /s/ Sampson Jenkins. Proven Columbia County, Georgia, 12 Feb1818 by Elias Baggett; Stephen Hoge JP. Rec 14th March 1818.

p.92   Henry G Harden et al to George Parker, Receipt. Received 1st January 1818 of George Parker One thousand Dollars in part of the within Bond $1000. /s/ Henry G Harden. Received 11th March 1818 of George Parker (acting agt for Isaac Parker trustee for Elizabeth Parker) Eight hundred seventy five Dollars in part of this bond. $875. /s/ Henry G Harden. Received 11 March 1818 of George Parker (acting agent for Isaac Parker trustee to Mrs Geo Parker) one thousand and ninety three Dollars 37 1/2 cts in part of this Bond. $1093.37 1/2. /s/ William C Harden. Rec 11 March 1818.

p.93   Jesse McClendon to His Children, Deed of Gift, 4 May 1818, love toward my four children viz Arthur W Cox, Eliza Ann Cox, James M Cox and Jesse Cox begotton on body of Sarah Cox lawful wife of George Cox, 130 acres on Turkey Creek adj lands of Gasper Gaulman, Allen McClendon and one Negro girl Hannah about 14 yrs of age with her future increase, my household and kitchen furniture, plantation tools, cattle, hogs, horse, share and share alike after my death. Wit John S Jeter, Wm Lindsay. /s/ Jesse (x) McClendon. Proven 15 May 1818 by John S Jeter; M Mims CCP. Rec 15 Mar 1818.

p.94   Jacob Martin to David Murray, Abbeville District, Deed, 26 March 1818, Two hundred Dollars, 103 acres being part of 1000 acres originally granted to William Moore, conveyance to me by James M Butler as sheriff 24 May 1814. Wit Joseph Black, Polly Miller. /s/ Jacob Martin. Proven 26 March 1818 by Polley Miller; Joseph Black JQ. Abbeville District: Justice Joseph Black certifies relinquishment of dower rights by Nancy Martin wife of Jacob Martin, 26 March 1818; /s/ Nancy Martin. Rec 31 March 1818.

p.94   William Hill Senior to William S Johnson and John Mixson Junr of Barnwell District, Deed, 22 November 1817, Eight hundred Dollars, 814 acres being land whereon sd Hill and son now live, on waters of Horns Creek, Marshalls Creek and Beaverdam, joining lands of John Gray Senr, heirs of Samuel Walker decd, Ryans lands, Starling Mitchell, heirs of Frederick Tilman decd, Benjamin Lindsay & Thomas Terry. Wit Christian Breithaupt, Edward Jones, William Hill junr, Travis Hill Junr, Millenton Blalock. /s/ William Hill Senr. Justice Christian Breithaupt certifies relinquishment of dower rights by Anne Hill wife of William Hill, 22 November 1817; /s/ Anne (x) Hill. Proven 6 April 1818 by Christian Breithaupt; M Mims CCP. Rec 6 April 1818.

p.96   Richard Findlay to his son Charles Findlay, Deed, 11 February 1812, One hundred Dollars, 54 acres on Savannah River adj lands of John Kilcrease, Richard Findley, plat certified by John Boyd D S, whereon sd Charles Findley now lives. Wit John Boyd, Ed^d Keeling, Anselm B Newsom. /s/ Richd (R) Findley. Proven 31(sic) November 1812 by Edmund Keeling; Charles Hammond QU. Rec 6 Apr 1818.

p.97   Richard Findley to Charles Findley, Deed, 4 July 1814, Fifty Dollars, 30 acres on Savannah River adj lands of Charles Findley, John Kilcrease, Paces old Ferry road, Richard Findleys Spring branch. Wit Edmund Keeling, Abraham Kilcrease, Robert Crawford. /s/ Richd (x) Findley. Proven 9th Feb 1818 by Robert Crawford; Thomas Price J P. Rec 6 April 1818.

p.98   Jesse Jay to John Mobley, Deed, 16 February 1818, One hundred thirty Dollars, 100 acres on Burrels Creek of Little Saluda, adj lands of sd Mobley, Anne Vaughan, line run by John Pope for Jesse Jay, Augusta Road, Arthur Simkins. Wit R Newport, Anson Mobley. /s/ Jesse (x) Jay. Justice Thomas Dozier certifies relinquishment of dower rights by Christian Jay wife of Jesse Jay, 14 March 1818; /s/ Christian Jay. Proven 14 March 1818 by Robert Newport; Thomas Dozier JQ. Rec 6th April 1818.

p.99   John Blocker to Francis Clement, Deed, 16 January 1818, Four hundred seventy seven Dollars twelve and half cents, 954 1/4 acres on Jinn branch and Rockey Creek, granted to John Blocker, and part granted to Alex Jillson, part sold off by John Blocker to David Parkman. Wit William Johnson, Haly Johnson. /s/ John Blocker. Justice Jesse Blocker certifies the relinquishment of dower rights by Mary Blocker wife of John Blocker, 19 January 1818; /s/ Mary T Blocker. Proven 19 January 1818 by Haly Johnson; Jesse Blocker JQ. Rec 6th April 1818.

p.100   Littleberry Franklin to Miles Buzbee junr, Deed, 23 March 1816, Fifteen Dollars, 125 acres being part of 705 acres granted to Berry Franklin 5 October 1812 on Little Bull Branch. Wit Benjamin Buzbee, Mary Ann (x) Buzbe. /s/ Little Berry Franklin. Proven 20 July 1816 by Benjn Buzbee; Lewis Holmes JP. Rec 6 Apr 1818.

p.101   David Gurganus to Chaney Farrar, Deed, 9 January 1818, Four hundred Dollars, 60 acres on Beaverdam Creek, part of land originally granted to Anguish McDaniel adj lands of James Beams, Matthew Mims, David Gurganus, William Blackborn. Wit James Beams, Rebeccah Beams. /s/ David Gurganus. Justice Matthew Mims certifies relinquishment of dower rights by Rebecca Gurganus wife of David Gurganus, 7 April 1818; /s/ Rebecca (x) Gurganus. Proven 16 April 1818 by James Beams; M Mims CCP. Rec 16 April 1816.

p.102   Burrel Arrington to John Glauzier, Deed, 22 January 1817, One hundred Dollars, 71 ½ acres on Mountain Creek of Turkey Creek adj lines of John Glauzier,

Jesse Holloway, Peter Dorn, William McDaniell, Henry Timmerman. Wit Ransom Holloway, Jonathan Clegg, Jesse Holloway Senr. /s/ Burrell Arrington. Proven 30 March 1818 by Ransom Holloway; Jourdan Holloway JP. Rec 16ᵗʰ April 1818.

p.103 Susannah Richardson, Wineford Richardson, John Wootan, Jesse Pitman, Absalom Moseley, Daniel Richardson, William May, Abraham Richardson, Hammond Richardson heirs of Abram Richardson to Richard Blalock senr of Barnwell District, 17 January 1818, Two hundred fifty Dollars, 400 acres on Bridge Creek of Big Horse Creek adj lands of Absalom Napper, sd Abraham Richardson's original line, M G Hautton. Wit Wm Smith, Beaufort Norwood. /s/ Wineford (x) Richardson, John Wootan, Jesse Pitman, Absalom Mosley, Daniel (x) Richardson, Jas Reynolds for Wm May, Susannah (x) Richardson, B Richardson, Hammond (x) Richardson. Proven 28 January 1818 by Beaufort Norwood; John Randall J P. Rec 16 Apr 1818.

p.104 Edmund Bacon to Matthias Jones, Deed, 7 February 1817, One hundred twenty Dollars, 4 3/4 acres on Beaverdam Creek, being part of land originally granted to Elias Blackborn, from him conveyed unto William Blackborn, from him to afsd Edmund Bacon, on road to Higgins Ferry on Saluda River. Wit John Martin, Robert Perrin. /s/ Edmund Bacon. Justice Matthew Mims certifies relinquishment of dower rights by Mary Blackborn wife of William Blackborn, 17 April 1818; /s/ Mary Blackborn. Justice Matthew Mims certifies relinquishment of dower rights by Eliza Bacon wife of Edmund Bacon, 17 April 1818; /s/ Eliza Bacon. Proven 1 January 1818 by John Martin; M Mims CCP. Rec 17 April 1818.

p.106 Moses Walton to Mary Ellis, Deed, 13 March 1806, Six hundred Dollars, 200 acres originally granted to Samuel Abney senr, from him to his son Samuel Abney junr heir at law, and from Samuel Abney junr to Moses Walton. Wit William Spragins, Thomas Walton. /s/ Moses Walton. Proven 30 December 1817 by William Spragins; John Abney J P. Rec 17ᵗʰ April 1818.

p.106 Thomas S Oliver of Augusta, Georgia, to James Meyers of Edgefield, Deed of sale, 10 April 1817, Five thousand Dollars, 16 Negroes Jacob, Molly, Diannah, Rozetta, [patch obscured name], Lucy, Susasa[?], Clarasa, Robert, Dorces, Ephr[patch obscures this and next name], Will, Arther, Amy, Leavy with their future issue. Wit Richard Hampton, Clement Green. /s/ Thomas S Oliver. Proven 26 April 1818 by Richard Hampton; John Sturzenegger JP. Rec 29ᵗʰ April 1818.

p.107 Sheriff Jeremiah Hatcher to John Turpin of Augusta, Georgia, Shff's Titles, 18 February 1818, at suit of John Bolton agt John Longmire, land to be advertised and publicly sold to highest bidder for ready money at Edgefield Courthouse; struck off to John Turpin by his friend John Lyon for Twenty eight hundred Dollars, two tracts, 150 acres on Cuffeetown Creek adj lands of Matthew Barrett, sd John

Longmire decd, Jacob Shively. Wit Richd H Tutt, Josiah Allen. /s/ J Hatcher SED. A plat by Robert Carson D S surveyed 7 February 1805 for 530 acres being part of 2300 acres granted to Benjamin Tutt on Bee Tree branch of Cuffeetown Creek; the plat drawn here shows 153 acres on Bee Tree crossed by a road and adjoining lands of Thomas Bacon Esqr, Matthew Barrett, John Longmire Esqr, Jacob Shively, and road · from Lees Ferry. Plat dated 2 September 1802 by Robert Bradford D S by order of Capt John Longmire shows land laid out for Sarah Blakeley, 120 acres on Cuffeetown Creek adj lands of Matthew Barrett, Thos Bacon, J Shibbley, Thos Wilborn, crossed by Lick Creek and adj Cuffeetown. Justice John Lyon certifies relinquishment of dower by Hannah Longmire wife of John Longmire, 20 April 1818; /s/ Hannah Longmire. Proven 1 May 1818 by Richard H Tutt; M Mims, CCP. Rec 1ˢᵗ May 1818.

p.109   Charles Waldrum of Monrough County, Mississippi Territory to Joseph Smart, Deed, 1 October 1817, Five hundred Dollars, 165 acres on Loyds Creek of Stephens Creek. Wit John Morgan, Isaac (x) Vann. /s/ Charles Waldrum. Plat shows 165 acres, part of two surveys, one originally granted to Jos Thomas for 150 acres 5 May 1775; the other to Edmund Holleman for 85 acres 3 August 1795. Plat shows adj lands of Vallentine White decd, James Martin, John Lyon, estate of Henry Key, decd, and is titled land laid off on division between John Morgan and Isaac Vann, purchased from them by Henry Waldrum; 29ᵗʰ August 1817 by Stephen Tillman D S. Justice Charles Hammond certifies relihnquishment of dower by Mary Waldrum wife of Charles Waldrum, 21 October 1817; /s/ Mary (x) Waldrum. Proven 21 October 1817 by John Morgan; Charles Hammond JQ. Rec 2d May 1818.

p.111   Lee Blackborn to Henry Shultz of Augusta, Georgia, Deed, 21 November 1817, Five hundred thirty seven Dollars fifty cents, 255 acres, part of two tracts, one originally granted to William Frazier; other granted to Samuel Marsh the elder. First tract on branch of Beaverdam Cr of Turkey Cr; the other adj lands of James Frazier, William Frazier. Wit Edward B Machin, Augustus G Nagel. /s/ Lee Blackborn. Proven 4 May 1818 by Augustus G Nagel; M Mims CCP. Rec 4 May 1818.

p.112   Peter Herrin to John Herrin, Deed, 13 December 1817, Four hundred Dollars, 140 acres on Mine Creek surveyed by Joseph Dawson and granted to Charles Brown, adj by Stephen Daniel, William Herrin, Youngblood. Wit Wm McClendon, Levi Coxon. /s/ Peter Herrin. Proven 25 December 1817 by Levi McCoxon; John Lain J P. Rec 4ᵗʰ May 1818.

p.113   Mary Grubbs to Richard Covington, Deed, 13 April 1818, Four hundred fifty Dollars, 50 acres being the land that Henry Day Senr granted unto sd Mary Grubbs formerly Mary Day, it being part of land that sd Henry Day surveyed for himself now known as Henry Days Old Tract, adj lands of James Day bought of Susannah Covington, land Richard Covington bought of Levingston Gardner. Wit James Day,

Elizabeth (x) Day. /s/ Mary (x) Grubbs. Proven 18 April 1818 by James Day; Charles Bussey JP. Rec 4 May 1818.

p.114 James Stewart of Augusta, Georgia, to Richard Covington, planter, Mortgage, 18 April 1818, Two thousand Dollars paid by Covington, 200 acres on which sd Richard Covington now lives adj lands of Sarah Harden, James Day, Daniel Frazier, James Panton, Savannah River, Stephens Creek, Nobles. Nevertheless, hereby provided that if James Stewart pays Richard Covington before January next, these presents to be void. Wit James Panton, J H Bussey. /s/ James Stewart. Proven 18 April 1818 by J H Bussey; Charles Bussey JP. Rec 4 May 1818.

p.115 Levington Gardner to Richard Covington, Deed, 19 January 1818, One thousand six hundred Dollars, 150 acres on Savannah river adj lands of James Day, Daniel Frazier, Stephens Creek, Nobles, same being land willed to Levington Gardner by his father Robert Gardner at his decease. Wit J H Bussey, Joel Howerton. /s/ Levington (x) Gardner. Proven 18 April 1818 by Joel Howerton; Charles Bussey J P. Rec 4 May 1818.

p.116 William Caldwell of Newberry District to John R Hammond, Deed, 3 November 1813, Five hundred Dollars paid by Charles Hammond of Edgefield, father of John R Hammond, 140 acres on Martintown Road being part of land formerly held by Mjr John Williams adj Joseph Collier, Martin Bailey, Aquilla Miles, Reuben Beckham, plat by Robert Lang. Wit Geo Parker, Matthias Ardis. /s/ Wm Caldwell. Proven 5 April 1814 by George Parker; A Edmonds JP. Rec 4 May 1818.

p.117 Doct. James A Ward & John Ross exrs of Frederick Ward decd to James Coleman, Deed, 20 May 1815, Two thousand one hundred ninety one Dollars, 475 acres on Ninety Six Creek adj lands of sd Coleman, Wardleworth, Savage, Wm Shaw, James Wilson decd, Larkin Griffin. Wit Archey Mayson, Larkin Griffin. /s/ J A Ward exr, John Ross Exr. Proven 20 May 1815 by Archey Mayson; Thomas Anderson JQ. Plat by Thos Anderson D S certified 19 May 1815 shows road to Augusta crossing the property and a sketch of a possibly brick house. Rec 14th May 1818.

p.118 James Herrin to Freeman Goode, Deed, 4 November 1817, Six hundred fifty Dollars, 100 acres on Halfway Swamp Creek of Saluda River adj lands of Freeman Goode, Sugar Matthews, John Troop. Wit Mackerness Goode, Joseph Morris Junr. /s/ James Herring. Justice William Robertson certifies relinquishment of dower rights by Susan Herrin wife of James Herrin, 4th November 1817; /s/ Susan (x) Herrin. Proven 14 May 1818 by Joseph Morris junr; Catlett Conner JP. Rec 18 May 1818.

p.119 John Pool to Reeves Martin and Mackerness Pope Goode, Deed, 4 November 1817, Two thousand two hundred Dollars, 600 acres on Breshy fork of Halfway

Swamp Creek of Saluda River adj lands of Mr Morris, William Summers. Wit Freeman Goode, Sugar J Mathews. /s/ John Pool. Justice William Robertson certifies relinquishment of dower rights by Hulday Pool wife of John Pool 4 November 1817; /s/ Hulday (x) Pool. Proven 14 May 1818 by Freeman Goode; Catlett Conner J P. Rec 18 May 1818.

p.120 Eldred Simkins to James M Butler, Deed, 8 June 1813, Two hundred Dollars, 2 acres in village of Edgefield known in plan certified 22d October 1800 by Robert Lang as a beautiful eminence reserved for a public academy adj on lands of Eugene Brenan, sd Elbert Simkins, Monroe Street, Peter Laborde. Wit J Burton, Wm Wash Junr. /s/ Eldred Simkins. Plat certified 14 April 1813 by John Blocker for Eldred Simkins Esqr and Doct John Hart, shows lot sold to William Glover. Proven 11 June 1813 by John Burton; Ste Butler CCP. Rec 20 May 1818[1816?]

p.122 Matthew Mims to David Mims, Deed, 15 May 1818, Three hundred fifty Dollars, 250 acres on Beaverdam of Turkey Creek and Stephens Creek adj lands of John Mims, Levi Jester, John Hollingsworth and sd Matthew Mims, deed and plat from Drury Mims Senr to sd Matthew Mims. Wit John S Jeter, John Negel. /s/ M Mims. Justice Eldred Simkins certifies relinquishment of dower rights by Eliza Mims wife of Matthew Mims 21 May 1818; /s/ Eliza Mims. Proven 21 May 1818 by John S Jeter; Eldred Simkins QU. Rec 21 May 1818.

p.123 Josiah Nicholson to Samuel Marsh, Deed, 20 August 1817, Fifteen hundred Dollars, 230 acres whereon I now live on Rockey Branch of Rockey Ceek, Turkey Creek of Stephens Creek, adj land of Shemuel Nicholson, Josiah Horn, estate of Thomas Adams. Wit Jesse Blocker, Latisha Nicholson. /s/ Josiah Nicholson. Proven 21 May 1818 by Jesse Blocker; M Mims. Justice Jesse Blocker certifies relinquishment of dower rights by Elizabeth Nicholson wife of Josiah Nicholson 20 August 1817; /s/ Elizabeth (x) Nicholson. Plat at request of Shemuel Nicholson certified 1 October 1800 by Shadk Stokes D S shows 260 acres in a tract of 1148 acres surveyed 6 Nov 1771 by Moses Kirkland D S for Henry Middleton, at present in Edgefield on Little Rockey Creek, adj lands shown are Jonathan Dawson, Thomas Bratcher, Mecail Utz, Thomas Adams. Rec 21 May 1818.

p.124 Matthias Jones to William Read, Deed, 28 March 1816, Three hundred seventy five Dollars, 170 acres whereon William Reed now lives on old Cambridge road adj lands of John Warters, Arthur Rice Watson now Jones', Fowl/Fall Creek, Jesse Daniels. Wit Henry Spann, Allen C Perry. /s/ Matthias Jones. Justice Charles Oneal certifies relinquishment of dower by Clary Jones wife of Matthias Jones, 6 November 1816; /s/ Clary Jones. Proven 16 May 1816 by Henry Spann; John Lark JQ. Rec 22 May 1818.

p.125   Jonathan Gregory to granddaughter Esther Deas a cow, to her brother Charles Deas a heiffer, to his brother Squire Deas, heiffer,   Deed/Gift, 30 April 1818, love. Wit Thomas Cockroft, John Lovelace. /s/ Jonathan Gregory. Proven 30 April 1818 by Thomas Cockroft; John Loveless J P. Rec 22 May 1818.

p.136   James M Butler to Alexander B McWhorter, Deed, 4 February 1816, Nine hundred fifty Dollars, 2 acres in village of Edgefield known in plan drawn by Robert Lang on 22 October 1800, adj Eugene Brenan, Eldred Simkins, Monroe Street, Peter Laborde. Wit Barkley M Blocker, J Hatcher. /s/ J M Butler. Proven 25 May 1818 by J Hatcher; M Mims CCP. Rec 25th May 1818.

p.127   Aaron Phelps and wife Mary Ann to William English, Agreement, 23 August 1817, Four hundred Dollars to be paid by Wm English to Aaron Phelps on or before first January next, also one hundred to be paid by Wm English to Aaron Phelps annually on every first day of January thereafter until the expiration of this lease, 195 acres adj lands of Catlett Conner, William Robertson, Col John Moore, Mssrs Benskin Lightfoot, Wm Spikes and James McCracken, for full term of twenty one years next ensuing; condition should Mary Ann Phelps die the lease shall immediately cease and the tract return to Aaron Phelps or the heirs of sd Mary Ann Phelps agreeable to deed of settlement between William shaw Esqr and Hon Abram Nott & the Revd Benj R Montgomery as trustees apptd for sd Mary Ann and her late sister Elizabeth Wybergh decd dated 25 Nov 1812, provided that 6 acres of above land adj Augusta road leased to Wm Nibbs for three years is excepted from this agreement but at expiration the 6 acres are to go with the rest of the land to Wm English; also twenty acres of above land leased to William Spikes for 12 months go to sd Wm English; also that John C Mayson or Mason, Henry Tolbert to whom Mr John C Mayson has transferred his right to seven thousand rails for fences [provisions for taxes & upkeep here omitted]. Wit Catlett Conner, Garland Chiles. /s/ Aaron Phelps, /s/ Mary Ann Phelps. Proven 2 May 1818 by Garland Chiles; Charles Mayson J P. Rec 27 May 1818.

p.129   Cadwell Evans to Jacob Hibbler, Receipt, received 1 Decr 1817 of Jacob Hibbler One hundred Dollars in part for 600 acres part of which I now live upon, surveyed for my father Batt Evans and part of Tuckers survey bounding on Jonathan Glanton, Beverly Burton, Mrs Raney, Robert Evans, Spencer. /s/ Cadwell Evans. N.B. I grant possession 15th January next during which time sd Hibbler pays One thousand Dollars and twelve months after One thousand on first January 1819 and One thousand Dollars on 29th Decr 1819. Wit Jonathan Glanton. /s/ Cadwell Evans. Proven 28 May 1818 by Jonathan Glanton; E B Belcher J P. Rec 29 May 1818.

p.129   Wineford Richardson to John J Johnson, Relinquishment, 9 October 1817, Justice Eldred Simkins certifies relinquishment of dower rights by Wineford Richardson wife of Abram Richardson deceased, land sold by Abram Richardson decd

73

DEED BOOK 35

agreeable to deed from sd Richardson to sd Johnson. /s/ Wineford (x) Richardson.
Rec 30 May 1818.

p.130   William Bailey, planter, to William Burnett, Deed, 4 August 1817, Three
hundred fifty Dollars, 200 acres which land was conveyed to me by Abner Corley,
adj Gardners land, Horsepen Creek, Samuel Williams, John Freeman. Wit Lark
Abney, John Hamilton. /s/ William Bailey. Justice William Robertson certifies the
relinquishment of dower rights by Margaret Bailey wife of William Bailey, 20
November 1817; /s/ Margaret (x) Bailey. Proven 22 May 1818 by Lark Abney; Davis
Williams J P. Rec 1 June 1818.

p.131   John Collum to Thomas Deen, Deed, 13 September 1811, Two hundred fifty
Dollars, 100 acres on Moors Creek of Little Saluda adj lands of Thomas Warren,
Watson. Wit Samuel Deen, Andrew Heron. /s/ John (x) Collum. Justice Elijah
Watson certifies relinquishment of dower rights by Catarena Collum wife of John
Collum, 29 October 1811/ /s/ Catarena (s) Collum. Proven 29 October 1811 by
Samuel Deen; Elijah Watson JQ. Rec 1 June 1818.

p.132   Joseph Rarden, planter, to his wife Nancy Rarden of second part, and Jourdan
Holloway and Sanders Rareden, trustees,   Deed of Trust, 14 June 1818, love, for
management of property for support of Nancy Rarden and children, 400 acres on
Mountain Creek and nine Negroes: Tom, Darcas, Abel, Aaron, Cain, Lewis, Edmond,
Charles, Kezziah and her child and their future increase [livestock, equipment,
household goods], other provisions [here omitted]. Wit Dabney Parmer, Jesse
Mitchell, Lewellwyn Holloway. /s/ Joseph Rarden, /s/ Nancy Rarden, /s/ Jourden
Holloway, /s/ Sanders Rarden. Proven 4 June 1818 by Dabney Parmer; Jordan
Holloway. Rec 6th June 1818.

p.134   William Ferguson, planter, to Zebulon Rudulph of Columbia, Richland
District, merchant, Deed, 7 March 1818, Three thousand Dollars, 1500 acres whereon
I resided last year, on Beaverdam and Richland Creeks of Little Saluda, resurvey
made for me by John Pope 28 Jan 1817 and certified by Shepherd Spencer. Wit
Zebulon Rudulph Jr, Lewis Bowdon. /s/ Wm Ferguson. Justice William Hurt certifies
relinquishment of dower rights by Morning Ferguson wife of William Ferguson, 16
May 1818; /s/ Mourning (x) Ferguson. Proven 13 April 1818 by Lewis Bowdon;
Mumford Perryman JP. Rec 1st June 1818.

p.135   Charles Waldrum of Monrough County, Mississippi Territory, to Isaac Vann,
Deed, 1 October 1817, Five hundred Dollars, 165 acres on Loyds Creek of Stephens
Creek adj lands of Mrs Buckhalter, estate of Henry Key, Valentine White, plat
certified by Stephen Tillman. Wit Charles Hammond, John Lyon. /s/ Charles
Waldrum. Proven 21 March 1818 by Charles Hammond; A Edmonds J P. Justice

74

Chas Hammond certifies relinquishment of dower by Mary Waldrum wife of Charles Waldrum, 1 October 1817; /s/ Mary (x) Waldrum. Plat at request of Isaac Hammond and John Morgan, land conditionally purchased by Henry Waldrum Junr, 330 acres divided into two parts of 165 acres; plat shows land agreed upon by Morgan and Isaac Vann to be possessed by sd Vann, being part of three surveys, one originally granted to Joseph Thomas for 150 acres 5 May 1775, one to Christian Buckhalter for 200 acres, the other to Edmund Holleman for 85 acres 3 August 1795, on Loyds Creek, 29 August 1817; Stephen Tillman DS. Plat shows New Market Road, adj lands of Mrs Buckhalter, Flinn, estate of Valentine White, John Morgan, estate of Henry Key, Jesse Waldrums gate, Wm Howl. Rec 1st June 1818.

p.137 State vs Martin Will. Stark. Elllison. Constitutional Court at Columbia Spring meeting 1818. Motion for new trial in arrest of judgment. Moton granted. Certified by James Guignard, clerk. Rec 1st June 1818.

p.137 Whitfield Brooks, commr of Court of Equity, to John Loftin, Commissioners Deed, 4 May 1818, John McDaniel & wife 25 Sept 1815 complaint against Samuel Marshand & others admrs & admx of estate of Willliam Harden decd praying for division of land; lands to be sold at public auction 4 May, sold unto John Lofton, Robert Lofton for Two hundred sixty three Dollars, he being highest bidder; [number lost in binding] hundred seventy two acres on Horns Creek. Wit Andrew P Butler, John Blocker. /s/ Whit Brooks comr. Plat shows 172 acres crossed by Horns Creek, adj lands of Wm Johnson, John Mason, land sold by Wm Hill to Wm Johnson, estate of Benjamin Ryan decd, estate of Lacon Ryan; 24 Jan 1818 by Stephen Tillman D S. Proven 1st June 1818 by John Blocker; M Mims CCP. Rec 1st June 1818.

p.139 Samuel Savage, Patrick McDowall, William Ross, and Duncan Matheson exrs of William F Taylor decd to William Hall, Deed, 1st July 1812, Nine hundred [number lost in binding] six Dollars ninety three cents, 193 acres adj lands of Sarah Gardner, Leven Gardner, Nobles, on Stephens Creek. Wit Robert Campbell, A Stewart. /s/ Saml Savage, /s/ Patrick McDowall, /s/ Wm Ross. Proven 1 June 1818 by A Stewart; Wm Hagens J P. Rec 1st June 1818.

p.140 George Riley to Jacob Huiet, Deed, 12 February 1817, Four hundred Dollars, 125 acres on Crooked branch of Big Creek of Little Saluda, and lands of sd Jacob Huiet, Smith Brooks, Henry King, sd tract to sd George Riley by will of his decd father. Wit John Chapman, John Daly. /s/ George Riley. Justice Lewis Miles certifies relinquishment of dower rights by Rebecca Riley wife of George Riley, 29 Sep 1817; /s/ Rebecca (x) Riley. Proven 29 Sep 1817 by John Daly; Lewis Miles J Q. Rec 1 June 1818.

p.141 Hannah Harry and Benjamin Harry to Joel Roper, Deed, 3 February 1817,

Two thousand Dollars, 292 acres adj lands of John Hollingsworth, William Terry decd, Jacob Earnest, George Capehart, Mcpatrick and Moses, plat by John Blocker 18 April 1812. Wit Jacob Earnest Junr, David Tillman. /s/ Hannah (x) Harry, /s/ Benj (x) Harry. Justice John Hollingsworth certifies relinquishment of dower rights by Dorcas Harry widow of Benjamin Harry decd, 14 March 1818; /s/ Dorcas Harry. Proven 12 March 1818 by Jacob Earnest; John Cheatham J P. Rec 1st June 1818.

p.142 Benjamin Bowers to his brother David Bowers, planter, Deed, 30 December 1817, Twelve hundred Dollars, my undivided shares of land to which I have right by will of my father some time deceased: 150 acres bounded by John Black, heirs of James Jones, Joseph Woods estate, Savannah River; second 60 acres near Galphins Mills on Hollow Creek and Silver Bluff adj Jones and Beuner[Benner?], now in possession of Philemon Bowers my other brother; third 200 acres on Long Cane Branch and Town Creek on which my mother now lives adj lands of John Burgess and others; fourth land known as Pettices Tract 150 acres adj lands of James Panton in Barnwell District. Wit Thomas Brooks, Robert Lowry. /s/ Benj Bowers. Barnwell District: Justice John Heard certifies relinquishment of dower rights by Mary Bowers wife of Benjamin Bowers, [day lost in binding] April 1818; /s/ Mary Bowers. Proven 18 April 1818 by Robert Lowry; John Heard JQ. Rec 2d June 1818.

p.144 Robert Ashly to James Picket, Bond, 1 January 1817, Ashly bound to Picket in sum Two thousand Dollars; condition, division of estate of Joicy Mallet & Ashly has given Picket a Negro woman Lucy for his part of estate; Ashly promises to support Joicy Mallet with provisions suitable for a woman of her stand in life, and James Picket shall not be chargeable with any expence of maintenance of Mrs Mallet; when this obligartion is complyed with the obligation is null and void. Wit Thomas Price, John Cartledge. /s/ Robert Ashly, /s/ Abraham Mallet, /s/ Joycy (x) Mallet. Proven 29th April 1818 by John Cartledge; Thomas Price J P. Rec 2 June 1818.

p.144 Hugh Alexander Nixon to his wife Elizabeth Nixon and sons William Henry Nixon, Thomas Harris Nixon, and Alexander Gillon Nixon, Deed of Gift, 1 March 1816, love, all my goods and chattels of every kind, livestock, Negroes Diana and girl Ann with future increase. Wit James Freeman, Geo Rister. /s/ Hugh Alexr Nixon. Proven 6 March 1816 by James Freeman; Wm Hagens JP. Received 1 March 1816 Six hundred fifty Dollars being full consideration thereof.

p.145 Hugh A Nixon, planter, to William Henry Nixon, Thomas Harris Nixon, Alexander Gillon Nixon, Deed of Gift, [sum not stated] Thousand Dollars, 200 acres on Savannah River adj Catlett Corleys land, Middle Creek. Wit James Freeman, George Rister. /s/ Hugh Alexr Nixon. Proven 26 March 1816 by James Freeman; Wm Hagens JP. Rec 2d June 1818.

DEED BOOK 35

p. 146   Ann Sibell Tillman, widow, to George Tillman, Deed, 25 April 1818, Five hundred one Dollars, two tracts originally granted John Walker: one surveyed for Lott Warren 24 Sept 1785 and granted to sd Walker on 4 December 1786, 182 acres on Marshalls branch and adj at time of survey Dr Daniel Mazyck, Nathan White, Conrod Gallman. The other tract surveyed for sd John Walker 31 October 1786 and granted 1 February 1790, by original survey 260 acres on Beaverdam creek of Turkey Creek and bounded at time of survey by John Frazier, John Carter, Mazyck, Samuel Marsh, Burns, and [name lost in binding] Rogers, and reserving out of last 260 acres about 40 acres lying between Frazier land and Starks old road which parcel has already been sold by John Holmes to John Cotton as will appear by reference to deed made to Frederick Tillman by Wm F Taylor 14 November 1801 and is also intended to be included in this release which two tracts were conveyed and consolidated on 9 Nov 1801 by Robert Lang D S and plat thereof certified by him annexed to release from Wm F Taylor to sd Fredk Tillman by which it appears that sd two tracts contain, exclusive of sd part sold to John Cotton 485 acres. The above mentioned land having been sold 5 August 1816 by order of Court of Equity and conveyed to Ann Sibell Tillman by Whitfield Brooks Esqr commr in Equity, the 485 acres exclusive of the 40 acres sold by John Holmes to John Cotton. Wit John W Berry, Fielding Reynolds. /s/ Ann Sibel Tillman.   Proven 2 June 1818 by Fielding Reynolds; M Mims CCP. Rec 2 June 1818.

p. 148   John Whitley to Jerry Trotter, Deed, 17 June 1811, Two hundred Dollars 126 acres adj lands of John Whitley, Elizabeth Whitley, Wm Maz[lost in binding], Charles Cailer[?Carler?Cailes?]. Wit Lewis Whitley, Matthew Mays. /s/ John (x) Whitley. Justice Thomas Anderson certifies relinquishment of dower rights by Ann Whitley wife of John Whitley, 23 April 1813; /s/ Ann (x) Whitley. Proven 5 December 1812 by Lewis Whitley; Gideon Christian J P. Rec 2 June 1818.

p. 149   Covington Hardy to Willis Whatley, Jonathan Limbecker, James [May? Day?Ray?], and James M Scott, pastor and deacons of sd church known as Big Stephens Creek at Hardys Meeting house, Release, goodwill and affection I have to religious society of Baptist of which I am a member, one acre whereon meeting house now stands, bounded on all sides by land of sd Covington Hardy, for sole use as meeting house. Wit John Hardy, Christian (x) Limbecker. /s/ Covington Hardy. Proven 2d June 1818 by John Hardy; M Mims. Rec 2d June 1818.

p. 149   Hicks Jones to Douglass Holloway, Deed, 31 October 1816, Five hundred Dollars, 125 acres on road from Cambridge to Augusta, plat dated 6 March 1812 by Thomas Chiles Esqr D S adj lands of estate of Joseph Williams, Maj Wm Robertson, Philip Dillard, estate of John Bullock. Wit Abner McMillan, Joseph Walker. /s/ Hicks Jones. Justice Wm Robertson certifies relinquishment of dower rights by Quintina Jones wife of Hicks Jones, 21 March 1818; /s/ Quintina Jones. Proven 11 March

77

DEED BOOK 35

1818 by Abner McMillan; Robert Walker J P. Rec 3d June 1818.

p.151   Joseph Cunningham to Richard Jones, Deed, 2 June 1818, Two hundred Dollars, 95 ½ acres on Sweetwater Creek of Stephens Creek adj lands of Peter [Day?May? Ray?], John Pierce Senr, Banks heirs, John Pierce Junr, John Hardy; plat by Robert Lang 23 March 1786. Wit Robert Nixon, A B McWhorter. /s/ Joseph Cunningham. Justice Charles Hammond certifies relinquishment of dower by Sarah Cunningham wife of Joseph Cunningham, 2 June 1818; /s/ Sarah (x) Cunningham. Proven 5 June 1818 by Robert Nixon; M Mims CCP. Rec 5th June 1818.

p.152   Peter Hitt to John Hitt, Deed, 9 June 1818, valuable consideration, 105 acres on Beddingfields Creek of Savannah River. Wit Wm Price, Henry Hitt. Plat surveyed 23 March 1818 by James Thomkins D S shows 105 acres adj lands of Peter Hitt, Breazeal, Wm Price. Proven 9 June 1818 by William Price; Stephen Thomkins J P. Rec 11th June 1818.

p.153   Peter Hitt to his daughter Susanna Hitt, Deed of Gift, 9 June 1818, love, 126 acres on Beddingfields Creek of Savannah River being part of land originally granted to James Hammond and conveyed by him to sd Peter Hitt, adj McCoys Road, Peter Hitt. Wit Wm Price, Henry Hitt. Plat 2 February 1815 by Edward Collier D S, shows adj lands of Peter Hitt, Munday, Wm McKinney, Wm Price, Robert White, and road to McCoy's ferry. Proven 9th June 1818 by William Price; Stephen Thomkins J P. Rec 11th June 1818.

p.154   Mary Ann Ramsay, widow, to her granddaughter Mary Ann Barton dau of Willoughby Barton who is married to my youngest daughter Sarah, Deed of Gift, 30 May 1818, Negro woman Sally with her increase. Wit Charles Goodwin, Chas Goodwin Junr. /s/ M A Ramsay. Proven 13 June 1818 by Chas Goodwin; M Mims C C P. Rec 13th June 1818.

p.154   Jacob Tillman to William Ellison, Mortgage, 8 May 1818, Five hundred Dollars paid byWilliam Ellison, Tillman delivers to Ellison a Negro woman Molley about age 24; Tillman's note to Wm Ellison [details lost in binding]. If Tillman defaults the Negro woman Molly to be taken into Ellison's possession. Wit Robt Ellison. /s/ Jacob Tillman. Rec 15 June 1818.

p.155   Robert Scott to William Ellison, Mortgage, 16 January 1818, One hundred Dollars paid to Scott, sells Negro man Morris age 22. Robert Scott gives note for Eight hundred sixty one Dollars to be paid on or before 16 January next, if paid this deed to be of no effect. Wit Charles Barrentine. /s/ R H Scott. Rec 15 June 1818.

p.156   Jeane Marie Odette Lequinio Kerblay to Walter Leigh Esqr of Augusta,

78

Georgia, Deed, 15 April 1817, 398 acres on Savannah River opposite Augusta being part of the Chickesaw lands and known as Number Seventeen of 174 acres and Number Eighteen of two hundred twenty four acres, bounded by Numbers 19 and 20 lately in possession of Rebecca Willison and now rented by her heirs, Numbers 15 and 16 lately in possession of Lucilla Fair. Wit Thomas Rainsford, Richard Newman. /s/ J M Odette Lequinia Kerblay. Proven 25 May 181[year lost in the binding] by Richard Newman; Charles Hammond JQ. Rec 15th June 1818.

p.156   Richard Covington to James Stuart of Augusta, Georgia, Deed, 18 April 1818, Two thousand three hundred twenty seven Dollars, 200 acres adj lands of Sarah Harden, James Day, Danl Frazer[Fenzer?], James Panton, Savannah River, Stephens Creek and lands of Nobles. Wit James Panton, J H Bussey. /s/ Richard Covington. Proven 18 April 1818 by James Panton; Charles Bussey J P. Rec 27th June 1818.

p.157   William Swearingen to Noah Cloud, Deed, 18 June 1811, Twenty five Dollars, 19 3/4 acres, being part of 150 acres convaid from Van Swearingen to William Swearingen 2 February 1808, lying on Paces branch, Clouds land, near the path from Pinewood house to sd Clouds where the still now stands. Wit John Cloud, Van Swearingen. /s/ William Swearingen. Proven 18 January 1811 by John Cloud; Thos Swearingen J P. Rec 29th June 1818.

p.158   Richard Wilborn to Edward Holmes, Deed, 11 April 1818, Four hundred thirty eight Dollars seventy five cents, 87 1/4 acres, it being part of 100 acres granted unto William Minter by Gov Bull 23 June 1774 and fell to his son Macness Minter as part of his legacy and sd Macness Minter conveyed unto Richard Wilborn 29 April 1812, sd 87 1/4 acres on Turkey Creek of Stevens Creek of Savannah River, plat by John Blocker 14 February 1818. Wit Martin Burress, Ambrose (x) Price. /s/ Richard (x) Wilborn. Justice John Lyon certifies relinquishment of dower rights by Pamela Wilborn wife of Richard Wilborn 11 April 1818; /s/ Pamela Wilborn. Proven 11 April 1818 by Martin Burress; John Lyon Q U. Rec 6 July 1818.

p.159   Jonas Holmes to Edward Holmes, Deed, 20 June 1818, Nineteen Dollars, 60 acres being part of 100 acres formerly surveyed for William Wall and granted unto William Holmes decd by will of Wm Holmes; he bequeathed sd 60 acres being all of sd tract lying on SW side of Beaverdam Creek, plat by Wm Coursey D S. Wit Wm Coursey, Aaron Loveless. /s/ Jonas Holmes. Proven 6 July 1818 by Wm Coursey; M Mims C C P. Rec 6th July 1818.

o.160   Jonathan Moore to Willis Bostick, Mortgage, 15 June 1818, Two thousand five hundred thirty five Dollars, Negros: Queen about 26 year old and her four children Edmund, Kitty, Briton, and Abram. It is true intent of this deed that whereas sd Willis hath joined with sd Jonathan in a note to Walter O Beackley for above sum

DEED BOOK 35

$2,535 payable to him as Executor of ---athington Bostick decd on or before 1ˢᵗ
January next; if sd Jonathan shall pay sd note according to tenor thereof and save
harmless to all costs and damages he may sustain by reason of sd note, then this deed
to be void. Wit Joseph H Dogan, Waller OBickley. /s/ Jonathan Moore. Proven 4
July 1818 by Waller Obickley; Catlett Conner J P. Rec 8 July 1818.

p.161 Lewis Mobley of Wilkinson County, Georgia, planter, to Jeremiah Mobley,
Junr of Edgefield District, planter, Deed, 6 March 1818, One hundred fifty Dollars,
210 acres on Shaws Creek of Edisto River being part of land granted to Ann Bland
and conveyed from Ann Bland to Lewis Mobley adj land of Medlock. Wit Abner
Whatley, William Humphreys. /s/ Lewis Mobley. Proven 14 April 1818 by W
Humphreys; James Bell J P. Rec 6ᵗʰ July 1818.

p.162 David Williams, blacksmith, to John Boyd, Deed of Trust, Georgia, Columbia
County, [blank] November 1810, Four hundred fifty Dollars, to John Boyd of
Edgefield to provide for support of my dear wife Winnyford Williams, slaves, goods,
and chattels, all the estate I received with her at marriage: Negro boy age 18 Tobe,
girl Dorkas age 7 and increase. Wit Wade Bussey, Henry Boyd, Martha Bussey. /s/
David Williams. Proven 12 May 1815 by Martha Bussey; John Lovelace JP. Proven
12 June 1818 by Henry Boyd; J Edmunds. Rec 6ᵗʰ July 1818.

p.163   John Grice to John Murrell, Deed, 6 July 1818, Four hundred Dollars, 175
acres Turkey Creek at Aaron Weeks corner, Charles Barrentines line, Philip Raifords
land, widow Mileses corner, Herod Burts line. Wit Thos Deloach Jr, Isaac Bush. /s/
John (x) Grice. Justice Matthew Mims certifies relinquishment of dower rights by
Deborah Grice wife of John Grice, 6 July 1818; /s/ Deborah Grice. Proven 6 July
1818 by Thomas DeLoach Junr: M Mims CCP. Rec 6ᵗʰ July 1818.

p.165   John Grice to Thomas DeLoach Junr, Deed, 11 December 1816, Three
hundred Dollars, 100 acres being part of land originally granted to George --riel
Powell. Wit Isaac Bush, Abram Eddins. /s/ John (x) Grice. Justice Matthew Mims
certifies relinquishment of dower by Deborah Grice wife of John Grice, 6 July 1818;
/s/ Deborah Grice. Proven 6 July 1818 by Isaac Bush; M Mims CCP. Rec 6 July 1818.

p.166   John Jennings Senr to Jesse Jennings, Deed, 14 July 1810, Three hundred
Dollars, 80 acres on on Stayleys cr of Little Saluda River, adj Lewis Mathews, Spear
Price. Wit Spear Price, Judas Bishop. /s/ John Jennings. Proven 6 June 1818 by
Spear Price who saw Esaias Bishop also witness; Nat Corley JP. Rec 6ᵗʰ July 1818.

p.166   Phebe Carter to William Morgan, Deed, 5 December 1811, One hundred
nineteen Dollars, 59 ½ acres being part of [blank] on Chavis Creek. Wit Esther
Kelley, Patience Carter. /s/ Phebe Carter. Proven 7 December 1811 by Esther Kelley;

John Tarrance JQ. Rec 6th July 1818.

p.167   William Morgan of Barnwell District to Martin Kelley of Richmond County, Georgia, Deed, 25 May 1800, Fifty Dollars, 59 ½ acres, part of land formerly Thomas Carters on Chavis Creek. Wit B Hightower Sr, Thomas C Kelley. /s/ Wm Morgan. Proven 25 May 1818 by Thomas C Kelley; John Tarrance JQ. Rec 6th July 1818.

p.168   Richard Gantt to Christian Breithaupt, Deed, 24 March 1817, Four thousand Dollars, land I purchased of Richard Johnson commonly called the Wade Tract; also a tract purchased of Dennis Carpenter, and part of two other tracts purchased of George Miller and Samuel Crafton, a reservation of tract whereon Dennis Carpenter presently resides containing 129 acres; also land previously disposed of Judge Johnson not comprehended in present conveyance; Land herby to be conveyed unto Breithaupt containing 600 acres now known by appelation of Mount Vintage on Dry Creek adj at this time lands of Lewis Nobles senior, Mrs Mary Woodroof, John Fox, Dennis Carpenter, [name lost in binding] Fell, Richard Gantt. Wit Elizabeth (B) Reynolds, Thomas John Gantt. /s/ Richard Gantt. Justice Matthew Mims certifies relinquishment of dower rights by Sarah Gantt wife of Richard Gantt, 14 July 1817; /s/ Sarah Gantt. Proven 11 July 1818 by Elizabeth Reynolds; M Mims CCP. Rec 11 July 1818.

p.169   Enoch Singleton to John Cheatham, Deed, 30 December 1817, Fifty Dollars, 90 acres being part of two tracts, one granted to John Thurmond, the other to Miner Kilcrease on Camp Branch of Beaverdam of Savannah River adj land of Levi McDaniel that he sold to William Thomas, Childers field. Wit Wm R Crawford, Levi McDaniel, Edward McDaniel. /s/ Enoch (x) Singleton. Proven 29 January 1818 by Levi McDaniel; John Hollingsworth JQ. Rec 27 July 1818.

p.170   Ephraim Doolittle to Freeman Taylor, Deed, 17 August 1816, Three hundred fifty Dollars, 100 acres being part of land surveyed for David Thompson on 1[?], adj March 1788 adj John Dagnal, Jonas Holmes. Also 50 acres adj above tract adj sd Doolittle, Allen Bicker[?], Brown. Wit Josiah Taylor, Lucy (x) Drinkwater. /s/ E Doolittle. Justice Charles Hammond certifies relinquishment of dower rights by Agnes Doolittle, 17 August 1816; /s/ Agnes (x) Doolittle. Proven 17 August 1816 by Josiah Taylor; Chas Hammond JQ. Rec 31 July 1818.

p.171   Wright Bruce to Hannah Bruce, Deed, 12 January 1818, Two hundred Dollars, 200 acres being half of tract conveyed to Right Bruce and Moses Bruce decd from James Bruce Senr 18 August 1804 on Dry fork of Mine Creek being part of two tracts, one granted to James Barrentine and the other granted to Rolan Williams, both conveyed to sd James Bruce Senr, and the two acres round the meeting is excepted out of this deed. Wit Amos W Sotcher, Saml Sotcher. /s/ Wright Bruce. Justice John Lark certifies relinquishment of dower rights by Martha Bruce wife of Wright Bruce,

DEED BOOK 35

14 January 1818; /s/ Martha (x) Bruce. Proven 7 May 1818 by Amos W Sotcher; John Lark JQ. Rec 31st July 1818.

p.172 James Benight of Laurens District to Thomas Chappell, Deed, 12 February 1818, Five hundred seventy six Dollars, resurvey by Patrick Gibson D S 208 acres in Edgefield and Abbeville adj part of a grant sold to Elizabeth Dorris, William Morris, John Blocker, being part of tract originally granted to John Wideman for 990 acres. Wit Wm (x) Morris, John Blocker. /s/ James Bennight. Proven 3 August 1818 by John Blocker; M Mims C C P. Rec 3d August 1818.

p.173 Francis Burt of Pendleton District to Aquilla Miles, Deed, 13 March 1818, One thousand four hundred sixty seven Dollars, 293 ½ acres on ---ky Creek of Savannah River adj lands of estate of Wm Kairden[Randen?], widow Pews, Maj Johnson, estate of Edward Burt decd,, being part of 500 acres [blank]. Wit E B Benson, John P Benson. /s/ Francis Burt. Pendleton District, John T Lewis Clerk of the Court, certifies relinquishment of dower rights by Catharine Burt wife of Francis Burt, 13 March 1818; /s/ Catharine Burt. Proven 13 March 1818 Pendleton District by Enoch B Benson; John T Lewis CC. Rec 3d August 1818.

p.174 Abraham Rutland to Alexander Jinkins, Deed, 22 November 1817, Four hundred fifty Dollars, 200 acres whereon I now live on Mill Creek of South Edisto River. Wit John Wimberley, Levi Walker. /s/ Abraham Rutland. Justice Lewis Holmes certifies relinquishment of dower rights by Martha Rutland, 19 January 1818; /s/ Martha (x) Rutland. Proven 23 May 1818 by John Wimberley; Lewis Holmes QU. Rec 3d August 1818.

p.175 Daniel Bullock to his daughters Martha Bullock, Rachel Bullock, Deed of Gift, 22 October 1817, love, Negro man William, Negro woman Ruth and her three children Frances, Michiel, and Matildy and all increase; also four cows and calves, mare, mule and increase. Wit Thomas Bullock, Robert Walker, Absalom Welsh. /s/ Daniel Bullock. Proven 25 July 1818 by Thomas Bullock; Jesse Blocker JQ. Rec 3 August 1818.

p.176 Thomas Chapman executor of estate of John Hardwick decd of Georgetown District to John Key, Deed, 1 June 1818, Three hundred thirty three and two thirds Dollars, 166 2/3 acres being two thirds of 250 acres originally granted to Michael Keltison 17 February 1773 adj at time of original survey on James Hudson. Wit H Carnes, John Graham. /s/ T Chapman executor. Georgetown District, Justice Thos Skrine certifies relinquishment of dower by Elizabeth Campbell widow formerly widow Hardwick widow of John Hardwick, 2 June 1818; /s/ Elizabeth Campbell. Proven Georgetown District, 2 June 1818, by Henry L Carnes; Thos Skrine. Rec 3 June 1818.

p.177 Thomas Stewart and Daniel Stewart executors of William Stewart deceased to Fanney Stewart, Mary Stewart, Destimony Stewart, Rebeccah Stewart, and Sarah Stewart, 23 February 1818, Five hundred Dollars, 200 acres Tossity Creek of Saluda River, originally granted to Ebenezer Stubbs 17 February 1772[?] at present adj Paul Abney, estate of Jones Wills decd. Wit John Chapman, Wm Stewart. /s/ Daniel Stewart exr, /s/ Thomas Stewart exr. Proven 24 June 1818 by John Chapman; John Abney JP. Rec 3 August 1818.

p.178 Levi McDaniel to John Lyon, Deed, 2 June 1814[?], Seventy five Dollars, 63 acres on Gunnels Creek adj lands of estate of Henry Key, sd John Lyon, George Martin, Levi McDaniel, it being part of tract originally granted to John Thurmond. Wit Henry Waldrum Junr, Saml C Edmonds. /s/ Levi McDaniel. Proven 2 June 1817 by Henry Waldrum; A Edmunds J P. Rec 5ᵗʰ August 1818.

p.179 State of South Carolina, Greenville District, Power of Attorney, 11 August 1818. Seaborn J Youngblood of Cock County, East Tennessee, to Allen Marshall of Greenville District, to collect any money which is my part of my Fathers estate or whatever property is coming to me. Wit Henry Cannon, Thomas (X) Watson. /s/ Seaborn (x) Youngblood. Greenville District, Proven, 11 August 1818, by Henry Cannon; David Jackson JP. Geo W Earle, Clerk of Court, for district afsd certifies that David Jackson is a Justice of the peace, 14 August 1818; /s/ Geo W Earle CC. Rec 21 August 1818.

p.180 Joseph Thornton to Henry Weaver, Deed, 25 July 1815, One hundred sixty Dollars, 81 acres on Cuffeetown Creek of Stephens Creek. Wit Hugh Moseley, William Jordan. /s/ Joseph (x) Thornton. Justice John Lyon certifies relinquishment of dower rights by Mary Thornton wife of Joseph Thornton, 15 October 1816; /s/ Mary (x) Thornton. Plat certified by Wm Coursey D S 29 January 1814 shows 121 acres on Reedy Creek of Cuffeetown Creek, adj lands of Widow Dorras, James Hollingsworth, Henry Weaver, James Maulden. Proven 18 September 1815 by Hugh Moseley; Edmund Belcher J P. Rec 26 August 1818.

p.181 Henry Weaver to John Morgan, Deed, 15 October 1816, Three hundred Dollars,   on Reedy Branch of Cuffeetown Creek of Stephens Creek. Wit Robert Anderson, Edward Settle. /s/ Henry Weaver. Plat shows 76 acres adj lands of Manoah Weatherington, Wm Rayborn, Saml Gilliam, James Hollingsworth, surveyed 9 October 1816 by E Settle D S, Federick Weaver and John H Capehart chain carriers. Proven 15 October 1816 by Edward Settle. Justice John Lyon certifies relinquishment of dower rights by Martha Weaver wife of Henry Weaver, 15 October 1816; /s/ Martha Weaver. Rec 26 August 1818.

p.183 David Rush to Jacob Gable and Samuel Gallaher of Abbeville District, Deed, [day lost in the binding] August 1818, One hundred Dollars, 100 acres on Cuffeetown Creek adj lands of David Rush, John Shively, being a tract granted to Elizabeth Bowers. Wit William (x) Dorris, Joseph (x) Thornton. /s/ David Rush. Proven 26th August 1818 by William Dorris; Samuel Perrin JP. Rec 26th August 1818.

p.184   James G O Wilkinson to Lewis L Hammond. Bill of Sale, 22 March 1816, received of Hammond Two hundred twenty Dollars, Negro woman [no name]. Wit Douglas Huff. /s/ James G O Wilkinson. Proven 31 August 1818 by Douglas Huff; M Mims CCP. Rec 4 September 1818.

p.184   John Grice to Benjamin Gallman, Deed, 5 September 1818, Four hundred Dollars, mill seat of four acres on Horns Creek, being part of tract originally granted to William Henry Drayton; also the land on other side of creek that water in Pond may overflow, privilege of getting timber for building and rebuilding until timber shall get scarce, not to make any choice timber. Wit J Gray Junr, H G Harden, Wm B Mays. /s/ John (x) Grice.   Justice Matthew Mims certifies relinquishment of dower rights by Deborah Grice wife of John Grice, 7th September 1818; /s/ Deborah Grice. Proven 7th Sep 1818 by H G Harden; M Mims CCP. Rec 7th Sep 1818.

p.185   Reason Barnes to John Moore, 5 April 1810, Three hundred five Dollars sixty seven and quarter cents, Negro woman named Sicily about age 45. Wit John Glover, Henry Tate. /s/ Reason Barnes. Proven 7th September 1818 by Henry Tate; M Mims CCP. Rec 7 September 1818.

p.186   Jane Bird to her children John C, Patsey, and Clarisy, Division: Negroes appraised and divided by Jordan Holloway, Daniel Bird, James Blocker: Jerry, Washington, Arena, Violet, George, Writter, Draper, Matilda, and Gabriel, which they have divided as follows: to John: Washington, Jerry, Arena; to Patsey: Violet, George, and Writter; to Clarisy: Draper, Marilda, Gabriel. Wit Jordan Holloway, D Bird, James Blocker. /s/ Jane (x) Bird. Receipt 17 August 1818 signed by John C Rarden, Martha Abney, Clarisy W Palmore, and witnessed by James Blocker, John Nobles. Proven 17th [month omitted] 1818 by James Blocker; Jordan Holloway J P. Rec 7th Sep 1818.

p.186   Edward Holmes to Philip Ikener, Deed, 8 October 1817, One hundred seventy seven Dollars, 192 acres being part of 761 acres originally granted unto John Thurmond decd 2 December 1793, and from Philip Thurmond executor to estate of sd John Thurmond conveyed to Edward Holmes, 192 acres thereof on Rockey Creek of Turkey Creek of Savannah River adj lands of John Glanton, John Couch, Red, White, Lewis Clark. Wit Levi McDaniel, John Glanton. /s/ Edward Holmes. Proven 8th October 1817 by Levi McDaniel; Wm Hagens JP. Rec 7th Sep 1818.

DEED BOOK 35

p.187   Simon Beck to Philip Ikener Junr, Deed, 21 February 1818, Three hundred Dollars, 300 acres being part of 800 acres granted to John Thurmond decd by Gov Chas Pinckney 17 [month omitted] 1792 on Beaverdam and Gunnels Creek adj lands of Levi McDaniel, Federick Bush, Blaylock, Burrel Johnson, head of Lick branch, William Parmer, Christopher Cox, Richard Tillery. Wit Haly Johnson, Lewis Collins. /s/ Simon (x) Beck. Proven 7th September 1818 by Lewis Collins; John Cheatham J P. Rec 7th September 1818.

p.188   James Nelson to W R Nelson, Deed, 10 May 1818, Five hundred Dollars, [acreage not stated] on Hard Labour Creek of Stephens Creek adj lands of heirs of William [name lost in binding], Daniel Rountree, S Adams.   Wit Allen Burton, George Longmire. /s/ James Nelson. Proven 5 Sep 1818 by Allen Burton; John Lyon Q U. Rec 7th September 1818.

p.189   Isaac Kirkland to John Thomas, Deed, 12 October 1815, Thirty Dollars, 50 acres on Beaverdam of Shaws Creek, being part of 400 acres granted to sd Kirkland 4 September 1797 by Gov Chas Pinckney. Wit Silas Day, Zechariah Kirkland. /s/ Isaac Kirkland. Proven 12th October 1815 by Silas Day; Isaac Kirkland JQ. Rec 7th September 1818.

p.190   Atha Thomas to John Thomas, Deed, 18 May 1811, One hundred Dollars, 200 acres being part of 1000 acres granted to sd Atha Thomas 5 August 1793, the 200 acres on Bull branch. Wit Wm Parker, Samuel Thomas. /s/ Atha Thomas. Justice Isaac Kirkland certifies relinquishment of dower rights by Judy Thomas wife of Atha Thomas, 18th May 1811; /s/ Judy (x) Thomas. Proven [day lost in binding] May 1811, by William Parker; Isaac Kirkland JQ. Rec 7th September 1818.

p.191   Stephen Bettis to Stephen Federick, Deed, 23 May 1817, Twelve hundred Dollars, 525 acres being two tracts and part of one more; one tract for 200 acres originally granted to John Bettis 9 March 1773; also grant to Stephen Bettis 175 acres on three sides of above grant 25 September 1789; also part of tract granted to Federick Swearingen 31 August 1797 adj lines of Atha Thomas, Stephen Bettis. Wit Amos Landrum, Henry Day, Elisha Bettis. /s/ Stephen Bettis. Justice Peter Lamkin certifies relinquishment of dower rights by Mary Bettis wife of Stephen Bettis, 15 November 1817; /s/ Mary Bettis. Proven 22 August 1818 by Amos Landrum; John Loveless J P. Rec 7th September 1818.

p.192   Federick Swearingen to Stephen Bettis, Deed, 15 February 1800, Five Dollars, [number lost in binding] hundred fifty acres being part of 500 acres originally granted to sd Federick Swearingen 4 September 1797; the 250 acres on Beaverdam of Shaws Creek. Wit Isaac Kirkland, Emsley Lott, Francis Bettis. /s/ Fed Swearingen. Proven 5[sic] February 1800 by Isaac Kirkland; Van Swearingen JP. Rec 7 Sep 1818.

p.193 Benjamin Ryan Sr to Benjamin Frazier, Deed, 31 October 1812, Two hundred
Dollars, mill seat of four acres on Horns Creek, being part of land originally granted
to William Henry Drayton; also land on either sides of creek that the water in the
Pond may overflow, with priviledge of getting timber for building and rebuilding untill
timber shall get scarce, tho sd Frazier is not to make use of any choice timber trees.
Wit John S Glascock, Smith (x) Radford. /s/ Benj (B) Ryan. Proven 10 Sep 1818 by
John S Glascock; M Mims CCP. Rec 10 Sep 1818.

p.194 James Cox of Burke County, GA, to Jesse Brassell, Deed, 8 February 1814,
Two hundred Dollars, 100 acres on Rock Creek. Wit Joseph Walker, James Partin.
/s/ James Cox. Proven 14 October 1816 by Joseph Walker; Lewis Holmes JP. Rec
16th September 1818.

p.195 Sarah Quarles widow of Richard Quarles to John[?] Middleton, Deed, 23
May 1818, Five hundred and [lost in the binding] Dollars, several plantations
originally the moiety of sd [lost in binding] sister Polley Findley and which sd Polley
inherited at death of her father Hugh Middleton Senr, being one sixth of land
formerly owned by sd Middleton, on Savannah River including the reversion of two
sixths part of the widow Adness[sic] Middletons dower, one share inherited by sd
Sarah in her own right and one in right of her sister Polly Middleton, land laid off to
Widow Middleton consists of following: part of a tract originally granted to Richard
Meadows 134 ½ acres; also land known as Capses Tract 150 acres being part of tract
originally 200 acres granted to Nicholas Ware on Stephens Creek adj lands now
owned by sd Middleton on Buzzard Creek of Stephens Creek, near mills formerly
owned by George Graves but at present property of William Garrett. Wit Wm
Tennent, Delphy Hamilton, Polly Graves. /s/ Sarah Quarles. Proven 10 August 1818
by Polley Graves; Chas Bussey J P. Rec 18 September 1818.

p.196 Nancy Hernton to William Day, Relinquishment, Justice John Tarrance
certifies relinquishment of dower rights by Nancy Herndon wife of Abram Herndon,
her interest of 350 acres adj Hatchers Ponds formerly conveyed by sd Herndon to
James May. 30 September 1818; /s/ Nancy (H) Hernton. Rec 3 October 1818.

p.197 Thomas Kilcrease to Jonas Holmes, Deed, 6 September 1818, Three hundred
Dollars, 80 acres being part of 114 acres granted to sd Kilcrease lying on Stephens
Creek. Wit Wm Coursey, Edward Holmes. /s/ Thomas (I) Kilcrease. Proven 24th
September 1818 by William Coursey; M Mims CCP. Rec 24 Sep 1818.

p.197 Dennis Carpenter to Solomon Lucas, Receipt and discharge, Ordinary of E
District vs Solomon Lucas, Debt on admin Bond, I have lately purchased of Wm
Cannon judgt agt sd Solomon Lucas in name of Ordinary at suit of Benjamin Roebuck
& other representatives of Robert Roebuck decd, three of whom have sued on adms

bond & sold their claim to William Cannon, judgment amounts to [blank]; sd Solomon Lucas agreed to pay me One hundred Dollars in discharge of sd judgt, I acknowledge receipt of full amount, provided sd Solomon recovers amt of sd judgt agt representatives of John Roebuck and Robert Roebuck in the suit now pending in Court of Equity. Wit Wm Ellison. /s/ Dennis (I) Carpenter. Proven 23 October 1818 by Wm Ellison; M Mims CCP. Rec 23d October 1818.

p.198· Arthur Simkins Senr to John S Jeter, Deed, 31 August 1818, Five Dollars, 5 1/4 acres two poles lot in village of Edgefield adj Jefferson Street, sd Arthur Simkins, Josiah Allen, and Augustus G Nagel. Wit A S Moore, John Simkins; /s/ Arthur Simkins Sr. Plat certified 6 August 1818 by John Blocker C S shows a spring. Proven 3 October 1818 by Dr. A S Moore; M Mims CCP. Rec 3 Oct 1818.

p.199 Patcy Will Spragins to Elijah Worthington, Deed, 3 March 1807, One hundred fifty Dollars, 62 acres on Big Saluda River being land granted by Gov Wm Moultrie to Thomas Black 7 August 1786. Wit Nancy Hogan, Orsamus Spragins, Charles Parkins. /s/ Patty Will Spragins. Proven 18 March 1807 by Charles Parkins; Sampson Pope JQ. Rec 5 October 1818.

p.200 James Summers to Elijah Worthington, Deed, 29 September 1818, One thousand Dollars, 150 acres on Big Saluda River being part of 305 acres originally granted to me 6 April 1789 adj Joseph W Waldo, Elijah Worthington. Wit John Chapman, John H Barnes, John Bulger Jr. /s/ James Summers. Proven 29 September 1818 by John Chapman; John Abney JP. Rec 5th October 1818.

p.201 Whitfield Brooks comr Court of Equity to John Lipscomb, Titles, 5 October 1818. Whereas John Lipscomb & wife about 7 June last petitioned agt Thomas G Lamar guardian of minor children of Luke Smith decd stating that Joseph Smith died [day omitted] April [year omitted]. In his will he devised to children of Luke Smith and children of James Bonham his estate to be equally divided at death of his wife, one of the daughters of James Bonham, a devise under will of Jacob Smith; prayed for partition to divide afsd land among interested parties. Sd land sold at public auction toJohn Lipscomb for Twenty hundred seventy two Dollars he being highest and last bidder, land known as Mount Willing, 250 acres on Richland Creek adj lands of estate of Luke Smith decd, Isome Gilliam, estate of Jacob Smith decd; and another tract of 100 acres on afsd creek adj lands of estate of Jacob Smith decd, James Allen, and estate of Luke Smith decd. Wit J W Waldo, T G Lamar. /s/ Whitfield Brooks Comr. Proven 5 Oct 1818 by Joseph Waldo; Val Corley JP. Rec 5 October 1818.

p.203 John Ardis of Green County, GA, only son and heir of Isaac Ardis late of Beach Island, decd, to Capt Arthur Simkins Junr, Deed, 9 June 1817, Four thousand five hundred Dollars, 100 acres in Beach Island being the distributive part of Isaac

Ardis of his faathers estate agreeably to division made by Robert Lang [date blank] adj lands of Jacob Zinn Jr, Capt Miller. Wit Jacob Zinn, John Cross, D Atkinson. /s/ John Ardis. Georgia, Putnam County, Archd McKey J P certifies relinquishment of dower rights by Patcy Ardis, 1 June 1818; /s/ Patcy (x) Ardis. Proven 5 October 1818 by D Atkinson; M Mims CCP. Rec 5th October 1818.

p.204   Joel Deas Senr, Tabitha Deas, Joel Deas Junr, to Hezekiah Almon of Orangeburgh District, 15 September 1818, Three hundred Dollars, 200 acres where sd Joel Deas now lives on South Edisto River, adj lands of Mathew Jones, sd Hezekiah Almon, sd Joel Deas Sr. Wit Lewis Holmes, Nancy (x) Deas. /s/ Joel (x) Dees Senr, /s/ Tabitha (x) Dees, /s/ Joel (x) Dees. Justice Lewis Holmes certifies relinquishment of dower rights by Mary Deas wife of Joel Deas Senr, 15 September 1818; /s/ Mary (x) Deas. Proven 17 Sept 1818 by Nancy Dees; Lewis Holmes JQ. Rec 6 Oct 1818.

p.205   Esaias Bishop to Hezekiah Almon of Orangeburgh District, Deed, Orangeburgh District, 22 August 1818, Six hundred twenty five Dollars, 200 acres adj lands of heirs of Federick Holmes, James Mairhead, Matthias Jones, heirs of Bibby Bush. Wit Richd Jones, West (x) Patterson. /s/ Esaias (x) Bishop. Justice Lewis Holmes certifies relinquishment of dower rights by Elizabeth Bishop wife of Esaias Bishop, 15 September 1818; /s/ Elizabeth (x) Bishop. Proven 27 August 1818 by Richard Jones; George S D Smith. Rec 6th October 1818.

p.206   Joel Swearingen of Amite County, Mississippi, to Haley Cotten, Letter of Attorney, 29 September 1818, to ask and receive of Federick Swearingen and Ezekiel McClendon exrs of will of Van Swearingen decd, sums of money, owing to me by virtue of sd will. /s/ Joel Swearingen. Amite County, Miss, 29 Sept 1818, Thomas Batchelor notary publick certifies that Joel Swearingen signed foregoing ltr/atty to Haley Cotten, 29 September 1818; /s/ Thos Batchelor Not Pub. Rec 17 Nov 1818.

p.207   Joel Deas to Esaias Bishop, Deed, 27 April 1816, Two hundred twenty five Dollars, 100 acres on Rocky Branch of south Edisto River adj Mathias Jones, James Mohead. Wit William D Milton, James Don. /s/ Joel (+) Deas. Proven 27 April 1816 by James Don; John Loveless JP. Rec 5th October 1818.

p.208   Mason Ezard to Esaias Bishop, Deed, 24 November 1814, Two hundred Dollars, 100 acres on south fork of Edisto River on road from Columbia to Augusta, adj lands of Charles Williamson, Matthias Jones, heirs of Bibby Bush, heirs of Frederick Holmes. Wit John Bell, James (x) Whitehead. /s/ Mason (x) Ezard. Proven 12 December 1814 by John Bell; John P Bush JP. Rec 6th Oct 1818.

p.209   Expenetus Stephens of Franklin County, TN, to Solomon Adams, Deed, 3

October 1815, Fifteen Dollars, 15 acres on Rocky Creek of Stephens Creek adj lands of afsd Adams, David Nicholson, John Adams. Wit Eugene Brenan, David W Thompson, James Coats. /s/ Expenetus (x) Stephens. Proven 3 October 1815 by David W Thompson; Jesse Blocker JP. Rec 7th October 1818.

p.209 Solomon Adams to John Bolger, Deed, 10 November 1816, Fifty Dollars, 15 acres on old Long Cain Road to Charleston, conveyed by Epenetus Stephens to sd Adams, adj lands of Davis Nicholson, John Bolger, John Adams Sr, and Solomon Adams. Wit Sampson Pope Junr, Jesse Forrest. /s/ Solomon (x) Adams. Proven 19th January 1818 by Jesse Forrest; Thomas Dozier JQ. Rec 7th October 1818.

p.210 Reuben Cooper, farmer, to Campbell Cooper, Deed, 8 August 1818, Five hundred Dollars, 50 acres sd Cooper purchased from Jonathan D Watson, on Stephens Creek where sd Campbell Cooper now lives. Wit Hugh Balentine, Loyd Barnes. /s/ Reuben (x) Cooper. Proven 29 August 1818 by Loyd Barnes; Chas Bussey JP. Rec 4 Oct 1818.

p.211 William Pike to John Wable, Deed, 22 December 1814, One hundred fifty Dollars, 125 acres on Richland Creek of Little Saluda River being part of 500 acres granted to Jacob Smith 7 March 1796 and conveyed by him unto John Salter Senr and by sd Salter to sd Wm Pike, on lines of Powel, and John Salter. Wit John Eidson, William Cockeroft. /s/ William (x) Pike. Justice John Lark certifies relinquishment of dower rights by Margaret Pike wife of William Pike, 22 December 1814; /s/ Margaret (x) Pike. Proven 22 December 1814 by William Cockeroft; John Lark JQ. Rec 8th October 1818.

p.212 Sarah Devall to Samuel Thompkins, 28 May 1818, Justice Edward Colier certifies relinquishment of dower rights by Sarah Devall wife or widow of Samuel Devall; /s/ Sarah Devall. Rec 8 October 1818.

p.212 Dildatha Odom to Benjamin Evans, Deed, 4 December 1817, One thousand Dollars, 565 acres being part of nine tracts, on Beach Creek adj lines of William Reads Bains, Bushes mill, John Chans[?] path, Augusta road, Andrew Gomillion, Henry Spann. Wit John P Bush, John Wimberly. /s/ Dildatha Odom. Proven [lost in binding] December 1817 by John Bush; Lewis Holmes JP. Rec 8th October 1818.

p.213 Buckner Blalock to Henry Meclendel, Deed, 28 December 1814(1816?), Four hundred Dollars, 313 acres, granted unto afsd Blalock in 1808. Wit Ezekiel Bishop, Francis Walker Junr. /s/ Buckner (x) Blalock. Proven 6 October 1818 by Ezekiel Bishop; H Williams JQ. Rec 8th October 1818.

p.214 Jordan Holloway to Rebecca Rardin, Deed, 17 July 1815, Five hundred fifty

DEED BOOK 35

five Dollars fifty six cents, 223 ½ acres being part of land formerly belonging to Moses
Kirkland which was confiscated, conveyed by commissioners of confiscated property
to Richard Johnston 8 & 9 July 1783, known as #2 on Turkey Creek, bounded by land
belonging to James Coats, heirs of Jones, James [surname lost in binding], Robert
Willis, Widow Johnston, and Francis Burt, Timothy Rardins half of a tract of 447 acres
purchased by Timothy and William Rarden from Armsted [surname lost in binding].
Wit Susannah Allen, Young Allen. /s/ Jordan Holloway. Proven 4[7?] October 1818
by Young Allen; [name of justice has been cut off page]. Rec 10th October 1818.

p.215   Bridges Brenan to Benjamin Frazier, Deed, 5 January 1810, One hundred
Dollars, 40 acres on Turkey Creek being part of a tract Mrs. Meginis now lives on adj
E by sd Frazier, NW by Mrs MeGinis. Wit Young Allen, D M Lovelace, Reuben
Tillman, Young Allen. /s/ Bridges (x) Brenan. Proven 8 October 1818 by D M
Loveless. Rec 10 October 1818.

p.215   James E Dawson to Lemuel G Dawson, Deed, 7 March 1818, Nine hundred
Dollars, 107 acres, one acre excepted whereon the ---gal Meeting House now stands,
with use of water out of the spring [word lost in binding] days of publick worship no
other person having any rights to sd acre. Wit John Cheatham Senr, John Cheatham
Jr. /s/ Jonas E Dawson(sic). Plat shows land crossed by a road, adj lands held by Mrs.
Winey Welsh, Luke Garner, Samuel Strum, Joseph Hough, John Terry. Proven 13
June 1818 by John Cheatham Sr; Jordan Holloway JP. Rec 26th October 1818.

p.216   William Borroum to Joseph West, 9 October 1815, Three hundred Dollars, 83
acres, it being part of 250 acres granted to William West 18 January 1763 and at
decease of sd West sd land fell to John West, conveyed from John West to Highdon
Barron and from Highden Barron to William Bourrom his father[brother?] by care
ship, lying on Little Saluda River and Clouds Creek. Wit Samson Pope, Elizabeth
Pope, Helen Pope. /s/ William Borroum. Proven 23 January 1818 by Sampson Pope;
Val Corley J P. Rec 13 October 1818.

p.217   Thomas Coleman to Charles Cooper, Deed, 24 April 1818, Three hundred
eighteen 1/4 Dollars, 67 acres on Rocky Creek of Ninety Six Creek. Wit John Finney,
Thos Anderson. Plat dated 26 March 1818 by Thos Anderson D S shows adj lands of
Chas Cooper, Wilson, Jas Ray, Thos Coleman. Justice Thomas Anderson certifies
relinquishment of dower rights by Edna Coleman wife of Thomas Coleman, 24 April
1818; /s/ Edna Coleman. Proven 24 April 1818 by John Finney; Rec 13 October 1818.

p.218   Elkanah Powel, planter, to Joseph West, planter, Deed, 30 November 1805,
One hundred twenty Dollars, 100 acres lyhing on Clouds Creek, that was granted to
Thomas Green 9 November 1774, adj [name lost in binding] Durkins land. Wit Hidon
Borrom, Edmund Etherage. /s/ Elkanah Powel. Justice Sampson Pope certifies the

90

relinquishment of dower rights by Rhody Powel wife of Elkanah Powel, [day lost in binding] December 1807; /s/ Rhody (x) Powel. Proven 30 November 1805 by Edmund Etheredge; Elkanah Sawyer J P. Rec 13th October 1818.

p.219   Eligah Chapman to Joseph West, Deed, 13 October 1814, Seven hundred Dollars, 100[?] acres originally granted to John [name lost in binding] on Little Saluda River binding NE on land of Thomas Davice, SE on Henry Etheridge and Charles Purkins, SW on John Davise, NW on Joshua Martin and Chapman. Wit Nathaniel Corley, Spear Price, Jacob West. /s/ Elijah Chapman. Justice Sampson Pope certifies relinquishment of dower rights by Elizabeth Chapman wife of Elijah Chapman, 27 November 1814; /s/ Elizabeth (x) Chapman. Proven 26 [month lost in binding] 1814 by Nathaniel Corley; Sampson Pope JQ. Rec 13th October 1818.

p.220   Marmaduke Coate of Newberry District to Joseph West, Deed, 6 May 1816, Five hundred Dollars, 200 acres being part of land granted to sd Marmaduke Coate for 228 acres 1st June 1812 on Little Saluda River adj line of sd Joseph West and William Flecher, Widow ---man, Daniel Mathews. Wit Hugh Oneall, Jacob Lorick, Austin Eskridge. /s/ Marmaduke Coate. Proven 21 October 1816 by Hugh Oneall; John Gante JP. Rec 13th October 1818.

p.221   Edward Homes to Wyett Homes, Deed, 29 August 181[lost in binding], One hundred thirty Dollars, 30 acres on Beaverdam Creek, plat by William Coursey, part of 100 acres granted unto Obediah Ritchardson 1771; also 36 acres adj afsd 30 acres bounded by Daniel Brunson, Amos Homes. Wit William Coursey, Jeremiah Holmes. /s/ Edward D Holmes. Proven 14 October 1818 by Wm Coursey; John Cheatham JP. Rec 14th October 1818.

p.222   Hardy Fluker to William Fluker, Deed, 15[?] July 1818, Twelve hundred Dollars, 156 acres on Clouds Creek of Little Saluda, being part of land purchased by me of Ezekiel Walker and the other by George Fluker, adj George Fluker, David Lagrone, the road, a spring, Joseph West to Beaverdam Creek, William Fluker. Wit John Barrett, George Fluker. /s/ Hardy Fluker. Justice Henry Coate certifies relinquishment of dower rights by Sophia Fluker wife of Hardy Fluker, 2 September 1818; /s/ Sophia Fluker. Proven 2 Sept 1818 by George Fluker; Henry Coate QU. Rec 14th October 1818.

p.223   Richmond Watson to Amos Watson, Deed, [blank] November 1816, Two hundred Dollars, 100 acres on a branch of Clouds Creek granted to William Odum adj lines of Jiles Chapman, Elijah Watson, Runnels, Widow Cates. Wit Amos W Satcher, Richard Howard Jr. /s/ Richmond Watson. Proven 25 November 1817 by Amos W Satcher; John Loveless JP. Rec 27th November 1818.

p.224   Joseph Moris to Joseph Moris junior, Deed, 27 April 1818, Four hundred Dollars, 100 acres on Halfway Swamp of Saluda River being land first granted to Thomas Farrier 1793 now belonging to Joseph Morris Sr, adj lands of Joseph Morris Sr, John Holloway. Wit John Allen, Jordan Morris. Proven 27 August 1818 by Jordan Morris; Ch Mayson JP. Rec 14 October 1818.

p.224   Cadwell Evans to Jacob Hibler, 11 June 1818, Three thousand Dollars, 600 acres on head branches of Cyper Creek but on resurvey found to contain 760 acres, being part of three tracts granted to Batt Evans, Joseph [name lost in binding] and Carson, now bounded by Jonathan Glanton, Mathew Devore, L Glanton, estate of Wm Terry, Jno Lyon Esqr, Mrs Raney, estate of Moses Tullis, Robert Evans, Shepherd Spencer. Wit Edmund B Hibler, Thos J Hibler. /s/ Cadwell Evans. Receipt of Jonathan Glanton, 11 June 1818 for One Dollar to him paid by Jacob Hibler for his claim to title of land sold by Cadwell Evans to Jacob Hibler. Wit Edmund B Hibler, Thos J Hibler; /s/ Jonathan Glanton. Justice Jesse Blocker certifies relinquishment of dower rights by Elizabeth Glanton wife of Jonathan Glanton, [day lost in binding] June 1818; /s/ Elizabeth (x) Glanton. Proven 11 June 1818 by Edmund B Hibler; Jesse Blocker. Plat by Jesse Blocker D S 10 June 1818 shows 760 acres and names of adj owners. Rec 4 October 1818.

p.226   John Key to Reuben L Marberry, 12 January 1818, Three hundred ninety five Dollars, 197 acres on Still Water branch of Bird Creek of Stevens Creek. Wit Francis Tompkins, James Tompkins. /s/ John Key. Plat by James Tompkins D S 10 Sept 1817 shows land crossed by Cambridge Road and names of adj owners: James Smith, John Key, Henry Jenings, Charles Nix. Proven 13 October 1818 by James Tompkins; Stephen Tompkins J P. Rec 14th October 1818.

p.228   George Sawyer to Negroes Marmaduke and Dina, 3(?) October 1818, Deed of Manumission, Two hundred Dollars, Marmaduke a man aged about 60, about 5 ft 10 inches high, black complexion; Dina about 45 years old, about four feet high, of black complexion. Wit Ansel Sawyer, John W Keel. /s/ George (G) Sawyer. Justice Nathan Norris and Nathaniel Burton, John Stone, John Deshazo, Ansel Sawyer, and William Grubs, freeholders, certify sd slaves are not of bad character and are capable of gaining a livlihood by honest means, 18 July 1818. Proven 15 October 1818 by Ansel Sawyer; Nathan Norris JQ. Rec 15 October 1818.

p.229   Rachel Humphries to her two children Margaret Pou Humphries and Robert Humphries, 11 March 1818, love, two Negro girls and their increase, Lucinda about age six and Sarah about age four, being the children of Mary now in my possession to be equally divided between my children. Wit William Humphries, James Wolf. Proven 13 March 1818 by James Wolfe; John Lark JQU. Rec 15 October 1818.

92

p.229   Starling Mitchel to Benjamin Frazier, Deed, 14 September 1815, Three hundred Dollars, 163 acres on Beaverdam Creek of Turkey Creek of Savannah River, plat made by John Loften D S 6 September 1815. Wit Eugene Brenan, Isaac Randolph. /s/ Starling Mitchel. Justice William Jeter certifies relinquishment of dower rights by Martha Mitchel wife of Sterling Mitchell; /s/ Martha Mitchell. Proven 19 October 1818 by Isaac Randolph; [justice's name illegible]. Rec 20 October 1818.

p.230   Abiah Jones to Ephraim Cook, Deed, 1 October 1818, One hundred Dollars, 62 acres on Log Creek adj lines of Wynn. Wit Sampson Butler, John Gomillion. /s/ Abiah (x) Jones. Justice Mathew Mims certifies relinquishment of dower rights by Mary Jones wife of Abiah Jones 20 October 1818; /s/ Mary (x) Jones. Proven 20 October 1818 by John Gomillion; M Mims CCP. Rec 20 October 1818.

p.231   Hannah McGinnis to Reuben Landrum, Deed, 13 April 1818, Thirty Dollars, 16(?) acres, it being the whole of Hannah McGinnis claim to sd land. Wit John Blocker, Haley Johnson. /s/ Hannah (x) McGinnis. Proven 14 August 1818 by Haley Johnson; John Blocker JQ. Rec 25ᵗʰ October 1818.

p.232   John Blocker to Reuben Landrum, 6 February 1814, Two hundred Dollars, 91 acres on Long Cain Road opposite John Loftins plantation adj on Reuben Landrum, John Loftin, and John Blocker. Wit Abner Blocker, Sanders Rareden. /s/ John Blocker. Justice John Blocker certifies relinquishment of dower rights by Mary T Blocker wife of John Blocker Senr, 26 February 1814; /s/ Mary T Blocker. Proven 28 February 1814 by Abner Blocker; John Blocker JQ. Rec 23ʳᵈ October 1818.

p.233   David Tillman to John Kenney, Deed, 17 November 1815, Twenty six Dollars twenty five cents, 7 ½ acres adj Cane brake branch of Horns Creek being part of a grant to Frederick Tillman Sr in August 1786 for 391 acres, conveyed to David Tillman 4 January 1802 and part to Lewis Tillman 14 Feb 1803. Wit Walter Boyd, Peter Robertson. /s/ David Tillman. Justice W Jeter certifies relinquishment of dower rights by Elizabeth Tillman wife of David Tillman 17 Nov 1815; /s/ Elizabeth (x) Tillman.   Plat certified 23 October 1812 by Stephen Tillman; land adj tract John Kenney bought from Lewis Tillman, part of the original survey. Proven 17 November 1815 by Peter Robertson; W Jeter JQU. Rec 25 October 1818.

p.234   John Kenney to Willoughby Williams of Georgia, Deed, 23 October 1818, One thousand eight hundred Dollars, 188 ½ acres on Cane break Branch of Horns Creek it being part of two surveys, one originally granted to Ephraim Jones 23 December 1771 and other granted to Frederick Tillman Senr [day lost in binding] August 1781 on Five Notch Road and Mrs Boyd. Wit James (x) Broadwater, Barsheba (x) Hollingsworth. /s/ John Kenny. Justice John Hollingsworth certifies relinquishment of dower rights by Rachel Kenny wife of John Kenny, 23 October 1818; /s/ Rachel

Kenny. Proven 23 October 1818 by James (x) Broadwater; John Hollingsworth JQ. Rec 23 October 1818.

p.236 John Kenny to Willoughby Williams of Georgia, Deed, 23 October 1818, Fifty Dollars, 7 ½ acres on Cain break branch of Horns Creek it being part of a grant to Frederick Tillman. Wit James (x) Broadwater, Barsheba (x) Hollingsworth. /s/ John Kenny. Justice John Hollingsworth certifies relinquishment of dower rights by Rachel Kenny wife of John Kenny, 23 October 1818; /s/ Rachel Kenny. Proven 23 October 1818 by James (x) Broadwater; John Hollingsworth. Rec 23 October 1818.

p.237 Harvey Drake to Eldred Simkins, Mortgage, 13 June 1818, Whereas Eldred Simkins hath endorsed a note in the Bank of the State for Six hundred Dollars, drawn by [lost in binding] and Dr. Abner Landrum and payable to his order, Now for purpose of securing sd Eldred, I convey to him for Ten Dollars two Negroes Dave about 17 years old, country born, and Eliza 18 or 20 years; Eldred to take possession and sell them to indemnify himself if necessary, he returning surplus to whoever is legally entitled. Wit E Thurston, Samuel B Marsh. /s/ Harvey Drake. Proven 26 October 1818 by Samuel B Marsh; M Mims CCP. Rec 26 October 1818.

p.237 Abner Landrum to Eldred Simkins, Mortgage, 26 October 1818, Whereas Eldred Simkins hath indorsed a note in the bank of the State for Six hundred Dollars on [blank] May 1818 [word in binding] Harvey Drake Dr Abner Landrum payable to his order with power of renewing sd note given by afsd to Dr Samuel Green and whereas sd Harvey Drake gave[?] mortgage to Eldred two Negroes Eliza and Dave to indemnify for any loss he might sustain by sd indorsement and sd [word in binding] being about to leave the state and sd Harvey having [word in binding] of parting with Negro Eliza and I being a copartner(?) In the business of a pottery establishment with sd Harvey (and?) Dr Abner and being willing to befreind them in securing sd Eldred for his indorsement and for consideration of the premises and Ten Dollars paid by Eldred do convey to sd Eldred 80 acres with a grist mill thereon lying on Shaws Creek of Edisto bounded by my land, Thomas Swearingen, John Landrum. Wit John S Jeter, Samuel B Marsh. Proven 25 October 1818 by Samuel B Marsh; M Mims CCP. Rec 26th October 1818.

p.238 Richard Blalock Senr of Barnwell District to Wade Blalock, Deed, 16 October 1818, Barnwell District, Four hundred Dollars, land in Edgefield District on Buck--- Creek, 904 acres granted to Absalom Napper in 1793 adj Man Hampton; one other tract surveyed for me January last 550 acres adj Blalock, Peter Hair, and Richardson; a tract granted in 1793 to Thomas Rogers for 98 acres adj the first tract, making in whole 1562 acres. Wit James Clark, John Wise Senr. /s/ Richard Blalock. Proven Edgefield District, 23 October 1818 by James Clark; John Tarrance JQ. Rec 30 October 1818.

p.239 William Butler to Thomas Cates, Deed, 21 August 1812, Three hundred thirty eight Dollars, [number in binding] hundred sixty nine acres on Clouds Creek adj lands of Daniel Smith, Wm Butler, being part of tract granted to Jonathan Richardson 18 May 1773. Wit William Butler Junr, John Scott. /s/ Wm Butler. Proven 16 Sept 1812 by John Scott; Elijah Watson JQ. Rec 2 November 1818.

p.240 Benjamin Faircloth to Thomas Cates, Deed, 31 January 1807, Fifteen Dollars, 100 acres adj lands of John Va---, Long Meadows Branch, Missors Branch, originally granted to Thomas Cates Senr 6 February [year lost in binding]. Wit Daniel Smith, Huldah (x) Watson. /s/ Benjamin (x) Faircloth. Justice Elijah Watson certifies the relinquishment of dower rights by Barbary Faircloth wife of Benjamin Faircloth, 31 January 1807; /s/ Barbary (x) Faircloth. Proven 31 January 1807 by Daniel Smith; Elijah Watson JP. Rec 2 November 1818.

p.241 James Parker to Gasper Gallman, Deed, 9 September 1818, Six hundred Dollars, 96 acres on Horns Creek originally granted to Andrew McGitton. Wit Christopher Vanner, Jesse Bettis, B Reid. /s/ James (x) Parker. Plat by Robert Lang surveyed 14 February 1793 shows 96 acres conveyed from Winfrey Whitlock to Daniel Parker with adj lands of John Sneed, John (Best?Rut?Rich?), John Ryan, Saml Walker. Justice W Jeter certifies relinquishment of dower rights by Elizabeth Parker, mother of James Parker, 31 October 1818; /s/ Elizabeth (-) Parker. Proven 1 November 1818 by Christopher Vanner; M Mims CCP. Rec 2 Nov 1818.

p.242 Jeremiah Hatcher to Aron Allen, Indenture, 28 July 1818, by virtue of writ of partition, R Goodwin deft; sheriff sold land publickly to highest bidder, sd Aaron Allen for One thousand Twenty five Dollars, 318 acres adj lands of estate of Stanmore Butler, estate of [blank] Campbell, of Jolly (Still?Gill?), Abraham Stephens, William Dean, Willy Berry. Wit John S Jeter, Richd H Tutt. /s/ J Hatcher SED. Proven [day lost in binding] November 1818 by Richd H Tutt; M Mims CCP. Rec 2 Nov 1818.

p.243 Richard C Lewis to Abner Landrum, 18 September 18[in binding], One hundred fifty Dollars, one acre on Cambridge Road. Wit Thomas (P) Presley, James Forgason. /s/ Richd C Lewis. Rec 3 Nov 1818.

p.244 William Andrews of Chesterfield District to Martin Witt, Deed, 14 September 1818, Three hundred Dollars, 300 acres on Clouds Creek of Little Saluda on both sides of Columbia Road adj lands of heirs of Michel Witt now held by heirs of Joseph Williams, James Edson. Wit John Lee, Mary (x) Lee (Jr), Mary (x) Lee(Sr). /s/ William (x) Andrews. Proven 5 November 1818 by John Lee; Arthur H Lort JP. Rec 9 November 1818.

DEED BOOK 35

p.245   Thomas Wynn to Ephraim Cook, 18 June 1818, Two thousand one hundred fifty Dollars, 700 acres with mill and other buildings adj lands of Edmund Bacon, Simkins, Richard Burton, sd Ephraim Cook. Wit Richd H Tutt, Edward C Ramsey. /s/ Thos Wynn. Justice Mathew Mims certifies relinquishment of dower rights by Elizabeth Winn wife of Thomas Winn, 10 November 1818; /s/ Elizabeth (x) Winn. Proven 10 November 1818 by Richd H Tutt; M Mims CCP. Rec 10 November 1818.

p.246   Abner Landrum to Mary Eddins, Deed, 31 December 1817, $1548.50; 948 ½ acres on Beaverdam and Shaws Creek adj lands of Benjamin Frazier, widow Jones, widow Eddins, Benjamin Darby, plat by John Frazier 1818, except 83 ½ acres sold to William Norton part on Flat Rock Br adj lands of Stephen Tillman, also except one acre above the mill which Abner Landrum reserves for chalk sand for his manufactory; understood that if chalk land should fail, right to sd acre vested in Mary. Wit Moses Swearingen, John Swearingen. /s/ Abner Landrum. M Mims certifies relinquishment of dower rights by [blank] Landrum wife of Abner Landrum, [blank] Nov 1818; /s/ Mekethelan Landrum. Proven 13 Nov 1818 by Moses Swearingen; M Mims CCP. Rec 13th November 1818.

p.247   John Thomas to Thomas Winn, Deed, 27 August 1818, Five hundred Dollars, 250 acres being part of two tracts, first of 200 acres on Bull Branch, part of 1000 acres originally granted to Arther Thomas 5 August 1793; the other of 50 acres on Beaverdam of Shaws Creek, being part of 417 acres granted to Isaac Kirkland 4 September 1797 by Gov Chas Pinckney. Wit Amos Landrum, Stephen Frederick. /s/ John (x) Thomas. Justice Lewis Holmes certifies relinquishment of dower rights by Lucy Thomas wife of John Thomas, 13 November 1818; /s/ Lucy (x) Thomas. Proven 7 September 1818 by Stephen Frederick; M Mims CCP. Rec 8 November 1818

p.249   Stephen Frederick to Thomas Wynn, 27 August 1818, Thirteen hundred Dollars, 525 acres being two tracts and part of another: 200 acres originally granted to John Bettis 9 March 1773; also 175 acres granted to Stephen Bettis 25 Sept 1789 adj first tract; also part of tract granted to Frederick Swearingen 31 August 1799 adj Stephen Bettis. Wit Amos Landrum, John (x) Thomas. /s/ Stephen Frederick. Justice Lewis Holmes certifies release of dower rights by Mary Frederick, 13 November 1818; /s/ Mary (x) Frederick. Proven 7 September 1818 by John Thomas; M Mims CCP. Rec 18th November 1818.

p.250   Shepherd Spencer to Zebulon Rudulph of Columbia in Richland District, Deed, 29 July 1817, Two thousand Dollars, 1500 acres on Beaverdam and Richland Creeks of Little Saluda River. Wit Sampson Pope Junr, Wade Allen. Acknowledgement that William Duncan who resides on part of above land is to continue during his life or until he may choose to remove and to be free from any charge or rent. Justice Jesse Blocker certifies relinquishment of dower rights by Hannah Spencer wife of Shepherd Spencer,

17 October 1817; /s/ Hannah Spencer. Proven 18 Nov 1818 by Sampson Pope Junr; M Mims CCP. Rec 18th Nov 1818.

p.251 John Cartledge to his children Martha Cunningham and Sarah Cartledge, Deed of Gift, 8 October 1818, love and Two hundred Dollars, [acreage lost in binding] whereon I now live; also seven Negroes: Pheby, Will, Phil, Randol, Winney, Allen, and Squire, reserving to myself and my wife income of land and labour, also reserving to Martha NegroWinny as her share and to Sarah girl Pheby; Squire I give to John Cunningham, rifle gun to John Cunningham. Wit Judith Griffis, Francis Griffis, Melinda Griffis, John Boyd. /s/ John Cartledge. Proven 18 Nov 1818 by John Boyd; M Mims CCP. Rec 18 Nov 1818.

p.252 William Moore to Negro Mary, Deed of Manumission, 3 November 1818, One Dollar, Mulatto slave age about eighteen named Mary and her male child named Andrew two years and her other male child Anderson two months of age. Wit Thos Anderson, Geo Butler. /s/ Wm Moore. Justices and freeholders certify sd slaves not of bad character and capable of gaining a livelihood by honest means, 3 November 1818. /s/ Thos Anderson JQ, Gilson Yarbrough, George L Partrick, Moses (x) Walton, John (x) Coleman Senr, Geo Butler. Rec 14th December 1818.

p.253 William Moore to Negro Susannah, Deed of Manumission, 3 November 1818, One Dollar, mulatto slave age fifteen named Susannah. Wit Thos Anderson, Geo Butler. /s/ Wm Moore. Justices and freeholders certify that Susannah is not of bad character and is capable of gaining a livlihood by honest means. /s/ Thos Anderson JQ, Gilson Yarbrough, George L Partrick, Moses (M) Walton, John (x) Coleman, Geo Butler. Rec 14 December 1818.

p.254 John Grumbles to George Anderson, Deed, 4 February 1815, Three hundred Dollars, 300 acres on Stephens Creek, Duleys road and Thomas Carters path. Wit John Trayler, Robert Frazer. /s/ John Grumbles. Proven 6 November 1818 by John Trayler; C Bussey JQ. Rec 20th Nov 1818.

p.255 William Nusom to his two sons Anselm B Nusom and William Hampson Nusom, Deed of Gift, 25 September 1818, all real and personal property, Negro fellow(Hnchan?), land I live on, stock, furniture, to be equally divided; Anselm to manage my business from this day forward; I am to be supported out of above property. Wit Richard (x) Findley, Charles (x) Findley. /s/ William (M) Nusom. Proven 18 November 1818 by Richard Findley; Thomas Price JP. Rec 21 Nov 1818.

p.256 Abigail Williams to John Bolger, Dower, 24 October 1818; Justice John Blocker certifies relinquishment of dower rights by Abigail Williams wife of Davis Williams Esqr; /s/ Abigail Williams. Rec 23rd Nov 1818.

p.256 William Fluker, planter, to Nicholas Siglar, planter, Deed, 16 November 1814, Seven Hundred Dollars, 244 acres adjoining lands of Sarah Boddy, John Williams, Allen Boddy, Abraham Michel, Zachariah Miller, William Fluker. Wit James Eidson Junr, Allen Boddy. /s/ Wm Fluker. Justice William Hurtt certifies relinquishment of dower by Isabel Fluker wife of William Fluker, 5 September 1818; /s/ Isabel (x) Fluker. Proven 2 November 1818 by James Eidson; Richd Williams JQ. Rec 27 Nov 1818.

p.258 William Jones to Nicholas Siglar, Deed, 17 November 1814, Five hundred fifty Dollars, 300 acres on Clouds Creek adj lands of Allen Bodie, Henson, Sarah Bodie, Martin Witt, W Jones. Wit Wm Fluker, John Williams, Isabella Fluker. /s/ William (U) Jones. Justice Elkanah Sawyer certifies the relinquishment of dower rights by Sarah Jones wife of William Jones, 1 September 1815. [No signature.] Proven [day lost in binding] Nov 1815 by John Williams; Elkanah Sawyer JQ. Rec 27 Nov 1818.

p.259 Richmond Watson to Charles Oneall of Charleston, Deed, 13 November 1812, One thousand Dollars, 266 acres being part of three tracts adj each other, one granted to Arthur Watson April 1792, one granted to Michael Watson 28 November 1711, the other granted to Robt Pringle, on Clouds Creek adj John Eidson's land. Wit Arthur Rice Watson, Ezekiel Perry Junr. /s/ Richmond Watson. Nov 15, 1812, certification that a line (surveyed?) By Amos Satcher between me and Richmond Watson shall be established. Wit Matthias Jones. /s/ Ezekiel Perry Junr. Elijah Watson certifies relinquishment of dower rights by Sarah Watson wife of Richmond Watson, 15 November 1812; /s/ Sarah (-) Watson. Proven 10 January 1813 by A Rice Watson; J P Bush JP. Rec 27 Nov 1818.

p.260 Richmond Watson to Charles Oneall of Charleston, Deed, 19 November 1812, Fifty Dollars, 350 acres, part of 530 acres granted to Arthur Watson 5 March 1792 on branches of Dry Creek of Little Saluda River, adj lines of Connik. Wit Arthur Rice Watson, Ezekiel Perry Junr. /s/ Richmond Watson. Justice Elijah Watson certifies relinquishment of dower rights by Sary Watson wife of Richmond Watson 13 November 1812, /s/ Sarah (x) Watson. Proven 10 January 1813 by A Rice Watson; JP Bush JP. Rec 27th Nov 1818.

p.262 John Azbell to Charles Oneale, Deed, 7 January 1814, Three hundred Dollars, 101 acres on Haw Branch and Fall Creek of Clouds Creek adj lands of John Eidson, Richmond Watson, Absalom Watson. Wit Matthias Jones, John Eidson. /s/ John Asbell. Justice Elkanah Sawyer certifies relinquishment of dower rights by Abigail Azbell wife of John Azbell, 14 April 1815; /s/ Abigail (A) Asbell. Proven 9 February 1814 by Matthias Jones, John P Bush JP. Rec 27 November 1818.

p.263 Charles Oneale to Nicholas Zeiglar, Deed, 27 January 1817, Three thousand three hundred Dollars, three tracts: one of 350 acres being part of 530 acres granted to Arthur Watson 5 March 1792 on branches of Dry Creek of Little Saluda River adj lines of Richard Howard, Connick; also 236 acres being part of three tracts adj each other one granted to Arthur Watson April 1792 one granted to Michael Watson 28 September 1771 the other granted to Robt Pringle situate on Clouds Creek, sd 266 acres bound on branches of Clouds Creek, John Eidson; also 101 acres on Fall Creek of Clouds Creek adj John Eidson, Richmond Watson, Absalom Watson, Fall Creek, Haw Branch. Wit Hardy Harris, Wm D Harris. /s/ Chs Oneale. Justice John Lark certifies relinquishment of dower rights by Mary C Oneale wife of Charles Oneale 28 Jany 1817; /s/ M C Oneale. Proven 27 January 1817 by Hardy Harris; Nathan Norris JP. Rec 27 November 1818.

p.264   Elijah Watson to Richmond Watson, Deed, 2 June 1818, One thousand Dollars, 252 acres on Clouds Creek of Little Saluda River being one tract of 200 acres granted to John ---alin and one tract of 35 acres granted to Arthur Watson 5 February 1787 & part of another tract granted to [blank] containing 300 acres.   Wit Amos Watson, Amos W Satcher. /s/ Elijah Watson. Justice Lewis Holmes certifies that Clowey Watson wife of Elijah Watson relinquishes dower rights, [day lost in binding] November 1818; /s/ Clowy (x) Watson. Proven [day lost in binding] November 1818 by Amos W Satcher; Lewis Holmes JQ. Rec 27th November 1818.

p.266   Gabriel Key to Tandy M Key, Deed, 26 October 1816, Three hundred Dollars, one third part of 300 acres originally granted to Henry Key and part originally granted to John Goff, sd land on Turkey Creek of Stephens Creek and adj Elisha Turnage, Stephen Thomas, estate of Lewis Martin, sd Tandy M Key, Chesly B Cochran, Turkey Creek. Wit Jesse Waldrum, William Key. /s/ Gabriel Key. Proven 30 November 1818 by William Key; M Mims CCP. Rec 30 Nov 1818.

p.267   Samuel Key now of Georgia to Tandy M Key, Deed, 4 August 1817, Three hundred Dollars, one third of 300 acres originally granted to Henry Key and part to Goff, sd tract on Turkey Creek of Stephens Creek and bounded by lands of Mackness Minter, Elisha Turnage, Lewis Martin, sd Tandy M Key, Chesly B Cochran, Turkey Creek. Wit William Key, Caleb Cooksey. /s/ Samuel Key. Proven 30 November 1818 by William Key; M Mims CCP. Rec 30th Nov 1818.

p.267   Nancy Bird to John Bird's children, Deed of Gift, love, to my grandchildren the lawful representatives of my son Eborn Bird by his now living wife Sarah and all which he may have by his wife Sarah, Negro girl named Ader, horse named Dick. Wit D Bird, S Rarden. /s/ Nancy Bird. Proven [date blank; no name, no official]

p.268   Daniel Hardy and John Hardy to George Delaughter Senr, Deed, 10 November 1818, Claim to land on Stephens Creek adj sd Delaughter, granted to John Hardy decd. Wit Henry W Barns, Dicy (x) Green. /s/ John Hardy, /s/ Daniel Hardy. Proven

DEED BOOK 35

2 December 1818 by Henry W Barns; Charles Bussey JQ. Rec 3 December 1818.

p.269   John Hardy to George Delaughter senior, Deed, 21 August 1818, Five thousand two hundred twenty Dollars, 348 acres it being part of land granted to [name lost in binding] Morgan and John Hardy and James Brewer on waters of Big Stephens Creek, on Martintown Road, Brewers branch. Wit James Day, Leroy Stringer, Shepherd Spencer. /s/ John Hardy. Proven 3 October 1818 by Leroy Stringer; Charles Bussey JQ. Justice Charles Bussey certifies relinquishment of dower rights by Clarissa Hardy wife of John Hardy, 3 October 1818; /s/ Clarissa Hardy. Rec 3 Dec 1818.

p.270   William Butler, planter, to George Riley, Deed, 11 November 1818, One hundred twenty Dollars, 50 acres on Halfway Swamp of Saluda River, same granted to William Hill July 14, 1785, conveyed to John Troop 1792, conveyed to Henry Weavour, from him to William Butler; adj lands of Denet Hill, William Butler, and by Persimmon branch. Wit Lewis Whitley, James ---grans, Henry (x) Weaver. /s/ William (x) Butler. Justice Thomas Anderson certifies relinquishment of dower rights by Elizabeth Butler wife of William Butler, 27 November 1818; /s/ Elizabeth (x) Butler. Proven 27 November 1818 by Lewis Whitley; Ths Anderson JQ. Rec 7 December 1818.

p.271   Gilson Yarbrough to John Riley Senr, Deed, 25 February 1818, Sixty(?) Dollars, saw mill on Persimmon Creek of Little Saluda River, it being part of tract purchased by Zacheriah Riley from Walter Abney and sold to sd Yarbrough. Wit Wm Barnes, Samuel (x) Abney. /s/ Gilson Yarbrough. Proven 28 February 1818 by Wm Barnes; John Abney JP. Rec 7th Decr 1818.

p.272   John W Berry to Tillman Hitt and Hamblen Quarles, Bill of Sale, 19 October 1818, One Dollar, Negro woman called Mariah and her child about age five named Louisa and their future increase, in trust for behoof of Agness Berry wife of John W Berry and heirs of her body hereafter to be born. Wit John Johnson, Lewis Nobles. /s/ John W Berry. Proven 6 November 1818 by John Johnson; Christian Britop J Q. Rec 7th December 1818.

p.273   Henry Weaver to George Riley, Deed of Gift, 12 August 1817, Bequeaths unto George Riley 100 acres on Halfway Swamp beginning at Persimmon Branch bounded by lands of Mathew Mays, Hesekiah Burnett. Wit Isaac Herring, Nathan Baker, Wm Johnson. /s/ Henry Weaver. Proven 23 Feby 1818 by William Johnson; Christian Britop JQ. Rec 7th December 1818.

p.274   James Panton, planter, to John Moore, planter, Deed, 29 October 1818, Three thousand five hundred Dollars, 338 acres, resurveyed by Leroy Hammond, lying below Stephens Creek on Savannah River adj the lands of Alexander Stewart, Thomas Judge,

DEED BOOK 35

W Thomas, estate of Reuben Frazer, Robert Gardner, Mrs Covington now James Dayes land, estate of William Howerton, being land on which I now reside, also my right to half the Fishery known by name of Old Field Fishery, and one third of Fishery known by name Head of Bull sluice; also my right to ten islands containing 45 acres conveyed by Robert Savage to William Covington. Wit James Wilson, Mary Ann Wilson. /s/ Jas Panton. Justice Charles Bussey certifies relinquishment of dower rights by Ann Panton wife of James Panton, 13 October 1818; /s/ Ann Panton. Proven 30 October 1818 by James Wilson; Chs Bussey JQ. Rec 7 Dec 1818.

p.275 Fielding Reynolds to Captain John Ryand, Deed, 13 October 1818, Three thousand five hundred Dollars, 352 acres on Dry Creek whereon my brother James Reynolds resides adj lands of Charles F Randolph, widow Cobbs, William Jeter, James Maul, land whereon I reside. Wit Reason Barnes, Wm Brazier Junr. /s/ Fielding Reynolds. Justice Christian Breithaupt certifies relinquishment of dower by Elizabeth Reynolds wife of Fielding Reynolds, 13 October 1818; /s/ Elizabeth (x) Reynolds. Proven 13 October by Reason Barnes; Christian Breithaupt QU. Rec 7 Dec 1818.

p.276 Francis Burt to Susannah Burt, Deed, 13 March 1818, Two thousand two hundred eighty two Dollars fifty cents, 4---ty6 ½ acres Turkey Creek being part of two tracts, one granted to [blank] Garrett, the other to Richard Johnson, whereon sd Susanna Burt now lives for her natural life or so long as she continues a widow, on her death unto Eugene Burt, Mary Ann Burt, Harewood Burt, Caroline Burt, Augustine Burt, Moody Burt, Amelia Burt, William Burt. If sd Susanna Burt should marry, she to hold one third part of premises, then to sd heirs. Wit Tho Harrison, Warren R Davis. /s/ Francis Burt. John T Lewis Clerk of Court, Pendleton District, certifies relinquishment of dower rights by Catharine Burt wife of Francis Burt, 13 March 1818; /s/ Catharine Burt. Proven Pendleton District 13 March 1818 by Warren R Davis; John T Lewis CC. Rec 7th December 1818.

p.278 Jacob Earnest to Stephen Terry Jr, Deed, 24 November 1817, Five hundred twenty Dollars, ---nty acres on Beaverdam Cr of Stevens Creek, being part of land originally granted to Daniel Stephens, adj lands of Jacob Earnest, Joel ---pers land. Wit Lewis Collins, Robert T Walker. /s/ Jacob Earnest. Justice John Hollingsworth certifies relinquishment of dower rights by Nancy Earnest wife of Jacob Earnest, 24 November 1817; /s/ Nancy Earnest. Proven 24 November 1817 by Robert T Walker; John Hollingsworth JQ. Rec 7th Decr 1818.

p.280 Mrs Eunice Reid to John Hughs, Mortgage, 10 November 1818, John deeds to Eunice land for Eighteen Hundred sixty Dollars, her note for $800 to be paid 10 November 1819, 258 acres in three tracts on Reedy Branch of Horns Creek adj lands of Stephen Tillman, M Ellison, Gosper Gallman, Reuben Reid; if Eunice pays the mortgage is void. Wit Stephen Tillman Senr, Jesse Bettis, Benj Harrison. /s/ E Reid.

DEED BOOK 35

Proven [day lost in binding] December 1818 by Stephen Tillman; M Mims CCP.

p.281 William W Olds, planter, to James Panton, planter, Deed, 15 December 1817, Three thousand three hundred Dollars, 338 acres on Stephens Creek adj lands of Alexander Stewart, estate of William Howerton, estate of John Covington, estate of Robert Gardner, estate of Reuben Fraser, estate of James Thomas, land of Thomas Judge being land on which [I?] now reside; also my interest in certain fisheries, half of Old Field Fishery, 1/3 of Head of Bull Sluice, also my islands containing 45 acres, conveyed by Robert Savage to William Covington. Wit Daniel Frazer, Philip (x) Frazer. /s/ Wm W Olds. Justice Charles Bussey certifies relinquishment of dower rights by Ann Old wife of William W Old, 16 December 1817; /s/ Ann Olds. Proven 16 December 1817 by Daniel Frazier; Charles Bussey JQ. Rec 7th December 1818.

p.282 Arthur Simkins to Henry Shultz of Augusta, Georgia, Deed, 26 March 1817, One hundred one Dollars security five cents, one half acre lot in village of Edgefield on the commons of Jefferson and Madison Street opposite lot of Peter Labourde, known in plan drawn by Robert Lang Esqr as No. 16; also one other half acre lot directly back of sd lot adj Madison St. Wit Eldred Simkins, Wady Thompson Jr. /s/ Arthur Simkins. Proven 27 March 1817 by Wady Thompson Jr; M Mims CCP. Rec 15th December 1818. Recd 24 June 1817 from Augustus G Nagle his note payable 1 January for One hundred thirty seven Dollars pd in full for the quarter acre lots we bought of Henry Shultz and do relinquish all rights to sd premises; Rob Lang & Co.

p.283 Sheriff Jeremiah Hatcher to John Morning, Deed, 7 December 1818, at writ of partition Richard Gibson and wife plf and John Morning and others dfts, land to be sold publicly to highest bidder; struck off to John(sic) Morning for Six hundred Dollars, 286 acres on Bog Branch which John Walker decd had at time of death. Wit Richd H Tutt, Edmd Harrison. /s/ J Hatcher. Proven 14 December 1818 by Edmd Harrison; M Mims CCP. Rec 14 December 1818.

p.285 Owen Dailey to William Furguson, Deed, 3 November 1818, Fourteen hundred Dollars, 130 acres adj lands of Doctor Charles ONeall, Jacob Hewit, Zachariah S Brooks on Big Creek; also adj to above tract the upper part of 70 acres conveyed by Jesse Summers to William Griffin and the lower part of 50 acres to William Griffin by will of his father and sd two parts of land conveyed by sd Wm Griffin to Owen Dailey 23 March 1813 containing 120 acres adj lands of Arthur Dillard, Zachariah S Brooks, Big Creek of Little Saluda River being 250 acres whereon I now live. Wit Henry Coate, William Eastland. /s/ Owen (x) Dailey. Justice Henry Coate certifies release of dower by Elizabeth Dailey wife of Owen Dailey 3 November 1818; /s/ Elizabeth (x) Dailey. Proven 3 Novr 1818 by Wm Eastland; Henry Coate QM. Rec 22 Nov 1818.

p.286 John Dailey to Wm Ferguson, Deed, 3 November 1818, Six hundred Dollars,

102

land I bought of Samuel [lost in binding] whereon I now live, 200 acres adj 21 ½ acres being the whole of my land adj Major Genl Wm Butler, James Butler, Wm Ferguson, granted by Gov Wm Bull 22 August 1771 to Mary Hines afterwards married to B[lost in binding] Izard; conveyed through sundry hands to [lost in binding] Davis and from him to myself, on Big Creek branches, Little Saluda. Wit Henry Coate, William Eastland. /s/ John Daley. Justice Henry Coate certifies the relinquishment of dower rights by Sarah Dailey wife of John Dailey 3 November 1818; /s/ Sarah (I) Dailey. Proven 3 Novr 1818 by William Eastland; Henry Coate QM. Rec 22 Dec 1818.

p.287 Jesse Summers to William Ferguson, Deed, 15 January 1818, Eleven hundred Dollars, 300 acres on Big Creek of Little Saludy River, composed of two adj tracts which I purchased of William Watts and William Blalock, adj lands of General Butler, William Riley, Owen Dailey, Doctor Charles ONeall, same whereon I now live. Wit Zah Brooks, J Martin, Jacob (H) Hewit. /s/ Jesse Summers. Justice Henry Coate certifies relinquishment of dower rights by Sarah Summers wife of Jesse Summers, 18 January 1818; /s/ Sally Summers. Proven 18 January 1818 by Zachariah Brooks; Henry Coate QU. Rec 22 December 1818.

p.289 John Blocker to James Morris, Deed, 8 [month lost in binding] 1818, Two hundred twenty nine Dollars fifty cents, 114 3/4 acres on Rocky Creek, being part of 1000 acres originally granted to William Logan 19 August 1774. Wit Abner Blocker, Haly Johnson. /s/ John Blocker. Justice Jesse Blocker certifies relinquishment of dower rights by Mary Tolbert Blocker wife of John Blocker, 14 June 1818; /s/ Mary T Blocker. Proven 14 June [year lost in binding] by Haley Johnson. Plat certified 21 May 1818 by John Blocker D S shows adj owners Peter Robertson, Morris, Chapell, Edmund Atchison.

p.290 James Kirby to Wilson Barontine, Received 26 February 1818 of Wilson Barontine Fifty Dollars in full payment for all my possessions except my dwelling house known by Thos Presley lease also bind myself, penalty $500 to give possession 25 December next. Wit Harvey Drake. /s/ James Kirby. I endorse within receipt to Moses Harris 18 July 1818; Wilson Baronton. Proved 29 December 1818.

p.291 Wilson Baronton to Moses Harris, Plat, shows drawing of house formerly occupied by James Cleveland, adj owners Abner Landrum, sd Wilson Baronton, John Lofton, Cambridge road, lots held by Nathan White and Charles Ferguson. Plat surveyed 1 July 1818 by John Lofton D S shows one acre on Northeast corner of pottery near Edgefield Courthouse. Rec 29th December 1818.

p.291 Charles Jones of Laurence District to Daniel Colvin, Deed, 10 December 1817, Six hundred fifty Dollars, 130 acres on Middle Creek of Savannah River, part of tract originally granted to James Clark. Wit William Jones, W H Nixon. /s/ Charles Jones.

DEED BOOK 35

Laurence District, Justice William Burnside certifies relinquishment of dower rights by Nancy Jones wife of Charles Jones, 1st January 1818; /s/ Nancy Jones. Proven 10 December 1817 by William Jones; Thomas Price JP. Plat surveyed [day lost in binding] December 1817 by James Tonby[?] shows adj owners Charles Jones, D Colvin, Hugh A Nixon, Stone & Bawden. Rec 30th December 1818.

p.293   Saxon Shaw of Jefferson County, Mississippi, to William Garrett, Deed on behalf of myself and as attorney on behalf of Thompson Shaw and Holson Shaw of same County and State, 13 December 1818, Five hundred twenty Dollars, [number lost in binding] hundred thirty acres surveyed for Ephraim Capts 16 July 1785 on Stephens Creek adj at time of survey William Longmire, James Smith, Edmund Whatley, Saxon Shaw's letter of attorney dated 30 October 1818. Wit John H Garrett, Henry Garrett. /s/ Saxton Shaw for Thompson Shaw, Hobson Shaw. Proven 1 January 1819 by John H Garett; M Mims CCP. Rec 1 January 1819.

p.294   Samuel Marsh Senr to Shemuel Nicholson, Deed, 1 January 1819, Twelve hundred Dollars, 230 acres on Rocky Branch of Rocky Creek, Little [lost in binding] Creek, Turkey Creek and Savannah River, adj lands of Shemuel Nicholson, Conrad Lowery Senr, heirs of Thomas Adams. Wit Jesse Blocker, Samuel Quarles. /s/ Saml Marsh. Justice Jesse Blocker certifies relinquishment of dower rights by Martha Marsh, 1 January 1819; /s/ Martha M Marsh. Proven 1 Jany 1819 by Samuel Quarles; Jesse Blocker JQ. Rec 1st January 1819.

p.295   Christopher Cox Senior to Pheraby Price, Deed, 21[24?] June 1817, Three hundred fifty Dollars paid by Pheraby Price on behalf of her three children Christopher Cox Price, Pamela Eleanor Price and Daniel William Price, 100 acres on Savanna River originally granted to William Brooks 3 Feby 1786. Wit Hugh A Nixon, Christopher Cox Jur. /s/ Christopher (x) Cox. Proven 28 December 1818 by H A Nixon; Thomas Price JP. Rec 4 January 1819.

p.296   Christopher Cox Senr, planter, to Gabriel Cox, Deed of Gift, 31 August 1816, parental love, 200 acres in two adj tracts; one tract of 150 acres being half of land originally granted to Richard Kennedy for 300 acres situate below mouth of Beding Field Creek running into Savannah river, sd 150 acres adj Bailey Cox, Henry [?] Cox, Philip Lightfoot, Jesse Stone, Solomon Beck, land formerly Charles Ashley; one other tract of fifty acres adj being part of sd Charles Ashleys survey adj lands of estate of Daniel Price decd, John Cox, Michell Cox. This deed does not take effect during natural life of Mary Cox wife of sd Christopher Cox Senr. Wit [name lost in binding] Nixon, James Freeman, William Shannon. /s/ Christopher (x) Cox. Proven 28 December 1818 by H A Nixon; Thomas Price J P. Rec 4th January 1819.

p.298   Benj Ryan to Reuben Reid, Deed in Trust, 2 Nov 1818, in trust for E Reid, my distributive share of intestate estate of Benj Ryan decd, all Negroes denominated free by will, all the lands purchased after the will, all other such property, and sd Reid has full power to sue for and collect same [other provisions here omitted]. Wit C Vanner, Jesse Bettis. /s/ B Ryan. Proven 4 January 1819 by Jesse Bettis; M Mims CCP.

p.298 Conrod Lowery Sr to Jacob Lowery, Deed, 10 December 1818, [number lost in binding] hundred Dollars, 70 acres in fork of Little Stevens and Rocky Creeks, it being part of 82 acres originally granted to Daniel Bird Sr, adj lands of sd Jacob, Stephenson Campbell, Shemuel Nicholson. Wit Shemuel Nicholson, George Mosley. /s/ Conrod Lowery. Justice Jesse Blocker certifies relinquishment of dower rights by Elizabeth Lowery wife of Conrod Lowry, 23 Decr 1818; /s/ Elizabeth (x) Lowery. Proven 10 December 1818 by George Mosley; Jesse Blocker JQ. Rec 4th Jan 1819.

p.299 [second of two pages with this number] James J Still to Jacob Lowery, Deed, 10(?) Novr 1815, One hundred ten Dollars, 30 acres on Rocky Creek, being part of 166 acres now in possession of Robert Scott and widow Glausier. Wit James Goudy[Gonsly?], George Mosley. /s/ James J Still. Proven 10 Decr 1818 by George Mosley; Jesse Blocker JQ. Rec 4th January 1818.

p.299 Davis Williams to Shemuel Nicholson, Deed, 22 June 1803, One hundred Dollars, 149 acres on Little Stevens Creek of Savannah River being part of 319 acres granted to sd Williams in 1792 adj lands of sd Nicholson, Thomas Eliot. Wit Stephenson Campbell, William (x) Morris. /s/ Davis Williams. Subscribers certify 4 January 1819 that they heard Davis Williams acknowledge above instrument; Jesse Blocker, John Buckhalter. Proven 4 Jany 1819 by John Buckhalter; Jesse Blocker JQ. Rec 4th January 1819.

p.301 James Sprott to Ransom Holloway, Bill of Sale, 9th June1818, One hundred four Dollars fifty cents State money Negro man Polladore. Wit J Holloway. /s/ James Sprott. Proven 4 Jan 1819 by Jordan Holloway; M Mims CCP. Rec [no date]

p.301 Henry Martin to Thomas Martin Junr, Deed, 1 October 1817(?), Five hundred Dollars, 153 acres on branch of Bird Creek of Stevens Creek. Wit Moab Martin, Temple (x) Martin. /s/ Henry Martin. Plat 19 September 1817 by James Tomkins shows adj owners Henry Martin, Thomas Martin, land granted to Francis. Proven 1 January 1818 by Moab Martin; Ansel Tolbert JP. Rec 4th January 1819.

p.303 Herrin Bush to Henry Waite, Deed, 26 April 1817, Three hundred Dollars, 359 acres, Cuffytown Cr, Five notch road. Wit James Sproul, Hugh Mosley. /s/ Herrin Bush. Proven 26 April 1817 by Jas Spowl(sic); Robt Walker J P. Rec 4th Jan 1819.

p.304 Jacob Lowery to Shemuel Nicholson, Deed, [day lost in binding] Decr 1818,

DEED BOOK 35

Four hundred Dollars, 100 acres whereon I now live in fork of Little Stevens Creek and Rocky Creek, it being part of two tracts originally granted to Daniel Bird, adj Margarett A(?) Smiths land, Stephenson Campbell. Wit Conrod Lowery, George Mosley. /s/ Jacob Lowery. Justice Jesse Blocker certifies relinquishment of dower rights by Elizabeth Lowery wife of Jacob Lowery 23 Decr 1818; /s/ Elizabeth (x) Lowery. Proven 10th Dec 1818 by George Mosley; Jesse Blocker JQ. Rec 4 Jan 1819.

p.305 Charles ONeall to Lark Abney, Deed, 17 July 1818, Deed in security of Twelve Hundred forty Dollars fifteen cents to me paid by Lark Abney, 330 acres on Big Creek of Little Saluda River whereon sd Charles ONeall lives, part of which was granted to Joachim Bulow 10 June 1786 and part to Elijah [surname lost in binding] 4 March 1811 adj lands of estate of William Hogan decd, Ridgeway Hogan, Joshua Martin, William Ferguson. ONeall to pay $1240.15 with interest before 1 January 1820 and within deed to be void. Wit Herrin Bush, Jacob P Abney. /s/ Chs Oneall. Proven 12 Sept 1818 by Jacob P Abney; Das Williams JQ. Rec 4 January 1819.

p.306 Joseph Fuller to Noney F Atkinson, Deed, 2 January 1819, One hundred Dollars, 100 acres granted to Asa Hix and conveyed from him to ---mes Hunter and John Rountree and from them to Joseph Fuller, being part of 1000 acres on Town Creek. Wit John L Atkinson, Seborn Powel. /s/ Joseph Fuller. Proven 4 January 1819 by Seborn Powel; John Sturgenegger JP. Rec 5th January 1819.

p.307 Joseph Fuller to Noney Atkinson, Deed, 2 January 1819, Four hundred Dollars, three thousand seven hundred seventeen acres lying all round the plantation called the Haw Pond granted to Moony Gordin, [word lost in binding] by land granted to Asa Hix, Lang, by land granted to Philip Lamar and Thos Lamar of Bellmount. Wit John L Atkinson, Seborn Powel. /s/ Joseph Fuller. Proven 7 January 1819 by Seborn Powel; John Sturzenegger J P. Rec 5 Jany 1819.

p.308 Joseph Fuller to Noney F Atkinson, Deed, 3rd November 1818, Two hundred Dollars, 988 acres surveyed for John Carter but granted to Joseph Fuller between Rablow and Town Creeks; likewise 934 acres and 917 acres, likewise 992 acres and 989 acres all surveyed for John Carter between Hollow Creek and Town Creek, Barnwell District, and granted to Joseph Fuller. Wit John L Atkinson, Seborn Powel. /s/ Joseph Fuller. Proven 7th January 1819 by Seborn Powel; John Sturzenegger JP. Rec 7(?) January 1819.

p.309 John Mackey of Barkley County, planter, to Joseph Messer, Deed, 27 August 1765, Five hundred pounds lawful money of province, Mackey to make title before last October next conveying unto Joseph 100 acres on a branch of Santee River at Clouds Creek adj vacant land. Wit William Saxon, Thomas Scurry. /s/ John Mackey. I endorse within bond to Isaac Bell 6th January 1808; /s/ Joseph (x) Messer. Proven 28

106

April 1808 by Nathan (N) Body who was present along with John Herrin when Joseph Messer indorsed within bond to Isaac Beal; Wm Hurtt JP. I do indorse within Bond to Basel Wooley 5th January 1809; wit Rezin Wooley, Wm C Michell. /s/ Isaac (I) Beal. Proven 5 January [year lost in margin] by Rezin Woolley; Wm Hurtt J P. I Indorse within Bond to John Williams for value recd, 8 Febnruary 1811; Basil Woolley; Jesse Williams. Proven 28 December 1811 by Jesse Williams: Wm Hurtt JP. I indorse within Bond to Zachariah Miller for value recd 28 December 1811; wit Moses Prescoat; /s/ John Williams. Proven 28 December 1811 by Moses Prescoat; William Hurtt JP. Rec 11 January 1819.

p.310 John Williams to Zachariah Miller, Deed, 28 December 1811, Fifty Dollars, 10 acres on Clouds Creek being part of land originally granted to John Bodie by his Excy William Multree, adj Mackeys old line, where sd John Williams now liveth including the house and spring. Wit Moses Prescoat, Adam Coon. /s/ John Williams. Proven 28 December 1811 by Moses Prescoat; Wm Hurtt JP. Rec 11 January 1819.

p.311 William C Mitchell to Zachariah Miller, Deed, 6 October 1818, Forty Dollars South Carolina money, 60 acres on Clouds Creek being part of land formerly granted unto William Mitchell by patent 7 August 1809 and signed by Gov [illeg]. Wit Sion Mitchell, Forrest Mitchell. /s/ Wm C Mitchell. Proven 11 January 1819 by Sion Mitchell; Wm Hurtt JQ. Rec 11th January 1819.

p.312 William Fluker to Zachariah Miller, Deed, 26 March 1814, Fifty Dollars, 133 acres in original grant but part sold to Nathan Body, lying down Mosses branch from Seglars corner in Megees old field, near Clouds Creek, land formerly of John Body, Martin Fouts, Nicholas Segler. Wit Moses Prescoat, Joel Foster. /s/ Wm Fuller(sic). Proven 11 November 1815 by Moses Prescoat; Nathan Norris JP. Rec 11 Jan 1819.

p.313 John M Lansdon to Zachariah Miller, Deed, 24 December 1814, One hundred Dollars, 50 acres on Clouds Creek adj Starks land, lands of Miller, Tipson, Abram Mitchell. Wit Moses Prescott, Wm Fluker. /s/ John M Lansdon. Proven 11 Nov 1815 by Moses Prescott who saw John M Langdon sign; Nathan Norris JP; Rec 11 Jan 1819

p.314 Abram Raleigh to Stephen Pixley, Deed, 10 October 1817, Twelve hundred Dollars, 700 acres on Sleepy Creek of Little Stephens Creek of Stephens Creek on Mathews road and known as Drury Mathews old Place, originally granted to Drury and William Mathews; other part originally granted to Joseph Thomson. Wit John Jeter, Wm W Williams. /s/ Abram (x) Raleigh. Justice William Robinson certifies release of dower by Sarah Raleigh, 23 October 1817; /s/ Sarah (x) Raleigh. Proven 12th January 1819 by John S Jeter; M Mims CCP. Rec 12th January 1819.

p.315 Richard Blalock to Waide Blalock, Receipt, 3 November 1818, [number lost in binding] hundred seventy Dollars in full for Negro girl Kissey about 15 or 16 yrs old. Wit Henry Wise, Richard Blalock Junr. /s/ Richard Blalock. Proven 9th December 1818 by Henry Wise; John Tarrance JQ. Rec 12th Jan 1819.

p.316 Richard Blalock to Waide Blalock, Receipt, 3 November 1818, Two hundred seventy Dollars in full for thirty head cattle on Shaws Creek. Wit Henry Wise, Richard Blalock Junr. /s/ Richard Blalock. Proven 9th December 1818 by Henry Wise; John Tarrance JQ. Rec 12th Jan 1819.

p.316 Arthur Simkins the elder to Sarah Pardue, Deed, 13 June 1818, Seventy five Dollars, lots of ½ acre each, the first fronting on Jefferson Street near Peter Laborde, Cloud; the other half acre lot back of sd lot. Wit Eldred Simkins, Stephen Clement. /s/ Arthur Simkins. Proven 12th January 1819 by Stephen Clement; M Mims C C P. Rec 13th Jany 1819.

p.317 Chaney Farrow to John S Glascock, Receipt, 15 January 1819, received Five hundred Dollars in full for 70 acres adj lands of Hinchey Mitchell, James Beams, Eldred Simkins. Wit Beverly Samuel, Waters Farrow. /s/Chaney Farrow. Proven 13 Jan 1819 by Beverly Samuel; M Mims C C P. Rec 15th Jan 1819.

p.318 Jane Cobbs, John Cobbs, Cynthia Ohara and James Ohara to John Ryan, Deed, 14 January 1819, One thousand forty Dollars, 208 acres on New Market Road on a spring branch of Dry Creek it being part of land formerly owned by Walter Jackson and since sold by Lawrence Rambo to James Cobbs. Wit Sampson Butler, Stephen Tillman Senior. /s/ Jane Cobbs, John P Cobbs, James Oharrow, Cynthia Oharrow. Plat resurveyed 6 January 1817 by Stephen Tillman at request of Dr John Cobbs. Justice Mathew Mims certifies release of dower rights by Cynthia Ohara wife of James Ohara, 22 January 1819; /s/ Cynthia Ohara. Proven 22 January 1819 by Sampson Butler who saw Mrs Jenny Cobbs et al sign; /s/ Sampson Butler. Rec 22 January 1819.

p.320 Sarah Pardue to her son Fields Pardue, Deed, 14 January 1819, love and Five Dollars, one half of an acre lot in Village of Edgefield on Jefferson Street near Peter Laborde and lot formerly James Cloud but now Augustus G Wash; the other half of the acre lot is reserved for myself. Wit John Mills, E Harrison. /s/ Sarah (x) Pardue. Proven 15 January 1819 by Edmund Harrison; M Mims C C P. Rec 15 Jan 1819.

p.321 Betsy B Wright to her niece Sarah Ann S Drinkwater daugher of Josiah Drinkwater, Deed of Gift, 25 January 1819, property which I acquired of sd Josiah Drinkwater: two feather beds and furniture, one sow and pigs, eight sitting chairs and kitchen furniture, after the death of her mother Lucy Drinkwater but not before. Wit Edmund Harrison. /s/ Betsy B Wright. Proven 25 January 1819 by Edmund Harrison; M Mims C C P. Rec 25th January 1819.

DEED BOOK 35

p.322 Henry McClendon to Benjamin Frazier, Mortgage, 29 October 1818, Henry's note to Col Benjamin Frazier made payable to bearer for Two hundred sixty five Dollars 89 cents due 25 December 1819; secures payment 313 acres granted to Buckner Blalock 1808, from Buckner Blalock sold to me 28 December 1816, lying on South Edisto; provided if Henry McClendon's payment is made, deed to be null and void. Wit J Hatcher, M McHann. /s/ Henry McClendon. Proven 29 January 1819 by Jeremiah Hatcher; M Mims C C P. Rec 29 January 1819.

p.324 David Richerson to the reverent(sic) John Monk, 19 November 1790, One hundred pounds current State money, 150 acres on South Edisto River which was granted to James Harrison 8 July 1774, from James Harrison to David Richerson 24 March 1787. Wit John (x) Leek, Jacob (I) Richerson. /s/ David (I) Richerson. /s/ Susannah (x) Richerson. Proven 20 August 1791 by John Leek; John Thos Fairchild J P. Rec 1 February 1819.

p.325 Nathaniel Fooshe to Henry Holland junior, Deed, 13 July 1817, Ten Dollars, 200 acres adj road to Arther Thomases, lands of Stephen Bettis, Beach Island road, being part of 1000 acres granted to John Monk 2 September 1793 by Hon William Moultrie; John Monk granted sd 200 acres to Sary Monk on 6 January 1794. Wit Benj Kirkland junr, Isaack Monk. /s/ Nathaniel Foshee. /s/ Sary (x) Foshee. Proven 9 November 1818 by Isaac Monk; Lewis Holmes JQ. Rec 1 Feb 1819.

p.327 Little Berry Franklin to Henry Holland, 1 December 1817, One hundred forty Dollars, 103 acres on Bull Branch of Edisto River adj lands of Col Samuel Mays, Henry Holland, Buckner Blalock. Wit Jesse (x) Brasell, William (x) Holland, A McEackin. /s/ Little Berry Franklin. Proven 9 Nov 1818 by Jesse Brazil; Lewis Holmes JQ. Rec 1 February 1819.

p.328 David Fooshe of Pendleton District to Henry Holland, Deed, 12 September 1805, Two hundred Dollars, 100 acres on Edisto River being part of 200 acres originally granted to Whitehead 9 March 1774 by Lt Gov Wm Bull, conveyed by Whitehead unto Daniel Goggins decd 23 & 24 December 1779; William Goggins eldest son & heir to Daniel Goggins decd hath sold 100 acres it being part of above 200 acres bounded on James Harrison at time of original survey... unto Henry Holland. Wit Joshua Monk, Moses Armstrong. /s/ David Fooshee. Proven 1(?) November 1818 by Joshua Monk; Lewis Holmes JQ. Rec 1 Feb 1819.

p.329 David Fooshe of Pendleton to Henry Holland, Deed, 20 September 1805, $10, 40 acres East side Long & Butlers Br adj sd Fooshe & Monk, part of land conveyed from Garret Buckler to John Stone senior and sd Stone conveyed same to David Fooshe. Wit Joshua Monk, MosesArmstrong. /s/ David Fooshe. Proven [day lost in binding] November 1818 by Joshua Monk; Lewis Holmes JQ. Rec 1ˢᵗ Feb 1819.

p.330   Isaac Monk to Henry Holland junior, Deed, 15 October 1818, One hundred Dollars, 75 acres south Edisto River granted to James Harrison by Hon Wm Bull 8 July 1774, by sd James Harrison to David Richardson and David Richardson to John Monk 19 November 1790, John Monk granted same to Isaac Monk, together with fifty acres being part of land containing 319 acres granted to Absalom Posey on 1 May 1789 and adj old Harris line, sd Henry Holland now [name lost in binding], old road from Monks Mill to head of Bridge Creek, Wootan land. Wit Joshua Monk, Nathaniel Fooshe. /s/ Isaac Monk. Justice Lewis Holmes certifies relinquishment of dower rights by Sarah Monk wife of Isaac Monk 9 November 1818; /s/ Sarah (x) Monk. Proven 9 November 1818 by Joshua Monk; Lewis Hoomes JQ. Rec 1 February 1819.

p.332   Henry Jones to Henry Holland, Deed, 21 November 1807, Ten(?) Dollars, 279 acres lying on Long Branch of Edisto River adj Fooshe line, Still branch, Monks line, originally granted to Absalom Posey 7 September 1789 for [number lost in binding] hundred sixty nine acres, on south side of Edisto. Wit Joshua Monk, William (B) Posey. /s/ Henry (x) Jones. Proven 1 November 1818 by Joshua Monk; Lewis Holmes JQ. Rec 1 February 1819.

p.333   John Slone Senr of Spartanburg County to John Monk, Deed, 21 March 1798, 100 pounds State money, 100 acres it being part of tract of 150 acres originally granted to James Harrison 8 July 1774 by Hon William Bull, conveyed from James Harrison to David Richerson 24 March 1787 and from David Richerson to John Monk 19 January 1790 and from John Monk to John Slone 28 March 1795. Sd 100 acres on Edisto River. Wit William Hill, Solomon Hill, J Sloan Junr. /s/ John Sloan. Proven 15 October 1804 by John Sloan junior; Isaac Freeman J P. Rec 1 February 1819.

p.334   John Sloan Senr of Spartanburg County to Armsted Hicks, Deed, 1 January 1803, One hundred twenty Dollars, 229 acres on Long Branch of Edisto River adj Foshees line, Still Branch, John Monks line, originally to Absalom Posey 7 September 1789. Wit Joshua Monk, Moses Armstrong. /s/ John Sloan. Proven 2 August 1805 by Moses Armstrong; Thos Swearingen JP. Rec 1st February 1819.

p.335   Armsted Hix to Henry Jones, Deed, 14 December 1804, One hundred Dollars, 229 acres on Long Branch of Edisto River adj lines of Fooshe, Still Branch, John Monk, sd land originally granted to Absalom Posey 7 September 1789. Wit Thos Marsh, Theophilus Jones. /s/ Armsted (H) Hix. Proven 2 August 1805 by Theophilus Jones; Thos Swearingen J P. Feb 1st February 1819.

p.336   John Monk to Sarah Monk, Deed, 6 January (year lost in binding), Ten Dollars, 200 acres adj road toArther Thomas, land of Stephen Bettis, Island Road, same being part of 1000 acres granted to sd John Monk 2 September 1793 by Hon William Moultrey. Wit Joshua Monk, David Foshe. /s/ John Monk. Proven 3 June 1812 by

Joshua Monk; J P Bush J P. Rec 1ˢᵗ February 1819.

p.337 Isaac Monk to Henry Holland junior, Deed, 15 October 1818, Ten Dollars, 24 acres on Long Branch of South Edisto River adj Beach Island Road, Holland's land, being part of 1000 acres granted to John Monk 2 Sept1793 by Hon Wm Moultrie, from sd John Monk to Isaac Monk 3 June [year lost in binding]. Wit Joshua Monk, Nathaniel Fooshe. /s/ Isaac Monk. Justice Lewis Holmes certifies relinquishment of dower rights by Sarah Monk wife of Isaac Monk 9 November 1818, [no signature]. Proven 9 November 1818 by Joshua Monk; Lewis Holmes JQ. Rec 1 Feb 1819.

p.338 Rebecca Minter to William Minter, Deed, 1 February 1819, One Dollar, [word lost in binding] the heirs of sd Estate, [word lost in binding] acknowledged have agreed to take only a childs part of her husband Mackeness Minter's estate, both real & personal, share & share alike with the following persons: William Minter, Permelia Wilburn formerly Permelia Minter, Martha Ann Key formerly Martha Ann Minter, Mackerness Minter, James Minter, Ebenezer Minter, and John Minter. Wit Champin Wilburn, John S Glascock. /s/ Rebecca (x) Minter. Proven 1 Feb 1819 by Champin Wilburn; M. Mims C C P. Rec 1ˢᵗ February 1819.

p.339 Allen B Addison to William Brazier, Mortgage, $1500, 900 acres adj Sanders Day, Christian Breithaupt; if Allen B Addison pays sd William at time specified, this instrument to be void. Wit Samuel Marsh. /s/ A B Addison. 1 February 1817 Mortgage assigned to James Longstreet. Wit Wm Brazier, John Brazier. /s/ Wm Brazier. Proven 1 February 1819 by Samuel Marsh; M Mims C C P. Rec 1 February 1819. Written across page 339: Satisfied in full 6ᵗʰ Feb 1821. James Longstreet.

p.340 John Cheatham to Casimir Delavigne, Deed, 23 January 1819, One thousand Dollars, 184 acres on Chaps Branch of Beaverdam creek of Turkey Creek of Stephens Creek originally granted unto Chapman Taylor by Hon Charles Greenville Montague 28 November 1771, conveyed by Chapman Taylor unto my father Peter Cheatham in December 1781, two thirds of sd tract came unto me, surveyed by John Blocker D S 11 January 1819. Wit Wm Garrett, David Outz, Emile Delavigne. /s/ John Cheatham. Justice John Collingswroth certifies relinquishment of dower rights by Fanny Cheatham wife of John Cheatham, 23 January 1819; /s/ Fanny (x) Cheatham. Proven 23 January 1819 by David Outz; John Hollingsworth J Q. Plat shows adj lands of Daniel Burnsell, John Buck, Davis. Rec 1ˢᵗ February 1819.

p.342 William Fletcher, Ezekiel Fletcher, John Lee to Reuben Lee, Deed, 26 January 1818, Two hundred twenty Dollars, rights to 106 acres being 2/3 of tract granted to Edward Fletcher adj lands of J Bussey, J Delaughter, William Fletcher, Stevens Creek Wit Micajah Bussey, William Mark Whatley. /s/ Ezekiel Fletcher, /s/ John Lee, /s/ Wm Fletcher. Proven 2 February 1818 by Micajah Bussey; Charles Bussey JQ. Rec 1

February 1819.

p.343   William Merit of Orange Burgh to Robert Johns, Deed, 24 January 1818, Three hundred fifty Dollars, 50 acres on Little Stevens Creek of Turkey Creek of Big Stephens Creek, being part of 1500 acres formerly granted unto Hugh Rose. Wit Reuben Landrum, Sally Burns. /s/ Wm Merrit. Proven 24 April 1818 by Reuben Landrum; Jesse Blocker JQ.

p.344   Seth Butler to John Butler, Deed, 31 January 1818, Eighty Dollars, my part of my father's undivided lands on Chaverses Creek adj lands of John Glackler, John Day, John Butler, Thomas L Shaw. Wit Hugh Ballantine, Thomas L Shaw, Henry Mathis. /s/ Seth Butler. Proven 18 February 1819; Hugh Balentine; Jesse Blocker JQ. Rec 1 February 1819.

p.345   Henry G Harden to James Longstreet, Assignment of Mortgage, November 23, 1818, Harden assigns mortgage to Longstreet. Wit Benj Gallman. /s/ Henry G Harden. Proven 1 Feb 1819 by Benjamin Gallman; Wm Hugens JP. Rec 1ˢᵗ Feb 1819.

p.345   Abner Butler to John Butler, Deed, 26 January 1818, Eighty Dollars, my part of my father's undivided lands on Chaverses Creek adj lands of John Glackler, John Day, John Butler, Thomas L Shaw. Wit Hugh Balentine, Frederick Day. /s/ Abner Butler. Proven 18 Feby 1819 by Hugh Balentine; Jesse Blocker JQ. Rec 1 Feb 1819.

p.346   John Couch to Aaron Loveless, Deed, 19 January 1816, One hundred thirty Dollars, 63 acres originally granted unto John Thurman decd by Gov Wm Moultrie 2 December 1793, and from Philip Thurman executor of estate of John Thurmon decd conveyed to Hem--- (Hem---) part thereof lying on Rocky Creek of Turkey Creek of Savannah River adj land of [name lost in binding] Hill, Philip Ikner. Wit Middleton Blalock, Henry Capehart. /s/ John Couch. Justice Charles Hammond certifies release of dower rights by Sarah Couch wife of John Couch 1 February 1819; /s/ Sarah (x) Couch. Proven 1 February 1819 by Henry Capehart; Charles Hammond JQ. Rec 1ˢᵗ February 1819.

p.348   William Seibles to William White of Augusta, Georgia, Deed, 1 July 1818, Two thousand Dollars, 129 acres near Savannah river on Stouks Gully. Wit Jacob Smith, Meline C Leavenworth. /s/ Wm Seibles. Justice James Hunter certifies release of dower rights by Martha Seibles wife of Wm Seibles, 1 November 1818; /s/ Martha J Seibles. Proven 2 February 1819 by Meline C Leavenworth.

p.349   Sophia Bonham to Negro Fanney, Deed of Emancipation, [day and month blank] 1819, sets free a mulatto woman Fanny otherwise called Fan about 22 or 23 years of age. Wit Wm Bledsoe, Ann Lewis. Proven 1 March 1819 by Wm Bledsoe.

Certification that Fanny late property of Sophia Bonham is capable of gaining a livlihood by honest means, 18 February 1819: /s/ John Lark J U Q, /s/ William Butler Senr, /s/ Mumford Perryman, /s/ Saml D L Loach, /s/ James (x) Hart, /s/ William Fox(Foy?) Rec 1st March 1819.

p.350 John Presley to Aaron Jackson, Deed, 3 March 1818, Four hundred Dollars, 556 acres on Turkey Cr of Savannah River adj lands of Joseph Minter, John Blocker Junr, Wm Strom. Wit Lee Blackbourn, Surles McCreless. /s/ John (P) Presley. Proven 27 Sept 1818 by Surles McCreless; Jesse Blocker JQ. Rec 1 Feb 1818.

p.351 Thomas Butler to John Butler, Deed, 24 November 1818, Eight hundred fifty Dollars, 75 acres where I now live adj lands of sd John Butler, Winefred Butler, Hugh Balentine, Thomas L Shaw. Wit Thomas L Shaw, Hugh Balentine. [No signature] Justice John Tarance certifies relinquishment of dower rights by Alley Butler wife of Thomas Butler, 24 November 1818; /s/ Alley (x) Butler. Proven 24 November 1818 by Hugh Balentine; John Tarance JQ. Rec 1st February 1819.

p.352 John Pope to John Lark, Deed, 16 January 1819, Three hundred Dollars, 174 acres on branches of Dry and Mine Creeks by resurvey of Amos Satcher D S, being part of three tracts granted to Drury Fort and conveyed by him to Edward Holmes and by him to me, adj lands of sd John Lark, William Humphries, and Charleston road. Wit Jonathan Fox, Andrew Lark. /s/ John Pope. Proven 1st February 1819 by Andrew Lark; Jesse Blocker. Rec 1st February 1819.

p.353 William Hollowa to Luke Devour, Deed, 14 January 1819, Fourteen hundred Dollars, 439 acres whereon I now live on head branches of Rock Creek of Turkey Creek of Stevens Creek of Savannah River adj lines of John Gibson. Wit Jonathan Devour, Abram Adams. /s/ Wm Hollowa. Justice Jesse Blocker certifies the relinquishment of dower rights by Margaret Hollowa wife of William Hollowa, 14 January 1819; /s/ Margaret (x) Hollowa. Proven 14 January 1819 by Jonathan Devour; Jesse Blocker JQ. Rec 1 February 1819.

p.355 Thomas Patton of Tennessee to John Butler, Deed, 21 October 1812, Twenty three Dollars, land entitled to Butler's wife Winnifred by heirship. Wit Thomas L Shaw, Hugh Balentine. /s/ Thomas Patton. Proven 1st February 1819 by Hugh Balentine; Jesse Blocker JQ. Rec 1 Feby 1819.

p.356 Mary Johnson to Hugh Balentine, Deed, 28 August 1818, Five hundred ninety Dollars, 59 acres on Five notched road adj sd Hugh Balentine, Thomas L Shaw. Wit Sarah Wade, James Miller. /s/ Mary (x) Johnson. Proven 6 October(?) 1818 by James Miller; C Bussey J Q. Rec 1 February 1819.

p.356 Sheriff Jeremiah Hatcher to Dawson Atkinson, 1 February 1819, at suit of John A[name lost in binding] against Jacob Zinn Junr, sheriff to sell land openly and publickly to highest bidder; struck off to Dawson Atkinson for Four thousand fifty Dollars, 114 acres adj Savannah River, and lands of Jonathan Dicks pr plat made 9th August 1806 by Robert Lang Esqr. Wit Jos Stallsworth, Richd H Tutt. /s/ J Hatcher S E D. Proven 2 February 1819 by Richd H Tutt; M Mims C C P. Rec 2 Feb 1819.

p.358 Jacob Zinn to Dawson Atkinson, planter, Deed, 20 January 1819, Five thousand Dollars, 114 acres on Beach Island and Savannah River adj lands of Arthur Simkins, Jonathan Dicks, resurvey made 9th Aug 1806. Wit Mary Simkins, Eliza Ardis, A Simkins. /s/ Jacob Zinn. Justice James Hunter certifies relinquishment of dower rights by Mary Zinn wife of Jacob Zinn, 30 January 1819. Proven 2 Feby 1819 by Col Arthur Simkins; M Mims C C P. Rec 2nd Feby 1819.

p.359 James Kilcrease, planter, to Stephen Smith planter, Deed, 23 January 1819, Five hundred forty Dollars, 100 acres being part of 640 acres granted unto Matt Martin and by sd Martin conveyed to Elijah Clakeler 28 October 1812 and by sd Clakeler to James Kilcrease 29 September 1815, 100 acres on Gunnels creek of Stephens Creek, plat by William Coursey D S 21 August 1796. Wit Matt Martin, Mathew Mayes. /s/ James Kilcrease. Justice Charles Hammond certifies relinquishment of dower rights by Mary Kilcrease wife of James Kilcrease, 3 January 1819; /s/ Mary (x) Kilcrease. Proven 25 January 1819 by Matt Martin; Charles Hammond JQ. Rec 2 Feb 1819.

p.361 Joseph Fuller to John Glover, Deed, 31 December 1818, One thousand Dollars, 100 acres between Horse Creek and Town Creek called the H[lost in binding] Pond, granted to Mary Gordon in 1789(?). Wit Dudley Rountree, Wade Glover. /s/ Joseph Fuller. Proven [day lost in binding] Feby 1819 by Wade Glover; A Edmunds JP. Rec 2nd Feby 1819.

p.362 John Kinard, farmer, to Jacob Long[Jacob Long Stiles?], Deed, 4 March 1818, [acreage not stated] on Lick Creek of Saluda River adj lands of Richard Rogers, Williams, John Kinard, Robert Atkins, Samuel Brooks, Benjamin Hughs, original grant containing 285 acres being the plantation whereon I now live. Wit Kesiah (x) Walker, Stephen Williams, Zachery Wooley. /s/ John M Kinard. Justice William Hurtt certifies relinquishment of dower rights by Christiana wife of John Kinard, 13 October 1818; /s/ Christiana (x) Kinard. Proven 13 October 1818 by Zachery Wooley; Wm Hurtt J Q. Rec 2nd Feby 1819.

p.363 Francis Taylor to Watts Mann, Receipt, 3 August 1816, received of Watts Mann Twenty one Dollars in full for land I was entitled by death of my father John Taylor decd in Edgefield, Lexington or elsewhere. Wit Herod (H) Thompson, Jno W Lee. /s/ Francis Taylor. Proven 30 January 1819 by Herod Thompson; Nathan Norris

JQ. Rec 2ⁿᵈ February 1819.

p.364 James Day to John Moore, Deed, 28 January 1819, Thirteen hundred fifty five Dollars, 391 ½ acres granted to William Hall on 6ᵗʰ August 1810, adj lines of Mrs Thomas, Col Leroy Hammond, Alexander Stuart, and William F Taylor. Wit A Stewart, Douglass Huff. /s/ James Day. Justice Charles Bussey certifies relinquishment of dower rights by Elizabeth Day wife of James Day, 30 January 1819; /s/ Elizabeth (x) Day. Proven 30 Jan 1819 by Douglass Huff; Charles Bussey JQ. Rec 3 Feb 1819.

p.365 Reuben Cloud to Easter Evans, Deed, 2 March1818, Two hundred Dollars, 178 acres on Shaws Creek adj lands of Ann Bland, Lacon Ryan on 8 July 1774, Morkley, granted to John Johnson 3 September 1808. Wit Henry Swearingen, John H Murphey. /s/ Reuben Cloud. Quit claim to above premises from me & my heirs. /s/ Barnabas (x) Grice. Proven 28 March 1818 by John H Murphey; John Loveless J P. Rec 4ᵗʰ February 1819.

p.366 Matthew Hamilton to Samuel Johnson, Deed, 21 September 1818, Eight hundred Dollars, 187 acres originally granted to Sarah Banks 16 Feby 1793 near old wells of Renns Fork adj William Hargrove, Charles Banks, Thomas Mosley, J Holsenback, William Hargrove. Wit Daniel Johnson, William Hamilton, John Elstre. /s/ Mathew Hamilton. Proven 24 Oct 1818 by William Hamilton; Christian Breightaupt NPQ. Rec 6ᵗʰ Feby 1819.

p.368 Henry Jennings to William Minter, planter, Deed, 28 October 1817, Five hundred Dollars, 100 acres on Bird Creek of Stephens Creek and Savannah River adj lands of Edward Settle, John Key, Charles Nix. Wit Triplet (x) Cason, John F Burress. /s/ Henry Jennings. Proven 8 Feb 1819 by John F Burress; M Mims CCP. Rec 8 Feby 1819.

p.369 Charles Nix to Henry Jennings, Deed, 6 August 1817, Five hundred Dollars, 100 acres on Bird Creek of Stephens Creek adj lands of Edward Settle, John Key, sd Nix. Wit John F Burress, James Key. /s/ Charles Nix. Justice John Lyon certifies the relinquishment of dower rights by Mary Nix wife of Charles Nix, 10 December 1817; /s/ Mary (x) Nix. Proven 10 December 1819 by John F Burress; John Lyon Q U. Rec 8ᵗʰ Feby 1819.

p.370 Benjamin Ryan to Negro Mary, Deed of Emancipation, 27 Decr 1809, Certification that Mary Scott is a free woman raised by me, born on my plantation, and served her due time with me; I pronounce Mary Scott a free woman of honest, good, industrious character, and her mother Jenny Scott was a free woman. Wit Benj Ryan Jr. /s/ Benj Ryan Senr. Proven 20 March 1819 by Benj Ryan; Christian Brightaupt NPQ. Rec 24 March 1817.

DEED BOOK 35

p.370   Edward Johnson to Jacob Tomlin, L&R, 17 & 18 May 1793, Fifteen pounds, ten shillings sterling money of sd State, 100 acres on road from Augusta to Congaree and on Clouds Creek of Edisto River, being part of 260 acres on main fork of Chincapin Creek, granted to Samuel Messer by Wm Moultrie Esqr in 1786, conveyed by sd Messer to Philip Gubs, adj lands of Widow McCartes, Kirkland. Wit Adam Efurt, John Vardell, Josiah (E) Nobles. /s/ Edward Johnson.   Orangeburg District, proven 10 August 1793 by Adam Efurt; Thomas Fairchild J P. Rec 9 Feb 1819.

p.374   William Messer to Jacob Tomlin, L&R, 30/31 December 1792, Twenty five pounds sterling money of State, 100 acres but plat of same specifies 112 acres; the 12 acres run into tract granted Saml Messer 1786 & are excepted; on the main road from the ridge to the Congarees, on head of Clouds Creek of Little Saluda River at Huckleberry Pond adj lines of Daniel Cannon, Jno Messer, Samuel Stephens, Jacob Read; the 112 acres were surveyed by Wm Howard, transferred by Wm Messer to afsd Jacob Tomlin. Wit Edward Johnson, Josiah (I) Nobles, Christian (C) Coonce. /s/ William Messer. Proven 15 February 1793 by Christian Coonce; Russell Wilson J P. Rec 9th Feby 1819.

p.378   Martin Powel to widow Milley Powel, Deed, 9 August 1818, Two hundred Dollars, 35 acres on West Creek of Saluda River adj lands of Widow Bates, Jacob Long, Anderson Mitchell, Bartlet Powel, being plantation where sd Martin Powell now lives. Wit Wm Hurtt Senr, William Hurtt Junr. /s/ Martin (P) Powel. Proven 21 August 1818 by Wm Hurtt Junr; Wm Hurtt JQ. Rec 16th Feby 1819.

p.379   Daniel Gallman to Benjamin Frazier and Harman Gallman, Deed of Trust, 1 January 1819, Ten Dollars, [livestock not here itemized] to hold sd Property in trust for benefit of affectionate wife Lydia Gallman during her natural life and my children Casper and Jemima Gallman and others that may be living. Wit Nicholas Fox, Hinchey Mitchell. /s/ Daniel (x) Gallman. Proven 18th February 1819 by Nicholas Fox; M Mims CCP. Rec 18 Feb 1819.

p.380   Edward Settle to William Minter, Deed, [blank] December 1817, Four hundred fifty Dollars, on Bird Creek of Stephens Creek and Savannah River. Wit Alexander G Nixon, William Logan. /s/ Edward Settle. Justice John Lyon certifies relinquishment of dower by Martha Settle wife of Edward Settle, 22 December 1817; /s/ Martha Settle. Proven 22 December 1817 by Wm Logan; John Lyon QU. Rec 8 Feb 1819.

p.181   Thomas Jennings to his sons Henry Jennings and Jeremiah Jennings, Deed of Gift, 9 November 1818, love, after my decease, Negro slaves to Henry boy Anderson; to Jeremiah boy Dick. Wit John Key, Levin Rardin. /s/ Thos Jennings. Proven 22 December 1818 by Levin Rardin; Thomas Price JP. Rec 18th Feb 1819.

116

DEED BOOK 35

p.182 John Pierce to John Traylor, Deed, 11 November 1817, Five hundred Dollars, 80 3/4 acres, part of land originally granted to John Hammond decd on Stephens Creek & Savannah River at Brewers Spring Branch. Wit Richard Covington, James Vann, John Pierce. /s/ John (x) Pierce. Proven 7 November 1818 by Richard Covington; Charles Bussey JQ. Rec 20 Feb 1819.

p.383 Frederick Swearingen to John Landrum, Deed, 27 August 1818, Fourteen hundred Dollars, 100 acres on the road from Augusta to the Ridge, originally granted to William Anderson 2 October 1786. Wit Benjn Medlock, Moses Swearingen. /s/ Fred Swearingen. Proven 6 February 1819 by Moses Swearingen; Stephen Williams JQ. Rec 20th Feb 1819.

p.385 Frederick Swearingen to John Landrum, Deed, 27 August 1818, One hundred Dollars, 100 acres, part of 140 acres originally granted to Rebecca Stark 21 September 1786 & conveyed by Rebecca to Ezekiel McClendon and by Ezekiel to Fr Swearingen adj 100 acres originally granted to William Anderson 2 October 1786. Wit Benjn Medlock, Moses Swearingen. /s/ Fred Swearingen. Proven 6th February 1819 by Moses Swearingen; Stephen Williams JQ. Rec 20th Feb 1819.

p.386 Morgan Mills of Orangeburg District to Richard Coleman, Deed, 29 October 1818, Five hundred Dollars, 200 acres on Little Saluda, being part of 1100 acres originally granted to James Brooks, adj lands of Samuel Mays decd, Jon Brown, Runnels Genty Richard Coleman. Wit William Mills, John Mills, Frederick Williamson. /s/ Morgan Mills. /s/ Barbary (I) Mills. Proven 2nd Nov 1818 by Wm Mills; Joseph Fannin JQ. Rec 25th Feby 1819.

p.388 John Pope to William Chipley, Deed, 13 July 1818, Four hundred sixty Dollars, 460 acres on Big Creek and Red bank Branches of Little Saluda River, being part of land originally granted to Thomas Dozier 1 September 1788; sd land adj sd Dozier, J & W Green, Richard Doziere. Wit James Gunter, Allen Elliot. /s/ John Pope. Proven 5 February 1819 by James Gunter; Wm Ferguson JQ. Rec 25th Feby 1819.

p.389 William Chipley to Richard Coleman, Deed, 14 January 1819, Four hundred Dollars, 460 acres on Big Creek, Red Bank of Little Saluda being part of land originally granted to Thomas Dozier 1 September 1788, adj sd Dozier J & Wm Green, John Pope, Richard Dozier. Provided that if William Chipley pay unto Richard Coleman the full sum of Four hundred Dollars on or before 19th instant, these presents to be utterly void. Wit Martha W Peterson, John G Peterson. /s/ Wm Chipley. Proven 19thFebruary 1819 by Martha Peterson; John G Peterson JP. Rec 25th Feby 1819.

p.390 Sheriff Jeremiah Hatcher to Mrs Sarah Q Hammond, Deed, 4 August 1818, by virtue of writ of partition Mrs Sarah J Hammond plf and F J Hammond and others dfts,

117

land to be sold publicly to highest bidder for cash; struck off for One hundred fifty Dollars to Sarah Q Hammond, 195 acres, parts of three tracts granted to Benjamin Allen of 96 acres, Elizabeth Mealer of 57 acres, and Simon Martin of 42 acres; and all estate which Leroy Hammond deceased had, sd three tracts to Sarah Quarles Hammond. Wit John Harrison, Richd H Tutt. J Hatcher S E D. Proven 3 February 1819 by Richd H Tutt; M Mims C C P. Rec 3 Feby 1819.

p.392   Sheriff Jeremiah Hatcher to William Garrett, Deed, 1 February 1819, at suit of Jeremiah Taylor against William D Cooper and Ann Meria his wife, land to be sold publicly to highest bidder for ready money; struck off to William Garrett, One hundred forty Dollars, 100 acres on Turkey Creek and Rocky Creek adj lands of Peter Labourd, John Terry Senr decd. Wit John Harrison, Richd H Tutt. /s/ J Hatcher S E D. Proven 3 Feby 1819 by Richd H Tutt; M Mims C C P. Rec 3rd Feb 1819.

p.393   Edward Hampton to Doctor Bunch, Deed, 19 December 1818, Two thousand five hundred Dollars, half of 16 1/2 acres formerly property of late James Lamar Senr adj Horse Creek, lands of Samuel Hammond, Thomas Oliver. Wit Melines C Leavenworth, Talliver M Cox. /s/ Edwd Hampton. Justice James Hunter certifies release of dower rights by Elizabeth Hampton wife of Edward Hampton, 23 Decr 1818; /s/ Elizabeth (x) Hampton. Proven 2 February 1819 by Melines C Leavenworth; M Mims C C P. Rec 2nd February 1819.

p.395   Thomas Coleman to John Hollowa, Deed, 15 September 1817, Thirty six hundred fifty two Dollars fifty cents, 608 3/4 acres on Henleys and Ninety Six Creeks, being part of land known as Recess. Wit Robert Hamilton, James Payne. /s/ Tho Coleman. Proven 27 March 1818 by James Payne; Thos Anderson JQ. Plat by Thos Anderson D S 30 August 1817 shows adj lands of Wm Burton decd, J Guffin, Thos Coleman, James Coleman, B Bunting, Moo[lost in binding]. Justice Thos Anderson certifies relinquishment of dower rights by Edna Coleman wife of Thos Coleman 26 March 1818; /s/ Edna Coleman. Rec 26th February 1819.

p.396   Obediah Johns to Robert Deshazo, Deed, 5 February 1803, Fourteen Pounds, 50 acres being part of 292 acres granted to sd Obediah Johns, on Clouds Creek of Little Saluda River adj lands of Elkanah Sawyer, Powel and vacant land. Wit Jonathan Owen, Nathan Norris. /s/ Obediah (W) Johns. Justice Jeremiah Williams certifies release of dower rights by Elizabeth Johns wife of Obediah Johns, 12 August 1803; /s/ Elizabeth (x) Johns. Proven 18 March 1817 by Nathan Norris; Wm Hurtt Q U. Rec 1st March 1819.

p.398   Elkanah Sawyer to Robert Deshazo, Deed, 5 February 1803, Thirty Dollars, 100 ac in three tracts on Mill Br, part of 150 acres on West Cr of Clouds Cr of Little Saluda River granted to James Warren 31 August 1774, adj lands of John Calwell,

DEED BOOK 35

John Sawyer, Lewis Powel, conveyed by James Warren to Elkanah Sawyer 26 November 1787. Wit Nathan Norris, William Deshazo. /s/ Elkanah Sawyer. Justice Jeremiah Williams certifies relinquishment of dower rights by Marium Sawyer wife of Elkanah Sawyer, 12th August 1803; /s/ Marium (x) Sawyer. Proven 12 August 1803 by Wm Deshazo; Jeremiah Williams JQ. Rec 1 March 1819.

p.399 Patty Newman to Nathan Norris, Deed, 16 March 1810, Two hundred eighty Dollars, 80 acres being part of 119 acres originally granted to Thomas Butler 7 January 1788, on Wattsman Pond, West Creek of Little Saluda, Hartwell Hart, from Hart to John Sawyer, to sd Patty Newman. Wit James Warren, Duke Hart. /s/ Patty (x) Newman. Proven 13 March 1810 by Duke Hart; Wm Hurtt JP. Rec 1st March 1819.

p.401 Robert Deshazo to Nathan Norris, Deed, 15 December 1809, Four hundred fifty Dollars, 150 acres on West Creek of Little Saluda, being part of two tracts, 100 acres part of 150 acres granted to James Warren 31 August 1774 and conveyed to Elkanah Sawyer 26 November 17887, from Sawyer to Robert Deshazo 5 February 1803; fifty acres part of 252 acres granted to Obediah Johns, conveyed from O Johns to Deshazo 5 February 1803. Wit Ezekiel Wooley, Ansel Sawyer. /s/ Robert Deshazo. Proven 26 February 1819 by Ezekiel Wooley; Wm Hurtt JQ. Rec 1st March 1819.

p.402 William Durham to Thomas Meriwether, Deed, 19 November 1818, Fourteen hundred Dollars, 130 acres being part of 225 acres granted to Charles Roberson 15 September 1785 adj lands of Robert Garrett and Thomas Meriwether; also two other tracts, one of 140 acres, the other 200 acres granted to William Swift 5 February 1747 adj George Groves, William Thomas, John Middleton. Wit Allen Tulley, Robert Garrett. /s/ William Durham. Proven 9 Decr 1818 by Robert Garrett: Charles Hammond JQ. Rec 1st March 1819.

p.403 John Pierce to David Bunch, Deed, 4 November 1818, Two thousand four hundred fifty six Dollars, 307 acres whereon I love adj Alec Stewart, Doc McWathee. Wit Joshua Key, Charles Bussey. /s/ John (x) Pierce. Proven 1 March 1819 by C Bussey; Loyd Barnes JP. Rec 1st March 1819.

p.404 Thomas Deen to Samuel Padget, Deed, 27 November 1818, Three hundred Dollars, 100 acres on Clouds Creek of Saluda River, Lamkin road, and land of Wilkin C Smith. Wit William D Loach, Peter Funderburk. /s/ Thos Deen. Justice William Hurtt certifies relinquishment of dower rights by Sarah Deen wife of Thomas Deen, 1 January 1819; /s/ Sarah (x) Deen. Proven 1 January 1819 by Peter Funderburk; Wm Hurtt JQ. Rec 1st March 1819.

p.406 Samuel Dunkin to Daniel Smith of Lexington District, Deed, 6 January 1818, Eight hundred Dollars, 385 acres on Saluda River joining the lands of John Colburn,

John Williams, Peter Dunkin, Harris. Wit Daniel Bouknight, Jacob Anderson. /s/ Samuel Dunkin. Justice William Hurtt certifies relinquishment of dower rights by Selah Dunkin wife of Samuel Dunkin, 12 January 1818; /s/ Seley (x) Dunkin. Proven 12 January 1818 by Daniel Bouknight; Wm Hurtt J Q. Rec 1ˢᵗ March 1819.

p.407   William Jones to Thomas Warren, Deed, 1 January 1810, Three hundred Dollars, 214 acres on prong of Double Branch, Messers Pond adj land of William Holston. Wit Jesse Johnson, Henry Fallow. /s/ William (W) Jones. Justice Elijah Watson certifies relinquishment of dower rights by Sarah Jones wife of William Jones, 9 December 1811; /s/ Sarah (x) Jones. Proven 1 January 1811 by Jesse Johnson; Elijah Watson QU. Rec 1ˢᵗ March 1819.

p.408   Thomas Cotton to John A Cotton of Georgia and Dedemia Cotton, Deed of Trust, 14 November 1818, One Dollar, love of wife Deadema M Cotton, furniture, crockery, livestock to John A Cotton, trustee for wife. Wit John S Glascock, Beaverly Samuel. /s/ Thos A Cotton, D M Cotton, John A Cotton. Proven 1ˢᵗ March 1819 by Beverly Samuel; M Mims C C P. Rec 1ˢᵗ March 1819.

p.410   Elisha Rumley and wife Nancy to Jeptha Sharpton, Deed, 12 February 1819, One hundred fifty Dollars, 240 acres run out on 4 March 1798 for John Kimber [Fimber?] and granted to me 4 April 1814 on Stephens Creek adj lands of James King, Saml Scott, Robert and John Boyd. Wit Snowdon Griffin, Armsted Burt. /s/ Elisha (x) Rumley, /s/ Nancy (x) Rumley. Justice John Middleton certifies relinquishment of dower rights by Nancy Rumley, 26 February 1819; /s/ Nancy (x) Rumley. Proven 27 February 1819 by Snowdon Griffin; Jno Middleton JQ. Rec 1ˢᵗ March 1819.

p.411   Daniel Smith to Samuel Padget, Deed, 20 September 1815, Three hundred Dollars, 100 acres being part of 458 acres on Moores Creek of Clouds Creek. Wit Mark Padjett, William D Loach. /s/ Daniel Smith. Justice Charles Oneal certifies release of dower rights by Rachel Smith wife of Daniel Smith 8 Feby 1816; /s/ Rachel (x) Smith. Proven by Mark Padget; Chas Oneal JQU. Rec 1ˢᵗ March 1819.

p.413   Daniel Smith to Samuel Padget, Deed, 20 September 1815, Fifty Dollars, 35 acres being part of 458 acres on Moores Creek of Clouds Creek, sd 35 acres adj Spring Branch, Moores Creek, lands of Thomas Deen. Wit Mark Padget, William D Loach. /s/ Daniel Smith. Justice Charles Oneal certifies relinquishment of dower rights by Rachael Smith wife of Daniel Smith 8 Feby 1816; /s/ Rachael (x) Smith. Proven 8 Feby 1816 by Mark Padget; Charles Oneale. Rec 1ˢᵗ March 1819.

p.414   Thomas Williams to Robert Allen, Deed, 29 October 1811, Fifty and half Dollars, 60 acres being part of land run by sd Thos Williams adj sd Allen, Weaver, Smiths old field, sd Allen, on Richland Creek of Little Saluda. Wit Levi Richardson,

Joel Bell. /s/ Thomas Williams. Proven 29th Octr 1811 by Levi Richerson; Shepherd Spencer JP. Rec 1st March 1819.

p.415   Joseph W Waldo to Jacob Smith, Anna L Smith, Sarah B Smith the children of my wife by her former husband Luke Smith decd, Deed, 5 October 1818, love and to be discharged of demands against the estate of sd Luke Smith, all the interest which I by marriage with the widow have acquired in the real estate of Luke Smith and also Negroes: Sealy, Phebe, Will, Davy, Jack, Amy, Nell, Delphy, Louis, Alsea, Andrew, Juno, Fanny, Lucy, Henry, Dolly, Bill, Lydia, [binding]leasen, James, Malinda. Condition sd Jacob, Anna L, and Sarah B Smith shall pay all debts which may hereafter arise against estate of sd Luke Smith decd. Wit J M Butler, Jno Lipscomb. /s/ Joseph W Waldo. Proven 3 April 1819 by John Lipscomb; Val Corley JP. Rec 3 April 1819.

p.417   William Spragins Senr of Abbeville District to Mark Black, Deed, 16 November 1818, Six hundred Dollars, 237 acres on Lasseter Creek of Saluda River, it being plantation Enoch Martin now lives on adj lands claimed by heirs of John Abney decd, Mary Bladen, Paul Abney. Wit John Meek, John Adkisson. /s/ Wm Spragins. Justice James Watts certifies release of dower rights by Martha Spragins wife of Wm Spragins, 4 January 1819; /s/ Martha (x) Spragins. Proven 18 November 1818 by John Meek; John Abney J P. Rec 1st March 1819.

p.418   Joseph Taylor to James Carson, Deed, 18 February 1819, Six hundred Dollars, 146 acres, being part of 250 acres originally granted to John Abney decd adj William Abney, John Taylor lying on Panther Branch of Big Creek. Wit Mark Black, James Abney, William (x) Abney. /s/ Joseph Taylor. Justice John Abney certifies release of dower rights by Mary Taylor wife of Joseph Taylor, 27 February 1819; /s/ Mary (x) Taylor. Proven 27 Feb 1819 by Mark Black; John Abney JQ. Rec 1st March 1819.

p.420   Hugh Balentine to Thomas L Shaw, Deed, 27 February 1819, Five Dollars, all land that he now has under fence which Balentine purchased of John Prior commonly called the Low Place. Wit John Butler, James Butler. /s/ Hugh Balentine. Proven1 March 1819 by James Butler; John Blocker JQ. Rec 1 March 1819.

p.421   Joseph Crafton of Columbia County, Georgia, to Thomas Meriwether, Deed, 31 December 1818, One thousand Dollars, 370 acres, granted to Thomas Evans 7 December 1807 on Stephens Creek; also 50 acres granted to Alexander Odon 1 February 1790 on Stephens Creek adj above tract and Jeff Sharpton. Wit J H Crafton, Samuel Crafton. /s/ Joseph Crafton. Proven 17 February 1819 by Samuel Crafton; C Bussey JQ. Rec 1st March 1819.

p.422   John Bladon, James & Margaret Carson, Allen and Whinea Corley to Mary Bladen, Deed, 27 August 1818, Two hundred twenty two Dollars, our claims as

121

legatees to land belonging to estate of William Bladen decd, 312 acres on waters of Saluda River. Wit John Meek, John Dkinson. /s/ John Bladen, /s/ Jas Carson, Marget Carson, Allen Corley, Whinea Corley. Proven 26 February 1819 by John Dkinson; Patrick Todd JP. Rec 1ˢᵗ March 1819.

p.423   Philemon Bozeman to Silas Hurst, Deed, 24 January 1818, Seven hundred Dollars, 350 acres adj lands of Drury Mathews, Joseph Morris Senr, John Hollowa, Rocky Branch, Jesse Rainey. Wit Dan Bozeman, Jesse Pitts. /s/ Philemon Bozeman. Justice Thomas Anderson certifies release of dower rights by Susannah Bozeman, 12 October 1818; /s/ Susanna (I) Bozeman. Proven 6 February 1819 by Jesse Pitts; James Bell JP. Rec 1ˢᵗ March 1819.

p.425   Robert Allen and wife Nancy Allen to Absalum Littlefield, Deed, 21 February 1801, Thirty pounds state money, 20 acres being part of 60 acres granted to William Butler 13 March 1788; also part of 140 acres granted to Robert Allen 2 March 1789 which supposed to be 80 acres. Wit Jacob Smith, Nathaniel Tate. /s/ Robert Allen, /s/ Nancy (x) Allen. Proven 14 March 1801 by Jacob Smith; Russell Wilson JP. Rec 1ˢᵗ March 1819.

p.426   John Weaver to Philip McCartey, Deed, 4 November 1815, Two hundred Dollars, 150 acres being part of tract originally granted to Thomas Williams, adj lands of Thomas Williams, Allen,Tate, Weaver, on waters of Richland Creek of Little Saluda River. Wit ames McCartey, Henry Tate. /s/ John Weaver. Proven 3 February 1816 by Henry Tate; John Lark JQU. Rec 1ˢᵗ March 1819.

p.427   Henry Barnes to Loyd Barnes, Deed, 27 Feby 1819, Six hundred Dollars, my undivided part of my fathers lands. Wit H W Bozeman, Wiley Glover. /s/ Henry Barnes. Proven 1 March 1819 by H W Bozeman; C Bussey JQ. Rec 1 March 1819.

p.428   Jesse Johnson to Thomas Warren senior, Deed, 13 February 1810, Two hundred Dollars, 95 acres on head of Double Branch of Clouds Creek of Saluda River adj lines of sd Thomas Warren, Jesse Johnston, being a part of land granted Levi Comming, plat 29 December 1809. Wit Andrew Heron, Nathan Norris. /s/ Jesse Johnston. Proven 24 Feby 1810 by Nathan Norris; Wm Hurtt JP. Rec 1 March 1819.

p.429   John P Bond of Lexington District to William Cates, Deed, 29 November 1817, Three hundred Dollars, 100 acres taken out of tract originally granted to Geo P Bond Esqr 5 May 1776 for 1250 acres but by resurvey of A B Stark found to contain 2293 acres and was by sd George P Bond given to his nephew Jacob Reese and by L&R deed 1 & 2 June 1793 Genl Jacob Reese conveyed same to Jno P Bond adj at present lands of Philip Johnson, John [blank], Thos Renolds, Robert Cates, Lewis Sawyer. Wit Jno P Bond, Andw Heron. /s/ Jno P Bond. Proven 10 Decr 1819 by

Andw Heron; Peter Lamkin JQU. Rec 2 March 1819.

p.430 Abram Tolison to Philip McCartey, Deed, 25 March 1812, Fifty Dollars, 100 acres on Gillians Branch adj lines of Edward McCarty, James Daniel, Amos Satcher, Hezekiah Watson. Wit James McCartey, Michael McCartey. /s/ Abraham (A) Tolison. Proven 31 March 1812 by James McCartey; Wm Hurtt JP. Rec 2 Mar 1819.

p.431 Christopher Cox Senr to his son Christopher Cox junr, Deed of Gift, 24 November 1815, love, 100 acres being part of two adjoining tracts, 50 acres from a survey of 100 acres originally granted to Francis Kitting; 50 acres originally granted to Francis Roff, the whole bounding on survey of Francis Kitting now property of Robert Jenning Jr, Savannah River, John Mosley, William Jennings, Bussy formerly estate of Nias Morgan. Wit Baily Cox, Jane Cox, Gabriel Cox. /s/ Christopher (x) Cox. Proven 13 February 1819 by Bailey Cox; Thomas Pierce JP. Rec 2 March 1819.

p.433 Richard Odom to William Cates [blank]

p.433 Jesse Blocker to John & Samuel Cameron of Petersburgh, Georgia, Deed, 17 April 1819, Two hundred fifty Dollars, 337 acres on Cuffeetown Creek of Stevens Creek adj Woolen Haupt, Roger McKinnie, Joseph Eaton, Freeman, Dyer Cook. Wit B M Blocker, John Blocker. /s/ Jesse Blocker. Justice Matthew Mims certifies release of dower rights by Eliza Blocker wife of Jesse Blocker, 21 April 1819; /s/ Eliza Blocker. Proven 21 April 1819 by John Blocker; M Mims CCP. Rec 20th April 1819.

p.434 Jesse Blocker to John and Samuel Cameron of Petersburgh, Georgia, Deed, 17 April 1819, Three hundred Dollars, 369 acres on Cuffeetown Creek of Stephens Creek adj lands of Robert Read, Pears on Holloways land, Widow Gray, Thos Ruston, widow Campbell. Wit B M Blocker, John Blocker. /s/ Jesse Blocker. Justice Matthew Mims certifies relinquishment of dower rights by Eliza Blocker wife of Jesse Blocker, 21 April 1819; /s/ Eliza Blocker. Proven 21 April 1819 by John Blocker; M Mims CCP. Rec 20th April 1819.

p.436 Jesse Blocker to John & Samuel Cameron of Petersburgh, Georgia, 17 April 1819, 266 acres on Beaverdam Cr of Cuffeetown Cr, Stephens Creek, granted to sd Jesse Blocker in 1818 adj lands of Thornton, Read, William Gray, Allen Burgher, Lark. Wit B M Blocker, John Blocker. /s/ Jesse Blocker. Justice Matthew Mims certifies release of dower rights by Eliza Blocker wife of Jesse Blocker, 21 April 1819; /s/ Eliza Blocker. Proven 21 April 1819 by John Blocker; M Mims CCP. Rec 20 April 1819.

p.437 Jesse Blocker to John & Samuel Cameron of Petersburgh, Georgia, Deed, 17 April 1819, Three hundred fifty Dollars, 349 acres on Cuffeetown Creek of Stephens Creek adj Frederick Slappy, John Anderson, James Harrison, Josiah Langley, estate of John McKeller decd. Wit B M Blocker, John Blocker. /s/ Jesse Blocker. Justice Matthew Mims certifies relinquishment of dower rights by Eliza Blocker wife of Jesse Blocker, 21 April 1819; /s/ Eliza Blocker. Proven 21 April 1819 by John Blocker; M Mims CCP. Rec 20ᵗʰ April 1819.

p.439 Jesse Blocker to John & Samuel Cameron of Petersburgh, Georgia, Deed, 17 April 1819, One hundred Dollars, 115 acres on Cuffeetown Creek of Stephens Creek adj lands of Wiley Kenp[Kemp], Abner Corley, Read. Wit B M Blocker, John Blocker. /s/ Jesse Blocker. Justice Mathew Mims certifies relinquishment of dower rights by Eliza Blocker wife of Jesse Blocker, 21 April 1819; /s/ Eliza Blocker. Proven 21 April 1819 by John Blocker; M Mims CCP. Rec 20 April 1819.

p.440 Richard Odom of Jones County, Georgia, to William Cates, Deed, 23 September 1809, One hundred Dollars, 100 acres on Moors Creek of Little Saluda River, being part of land run for John Watson Senr and given by sd Watson to Mary Odom and Richard Odom her lawful heir. WitWilliam Brassell, Green Wynn. /s/ Richard (R) Odom. Proven Jones County, Georgia, 1 August 1818 by William Brassell; Wm S Middlebrooks JP.

p.441 Robert Cates to William Cates, Deed, 22 August 1818, One hundred Dollars, 62 acres on Clouds Creek of Saluda River adj lands of William and Wiley Reynolds, Lewis Sawyer, Elizabeth Cates. Wit William D Loach, Wiley (-) Cates. /s/ Robert (x) Cates. Proven 5 September 1818 by William Dloach; Nathan Norris JQ. Rec 2ⁿᵈ March 1819.

p.442 Robert Cate to Elizabeth Cate, Deed, [blank] August 1818, One hundred Dollars, 65 acres on Clouds Creek of Saluda River on lines of Wm Reynolds, Huldah Cates, Blakey, Wm Cates. Wit William Dloach, William (x) Kate, Huldah (x) Kate. /s/ Robert (x) Kate. Proven 5 September 1818 by William Dloach; Nathan Norris JQ. Rec 2 March 1819.

p.444 Samuel Medlock Senr to his five grandchildren Leroy Singleton, Eliza Singleton, Benjamin Singleton, Samuel Singleton, James Singleton, Deed, 23 November 1818, love, Negro woman named Alley, boy named Jack, also Two hundred Dollars which property is now in hands of their stepsfather John H Walker of Putnam County, Georgia. [page torn]. Wit Phinehas Sutton, Moses Medlock. /s/ Samuel Medlock. Proven 23 Novr 1818 by Phineas Sutton; Lewis Holmes JQ. Rec 2 March 1819.

p.445 James Ruston to James Eidson, Deed, 21 February 1814, Four hundred eleven Dollars, 274 acres on Dry Creek of Little Saluda, crossed by Augusta Road, adjoining lines of Dempsey Weaver. Wit John Lark, John Eidson. /s/ James (x) Ruston. Justice

DEED BOOK 35

Elijah Watson certifies relinquishment of dower rights by Rachel Ruston wife of James Ruston, 22 Feby 1814; /s/ Rachael (x) Ruston. Proven 21 February 1814 by John Lark; Mathew Bettis JP. Rec 2d March 1819.

p.447 Washington Belcher of Abbeville District to Edmund Belcher, Deed, 15 February 1817, Twelve hundred Dollars, my moiety of a tract containing 374 acres on Cuffeetown Creek of Stephens Creek being the same plantation whereon Susannah Belcher decd formerly resided. Wit Allen Burton, Benjamin Burton. /s/ Washington Belcher.

p.448 [blank]

p.449 Justice Edmund Colier certifies release of dower rights by Mary Ann Belcher wife of Washington Belcher, 15 September 1818; /s/ Mary Ann Belcher. Proven 15 Novr 1818 by Allen Burton; John Lyon QU. Rec 2 March 1819.

p.449 Sterling Harrison of Abbeville District to Agness Letcher, Deed, 3 February 1817, Three hundred Dollars, 60 acres being part of land originally granted to Henry Key decd & conveyed to his daughter Willa Letcher and conveyed by her heirs to Sterling Harrison, on Bird Creek of Stephens Creek adj Jno Burress, Richard Hardy, Nicholas Griffin. Wit Richard Hardy, Ansel Talbert. /s/ Sterling Harrison. Justice John Lyon certifies release of dower rights by Louisa Harrison wife of Sterling Harrison, 17 November 1818; /s/ Louisa Harrison. Proven 17 November 1818 by Ansel Talbert; John Lyon QU. Rec 2d March 1819.

p.451 Agness Letcher to Martin Burress, Deed, 11 November 1818, Four hundred Dollars, 60 acres, part of land originally granted to Henry Key decd and conveyed to his daughter Willa Letcher by Deed of Gift, conveyed by her heirs to Sterling Harrison and by Sterling Harrison to Agness Letcher, and by Agness Letcher to Martin Burress, on Bird Creek of Stephens Creek adj land of John Burress, Richard Hardy, Nicholas Griffis. Wit John Key, John F Burress. /s/ Agness (x) Letcher. Proven 2 March 1819 by John Key; Charles Bussey JQ. Rec 2 March 1819.

p.452 Ogden & Jenny Cockeroft to daughter Mary Cockeroft, Deed of Gift, 4 December 1818, love, Negro girl Creese and heirs of her body, sd girl to remain property of Ogden and Jennie Cockeroft until their death. Wit Thomas Cockeroft, Susanah Cockeroft. /s/ Ogden Cockeroft, /s/ Jaen (I) Cockeroft. Proven 2 March 1819 by Thomas Cockeroft; Lewis Holmes JQ. Rec 2d March 1819.

p.453 Robert Cate to Polly Cate daughter of my son Joshua Cate deceased, Deed, [blank] November 1815, One hundred Dollars, 65 acres on Clouds Creek of Saluda River adj Elizabeth Cate, Elijah Watson, Blackley. Wit Hardy Harris, William

DEED BOOK 35

Wm Dloach. /s/ Robert (x) Kate. Proven 5 September 1818 by William Dloach; Nathan Norris JQ. Rec 2 March 1819.

p.454 Robert Cate to Huldah Cate, Deed, 5 August 1818, One hundred Dollars, 50 acres on Clouds Creek of Saluda River to Hulda Kate; land adj Betty Kate, Elizah Watson, William & Wiley Reynolds. Wit William Dloach, Keziah (x) Johnston, Libby Kate. /s/ Robert (x) Kate. Proven 5 September 1818 by William Dloach; Nathen Norris JQ. Rec 2 March 1819.

p.455 Nathaniel Tate to Philip McCartey, Deed, 22 January 1817, Fifty Dollars, [acreage not stated] on Richland Creek adj lands of Michael McCartey, estate of Jacob Smith, Robert Allen, James Allen. Wit Henry Tate, J F Musgrove. /s/ Nathaniel Tate. Proven 1 August 1817 by Henry Tate; Nathan Norris JQ. Rec 2 March 1819.

p.456 David Glover and wife Elizabeth to John Moore, 1 December 1818, One thousand Dollars, 100 acres on Savannah River near Bull Sluice adj land of estate of Col. Leroy Hammond, David Bunch, Sarah Thomas, being land by Court of Equity to Elizabeth Thomas now Elizabeth Glover, plat certified by John Boyd [too faded to read on microfilm]. Wit H K Boyd, Sarah Thomas. /s/ David Glover, /s/ Elizabeth Glover. Justice Charles Bussey certifies release of dower rights by Elizabeth Glover wife of David Glover, 18 December 1818; /s/ Elizabeth Glover. Proven 18 December 1818 by Henry K Boyd; C Bussey JQ. Rec 2nd March 1819.

p.458 Joseph Smart to James H Broadwater, Deed, 3 November 1818, Six hundred fifty Dollars, [acreage not stated] on Loyds Creek of Stephens Creek, adj lands of James Martin, John Lyon, Henry Key, J Vann, estate of Balentine White. Wit John Terry Sr, L B Lang. /s/ Joseph Smart. Justice John Hollingsworth certifies release of dower rights by Margaret Smart wife of Joseph Smart, 3 November 1818; /s/ Margaret Smart. Proven 3 November 1818 by John Terry Senr; John Hollingsworth JQ. Rec 2nd March 1819.

p.460 Jonathan Glanton to John Lowe of Newberry District, Deed, 23 January 1819, One Dollar, in fulfillment of a contract made between between Jonathan Glanton and John Lowe and others, sd company on 26 November 1817 purchased two tracts of land originally granted to James Carson, titles executed by Commrs of Equity in Charleston, Glanton makes titles to company according to agreement, 373 acres on Five notched road adj lands of Jonathan Devore, Cadwell Evans, Jonathan Glanton, being part of land originally granted to James Carson of 1000 acres. Wit David Williams, James Sanders. /s/ Jonathan Glanton. Justice William Thurmond certifies relinquishment of dower rights by Elizabeth Glanton wife of Jonathan Glanton, 7 February 1819; /s/ Elizabeth (x) Glanton. Proven 6 February 1819 by David Williams; William Thurmond JQ. Rec 2nd March 1819.

126

p.461 John Feaster to William DLoach, Deed, 18 October 1817, One hundred thirty Dollars, 50[further on deed says 52 acres] acres on Moores Creek of Clouds Creek and Saluda River being part of 114 acres originally granted to George Mee 5 June 1786 by Gov Wm Moultrie, land adj Dennis McCartie, sd William Dloach, Moses Holston, Elkanah Sawyer. Wit William Smith, Saml (x) Dloach. /s/ John (x) Feaster. Proven 12 October 1818 by William Smith; John Loveless JP. Rec 2nd March 1819.

p.463 Whitfield Brooks to Casper Nail Jr and Matthias Ardis Deed, 5 January 1819, at suit in Court of Equity against Eliza A Lamar and others showing that Robert Lamar Senr executed deed of gift to his natural son Thomas L Winfrey of several tracts of land, Negroes, deed confirmed; writ of partition issued, to be sold at public auction; Whitfield Brooks as commissioner having duly advertised the sale, disposed of sd tracts unto highest bidders Casper and Matthias for Eleven thousand twenty five Dollars, 300 acres on Savannah River being part of the Beach Island land, adj lands of Edward Rowel, John Clarke. Wit Geo Butler, Crad^k Burnell. /s/ Whit Brooks. Proven 1 March 1819 by Crad^k Burnell; C Bussey JP. Rec 2 March 1819.

p.465 Robert Kate to his daughter Sibby Kate, Bill of Sale, 5 August 1818, Fifty Dollars, black mare. Wit William Dloach, William (x) Kate. /s/ Robert (x) Kate. Proven 5 September 1818 by William Dloach; Nathan Norris JQ. Rec 2 March 1819.

p.466 John O Jordin to Wiley Kemp, Deed, 10 January 1818, Two hundred fifty Dollars, 140 acres adj lands of Wm Thomas, John Rabun, Wm Thomas Junr, Wm Davis, 97 acres being sold from the plat of same. Wit Ransom H Cloud, Richard Kemp. /s/ John O Jordin. Justice William Robinson certifies relinquishment of dower rights by Polly Ann Jordin wife of John O Jordin, 1 September 1818; /s/ Polly Ann (x) Jordin. Proven 1 Sept 1818 by Richard Kemp; Wm Robinson JQ. Rec 3 March 1819.

p.467 John Hargrove to Michael Corley, Mortgage, 17 March 1818, Three hundred seventeen Dollars thirty five cents paid by Corley, 270 acres on Sleepy Creek being all land granted to Drury Matthews and by him sold to sd John Hargrove, on Martin Branch; Hargrove indebted to Corley, note due on 1 January next, if Hargrove shall pay off sd note, then these presents to be utterly void. Wit James Burgess, B T Whitner. /s/ John Hargrove. Proven 3 March 1819 by B F Whitner; M Mims CCP. Rec 3rd March 1819.

p.469 Abner McMillian to Joseph Lake of Newberry District, Deed, 20 February 1818, Four thousand Dollars, 400 acres on Jack Branch of Savannah River. Wit Thos Chiles, William Muckle, Robert Red. /s/ Abner McMillian. Justice Wm Robinson certifies relinquishment of dower rights by Elizabeth McMilian wife of Abner McMillian, 4 May 1818; /s/ Elizabeth McMilian. Proven 4 May 1818 by Robert Red; Wm Robinson JQ. Rec 3 March 1819.

DEED BOOK 35

p.470   Robert Gilliam, Frederick Nance, Wilks B Waters, executors of will of Phileman B Waters decd of Newbury District to John Pope, Deed, 7 May 1810, Ninety Nine Dollars thirty seven and half cents, 265 acres being part of 840 acres originally granted to Phileman Waters decd 5 March 1787 by Gov Thos Pinckney; adj Sampson Pope, J Pope, John Pope, Aron Etheridge, Martin, Messer Merchant, plat made by John Colwell D S. Wit Aron Etheridge, John Summers, Elias (x) Boatner. /s/ Robert Gillam, /s/ F Vance, /s/ Wilks Berry Waters. Justice Sampson Pope certifies release of dower rights by Sarah Shepherd wife of Capt William Shepherd and widow of Philemon B Waters, 7 May 1810; /s/ Sary Shepherd. Proven 7 May 1810 by Aron Etheridge; Sampson Pope JQ. Rec 3 March 1819.

p.472   John Blalock, Rachael Park, and Mary King lawful heirs of estate of John Blalock Senr decd to John Pope, Deed, 26 December 1809, One hundred fifty Dollars, 110 acres on Big and Burnetts Creek originally granted to Arthur H Davis by Gov Wm Moultrie 8 July 1797; adj lands of William Little, Chesley [binding] and John Pope, estate of John Coats. Wit Sampson Pope, Mullican Norred, Jesse Christian. /s/ J Blalock, /s/ Rachel (x) Parke, /s/ Mary King. Proven 13 July 1812 by Sampson Pope; Samson Pope JQ. Rec 3 March 1819.

p.473   Lucy Conner to Daniel McKee jr, Power of Attorney, 25 April 1818, to receive property and use it to take care of me, to bring settlement with legatees of my Father's estate Daniel McKee deceased. Wit John Lyon, Emberson Bussey. /s/ Lucy (x) Conner. Proven 3 March 1819 by John Lyon; M Mims CCP. Rec 3 March 1819.

p.474   Joseph Griffin to Thomas Coleman, Deed, 24 April 1818,One thousand Dollars, 870 acres on Ninety Six Creek, granted to sd Joseph Griffin 4 April 1814. Wit John Finney, Thos Anderson. /s/ Joseph Griffin. Justice Thomas Anderson certifies release of dower rights by Parthenia Griffin wife of Joseph Griffin, 24 April 1818; /s/ Parthenia Griffin. Proven 24 April 1818 by John Finney; Thos Anderson J Q. Rec 3 March 1819.

p.475   John Summers, admr of Col Philemon Waters decd, and Wilks Berry Waters, both of Newbury District to John Pope, Deed, Newbury District, 7 May 1810, Ninety nine Dollars thirty seven and half cents, 265 acres in Edgefield District on Little Saluda, it being part of 845 acres originally granted to Colonel Philemon Waters afsd decd on 5 March 1787 by Gov Thos Pinckney; afsd land is bounded by lands of Sampson Pope, John Pope, Aron Etheridge, Martin, land claimed by Merchant, plat by John Caldwell D S. Wit F Nance, Aron Etheridge. /s/ John Summers admr, /s/ Wilks Berry Waters. Newbury District, Justice Sampson Pope certifies that Nancy Waters wife of Wilks B Waters relinquished dower rights, 7 May 1810; /s/ Nancy Waters. Proven Edgefield District, 7 May 1810 by Aron Etheridge; Sampson Pope JQ. Rec 3 March 1819.

128

DEED BOOK 35

p.478 John Blocker to Peter Robertson, Deed, 8 June 1818, Two hundred Dollars, 100 acres on Rockey, being part of land orignally granted to William Logan 19 August 1774 for 1000 acres. Wit Abner Blocker, Haly Johnson. /s/ John Blocker. Justice Jesse Blocker certifies relinquishment of dower rights by Mary Tolbert Blocker wife of John Blocker, 14 June 1818; /s/ Mary T Blocker. Proven 14 June 1818 by Haly Johnson; Jesse Blocker JQ. Plat certified 21 May 1818 by John Blocker shows adj lands of Al[faded] Robertson, James Harris. Rec 3 March 1819.

p.480 George Pope to John Pope, Deed, 20 November 1809, One hundred Dollars, 450 acres on Little Saluda River being the balance of land which contained 878 acres, surveyed for sd John & George by Jesse Blocker D S in 1808, conveyed through surveyor general's office 5 Dec 1808; above being all afsd 878 acres except the part that has been lately run off by direction of heirs of Col P Waters decd; afsd land now being sold my share or half share, the other half of sd estimated land belongs to sd John, copartner in sd survey, adj new line made by heirs of Waters on Sampson Pope, David Martin, Aron Etheridge, Jacob Pope, Sampson Pope; also a small parcel adj Merchant, Wheeler. Wit Lewis Mobley, Rebecca Corley. /s/ George Pope. Justice Sampson Pope certifies relinquishment of dower rights by Marget Pope, wife of George Pope, 26 November 1809; /s/ Marget (x) Pope. Proven 2 February 1810 by Lewis Mobley; Sampson Pope JQ. Rec 3 March 1819.

p.481 Lewis Clarke, hunter, and wife Catrin to Solomon Pope, merchant, Deed, 30 November 1774, Release, One hundred Pounds, 137 acres on Little Saluda in Collington County adj John Smeldes[?] and Arthur Tomkins, Dines Hays, Lewis Clark; granted 2 February 1773 by Gov Charles Montague unto Lewis Clarke; Wit Jno Davis, John (x) Smith. /s/ Lewis Clark, /s/ Cattrin (x) Clark. Proven 10 March 1777 by John Davis; John Fairchild J P. Rec 3 March 1819.

p.484 James Walker to Robert Gillam, Deed, 28 July 1817, One hundred Dollars, 25 acress it being part of land originally granted to Robert Spence adj lands of Robert Gillam, Elizabeth Thornton, James Walker. Wit John Roden, Henry Youngblood. /s/ James Walker. Justice William Robinson certifies relinquishment of dower rights by Christian Walker wife of James Walker, 9 August 1817; /s/ Christian (x) Walker. Proven 28 July 1817 by John Roden; Catlett Conner JP. Rec 3 March 1819.

p.485 Thompson Shaw and Hobson Shaw to Saxton Shaw, Letter of Attorney, Jefferson County, Mississippi, 30 October 1818, to sell land and give accurate account. Wit Hobson Shaw, Russell Puckett. /s/ Thompson Shaw, /s/ Hobson Shaw. Witnessed on date hereof by John Henderson Notary Publick in Natchez, Mississippi. /s/ John Henderson Not Pub. Rec 3 March 1819.

p.486 Stephen Frederick to Matthias Jones, Deed, 22 May 1817, Sixteen hundred

129

DEED BOOK 35

Dollars, 1543 acres on Clear Waters, Lotts, and Horse Creeks, being two whole tracts and parts of five others. Wit Amos W Satcher, Andrew T Perry. /s/ Stephen Frederick. Justice Peter Lamkin certifies the relinquishment of dower rights by Polly Frederick wife of Stephen Frederick, 23 August 1817; /s/ Polly (x) Frederick. Plat certified 22 May 1817 by Amos W Satcher D S shows shows adj landowners (faded): Betsy Bush, John Sanders, Alexander B Stark, Matthias Jones, Josiah Todd. Proven 23 August 1817 by Andrew T Perry; /s/ Peter Lamkin JQU. Rec 4 March 1819.

p.489   Boling Biship to Jonathan Devore, Deed, 26 December 1817, Four hundred Dollars, 300 acres on Turkey Creek of Savannah river known as Reedy Spring, adj lands of Jonathan Glanton, Sarah Gipsen, John Adams. Wit Joseph Runnels, John Bishop. /s/ Boling (x) Biship. Justice John Lyon certifies release of dower rights by Rebecca Bishop wife of Boling Bishop, 6 November 1817; /s/ Rebecca (x) Bishop. Proven 26 December 1817 by John Bishop; John Lyon QU. Rec 5 March 1819.

p.490   Daniel Hartley to his son Michael Hartley, Deed of Gift, 19 February 1819, love, 200 acres whereon I now live; also to have an equal share of the rest of my estate. Wit Richard Williams, Polenah Williams. /s/ Daniel (x) Hartley. Proven 20 Feby 1819 by Richard Williams; Geo F D Smith JP. Rec 5th March 1819.

p.491   William Anderson to William Hollowa, 28 November 1803, One hundred fifty Dollars, 148 acres originally granted to James Wilson 25 May 1774, descended to Alexander Wilson as heir at law by death of his brother James Wilson; at death of Alexander Wilson descended to his daughter Jean Wilson the only surviving heir of sd Alexander Wilson and now wife of Elijah Rogers, lying on branch of Rocky Creek of Savannah River. Wit James Harkins, Henry (x) Parkman. /s/ William Anderson. Justice John Lyon certifies relinquishment of dower rights by Elizabeth Anderson wife of William Anderson 31 March 1804; /s/ Elizabeth (-) Anderson. Proven 5 Feby 1819 by Henry (x) Parkman; Robert Walker, JP. Rec 6th March 1819.

p.492   John Holland Jur to John Lark, Mortgage, 19 February 1819, Five Shillings paid by John Lark, furniture, tools, and livestock; if sd John Holland pays John Lark Two hundred fifty Dollars with interest thereon by 25 December next, then this bill of sale to be void. Wit John L Rottin, A L Lark. /s/ John Holland. Proven 6 March 1819 by A L Lark; Lewis Holmes JQU. Rec 6th March 1819.

p.494   Anthony Low to Elizabeth Evans, 24 August 1818, Five hundred Dollars, 80 acres on Stevens Creek of Savannah River. Wit Edward Settle, Joshua Harris. /s/ Anthony (x) Low. Justice John Lyon certifies relinquishment of dower rights by Rebecca Lowe wife of Anthony Low, 24 August 1818; /s/ Rebecca Lowe. Plat shows Stephens Creek, land of Saml Price, [other words too faded to read on microfilm]. Proven 26 August 1818 by Joshua Harris; John Lyon QU. Rec 6th March 1819.

p.495   William Price to Anthony Lowe, Deed, 14 September 1816, [blank] hundred Dollars, 80 acres on Stephens Creek of Savannah River. Wit Robt Harrison, William Evans. /s/ William Price. Justice John Lyon certifies relinquishment of dower rights by Nancy Price wife of William Price, 14 September 1816; /s/ Nancy (x) Price. Plat shows adj lands of heirs of Jas Quarles, Joel Hill, Stephen [faded], heirs of Saml Price. Proven 14 September 1816 by William Evans; John Lyon QU.   Rec 6 March 1819.

p.497   John Bullock to Zachariah S[T?] Bullock, Deed, 10 October 1818, Five hundred Dollars, 371 acres whereon my father Dan Bullock now resides, being land devised by will of John Bullock to children of Dan & Jane Bullock to be equally divided between them, my claim to sd land to be sold, being the one undivided fifth part of same. Wit Thos Coleman, Robert Marsh, Wm Paine. /s/ John Bullock. Proven 27 Feby 1819 by Wm Paine Junr; Wm Robinson JQ.   Rec 6 March 1819.

p.498   Aron Ethridge to Jacob Pope, Deed, 28 December 1818, Four hundred Dollars, 103 acres resurveyed by John Pope D S, on branches of Indian Creek of Little Saluda, it being part of land originally granted to Philemon Waters by Chs Pinckney 5 March 1787 which contains 845 acres, sd land being part of a parcel granted that sd Philemon Waters conveyed to Jacob Pope Senr decd and in pursuance of his last will fell to his son Elijah Pope and was conveyed by sd Elijah to me, sd land adj John Pope.   Wit Thornton Coleman, Jacob Rambo, Sugar J Matthews. /s/ Aron (x) Ethridge. Proven 4 January 1819 by Thornton Coleman; Val Corley JP.   Rec 8 March 1819.

p.498 [second page of this number] William Abney to three granddaughters children of my son William, decd, Charlotte Abney, Susa, and Mary Ellen Abney, Deed of Gift, 28 January 1819, Love, 320 acres on Big Creek adj my own land, John Alson, John, Joseph, and William Culbreath, Ralf Scurry. Wit Wm Culbreath, Hazel Culbreath, Joseph Culbreath. /s/ W Abney.   Proven 6 March 1819 byWillliam Culbreath; John G Peterson JP.   Rec 8 March 1819.

p.500   William Cotney to William Hardy, Deed, 13 November 1818, Three hundred Dollars, 182 acres on Beaverdam branch of Clouds Creek of Little Saluda River, granted to Kezia Cotney in 1792, adj lands of James McCart, Jesse Jenning, Lewis[?] William Hardy, mouth of Muster ground Branch, plat made by John Pope D S on 12 November 1818. Wit Spear Price, William B Fortner. /s/ William Cotney. Justice Wm Ferguson certifies the relinquishment of dower rights by Margaret Cotney wife of Wm Cotney, 19 January 1819; /s/ Margaret (W) Cotney. Proven 4 January 1819 by Spear Price; Val Corley JP.   Rec 8 March 1819.

p.501   Ansibell Tillman widow of Frederick Tillman, Jacob Tillman and George Tillman sons of sd Frederick Tillman decd to Stephen Tillman Senr, Deed, 8 October 1818, Five hundred Dollars, 69 acres on Horns Creek including fork of Horns and

Marshalls Creeks and all lands which may be drowned by raising a mill dam at the old mill seat formerly owned by Lawrence Rambo, part of three original surveys, one of which was granted to Gasper Stroble for 100 acres, one to Joseph Nobles, and the other to Lawrence Rambo; sd 69 acres with adj lands was part of real estate of Frederick Tillman decd and was assessed by commissioners appointed by Court of Equity and given up to Annsibell Tillman, Jacob Tillman, Georgi Tillman and Frances Tillman on their paying to the other distributees their proportionable share of sum assessed; Frances Tillman having since conveyed her share to sd Annsibell Tillman. Wit Randolph Blackwell, Gasper Donalson. /s/ Ann S Tillman, /s/ Jacob Tillman, /s/ George Tillman. Plat shows adj lands of Stephen Tillman. Proven 1 March 1819 by Gasper Donalson; Jesse Blocker JQ. Rec 9 March 1819.

p.503   William Roberts to Presley Swillivan, Deed, 8 March [apparently a line of original deed here omitted], Four hundred Dollars, one seventh part of two thirds of 137 acres on Dry creek formerly property of Absalom Roberts decd adj lands of Jonathan Limbecker, Shear[binding] Watley senr, Frederick Watley, John [lost in binding]; also two other shares of sd land being moieties of David Roberts and Rachael Durham. Wit Murtle (x) Lasure, Absalom Roberts. /s/ William Roberts. Justice Charles Hammond certifies relinquishment of dower rights by Clarisa Roberts wife of William Roberts, 8 March 1819; /s/ Clarisa Roberts. Proven 8 March 1819 by Murtle (x) Lasure; Charles Hammond. Rec 10 March 1819.

p.505   James Butler to John Butler Snr, Deed, 4 March 1819, Eighty Dollars, my undivided part of land now in occupation of my mother Mrs [blank] Butler, same being the seventh part thereof. Wit H W Bozeman, Seth Butler. /s/ James Butler. Proved 11 March 1819 by Seth Butler; M Mims CCP. Rec 11 March 1819.

p.506   Sarah Bates and Daniel Goodman to William Johns, Deed, 8 November 1818, Four hundred Dollars, 145 acres on Clouds Creek adj lands of James Johns, Rasher Haney, Herod Thompson, Robert Tompson, being part of 665 acres originally granted to Elizabeth Mann, became lawful property of her sons Gilbert Mann and Watts Mann; from Gilbert and Watts Mann to others which has become property of Watts Mann again. Wit John W Lee, Rasha (x) Haney. /s/ Sarah (x) Bates, /s/ Daniel (x) Goodman. Proven 18 November 1818 by Rasha Haney; Nathan Norris JQ. Rec 11 March 1819.

p.507   William Moore to George Butler, Deed of Trust, 3 November 1818, land being part of my Big Creek lands and included in following bounds, line of Buffington, tracts I purchased of Korer & Lindsey, Dry Creek, Graham; also seven Negroes: Tom, Amey and her child Pascal, little Sarah and her child Jim, Ned little Sarah brother, Fanny and their future increase; same to be kept by George Butler in Trust for a Mollatto girl raised by me and called Susannah, for her and her heirs; in case of her death without heirs, land and Negroes to be divided between children of General William Butler. Wit

Behethland Butler, Gilson Yarbrough, Thos Anderson. /s/ Wm Moore. Proven 3 July 1819 by Gilson Yarbrough; Wm Furguson JQ. Rec 30 July 1819.

p.508   Moses Harris to Wilson Barentine, Deed, 15 March 1819, Twelve hundred Dollars, 150 acres originally granted unto Joseph Nobles lying on Cedar Creek, conveyed from sd Nobles to John Mock, from sd Mock to John Cheney, from Cheney to Tolaver Davis Senr, by sd Davis to Davis Moore, from Davis Moore to Moses Harris, being plantation whereon sd Harris now lives; agreement of Moses Harris with William Hagens on part of the boundary. Wit Daniel Robertson, Wm Robertson. /s/ Moses Harris. Proven 19 March 1819 by Wm Robertson; M Mims CCP. Rec 19 March 1819.

p.510   Jehew Carson to Edward Holmes, Deed, 15 March 1819, Fifty Dollars, 50 acres being part of 100 acres laid out of 538 acres granted unto Wm Jeter and conveyed by sd Jeter unto Nancy Mosley & George Mosley Jr, mother and son by his will, and by George Mosley Junr to Jehew Carson, on White Lick Branch of Gunnels Creek of Stephens Creek, on old road. Wit Wm Coursey Senr, Stephen (X) Carson. /s/ Jehew (x) Carson. Proven 22 March 1819 by Wm Coursey; Wm Hagens JP. Rec 22 March 1819.

p.511   Beverly Samuel to Walker G Samuel, Deed, 18 March 1819, Five hundred Dollars, 206 acres on Bakers Branch adj lands of Lucy Samuel, Robert T Samuel and others. Wit John Samuel, Maria Samuel. /s/ Beverly Samuel.

pp.512 and 513 are missing. Susequent pages are patched.

p.514   Charles Nix to Bartholomew Still, Deed. Wit John F Burress, Ansel Talbert. /s/ Charles Nix. Plat shows 155 acres on Bird Creek with adj lands of Charles Nix. Proven 8 May 1818 by John A Burress; Ansel Talbert JP. Rec 27 March 1819.

p.515[Page number obscured by a patch.] William Wash to Littleberry Cockran, 27 [month and year obscured by patch] Five hundred Dollars, 100 acres on Turkey Creek of Stephens Creek, adj lines of Capt Thos Jones, [patch] Cockran, William Wash, Hugh Moss. Wit Robert Cockran, Charles W Cockran. /s/ William Wash. Plat certified 22 Feby 1819 by James Tomkins. Proven 13 March 1819 by Charles Cockran; William Thurmond JQ. Rec 5 April 1819.

p.516[page number obscured by a patch] M Mims to John Gray Junr, Obligation, 1 January 1819, Three notes of hand: one payable1 July next for One thousand Dollars; second payable 1 July 1820 for Seven hundred fifty Dollars; third for sum of Seven hundred fifty Dollars payable 1 July 1821; upon full discharge of these notes I will execute good titles to John Gray Junr my house and lot in village of Edgefield opposite

133

to lot now occupied by Wm Brazier containing three acres whereon sd John Gray Junr now lives. Wit E Harison, Stephen Pixley. /s/ M Mims. Proven 12 January 1819 by E Harrison; Jesse Blocker JQ. Rec 5 April 1819.

p.517[Number obscured by patch] Wilken Smith to Richard Dunham, Deed, 8 December 18[lost in binding], Two hundred Dollars, 30 acres adj lands of Job Padget's mill, Clouds Creek. Wit Samuel Deen Senr, Nelson Durkins. /s/ W S C Smith. Justice Elijah Watson certifies relinquishment of dower rights by Jeney Smith, 8 December 18[binding]; Wit Elijah Watson, F Lee; /s/ Jeney Smith. Proven [patch] July 1813 by Samuel Deen; [name of justice oscured by patch]. Rec 5 April 18[binding].

End of Deed Book 35

---ALIN, John 99
---ANCE, Sarah 2
---, Armsted 90
---, Chesley 128
---, Elijah 106
---GAL MEETING HOUSE 90
---GAN, William 49
---grans, James 100
---, James 90
---, John 91 122 132
---, Joseph 92
---KY Creek 82
---man, Widow 91
---OKES GULLEY branch 51
---PERS, Joel 101
---, Samuel 103
---, Stephen 131
---, William 85
A---, John 114
ABBEVILLE DIST/CO 4 6 16 18-20 22-25 40 46 61 67 82 83 121 125+
ABBEVILLE ROAD 64
ABBOTT, Samuel 66
ABERDEEN, SCOT 13 15 16
ABNEY, Azariah 58 63 Charles 55
Charlotte 131Elizabeth 41 Emily 41 Jacob
14 106 James 121 John (official) 18 35 41
42 50 58 63 69 83 87 100 121 (personal)
49+ 50+ 53+ 54 58 121+ Lark 7 36 44 58
74 106 Martha/Patsey 84 Mary 41+ 42
131 Paul 58 83 121 Samuel 35 58 69 100
Susa 131 Thomas 41 W 4 Walter 100
William 2 28 41 49 50+ 53+ 121 131
Zachariah 2 41 --- 55
ADAMS, Abram 113 Charles 7 Drury 21
Jacob 42 43 James (official) 2 5 7 14 34
43 John 6 33 89+ 130 Joseph 41 Martha
33 S 85 Solomon 33 88 89 Thomas 7 51
59 72 104
ADDISON, Allen 111 Joseph 63
ADKINS, Benjamin 29 30
ADKISSON, John 121
ALDREDGE/ALDRIDGE, John 6 33
ALLAN, John 15

ALLEN, Aron 46 95 Benjamin 118 David 15
James 29 47 87 126 John 52 92 Josiah 70 87
Minarva 29 Nancy 122 Orsamus
(official) 19 Robert 12 27 120 122 126
Susannah 90 Wade 96 Young 34 43+ 46
56 67 90+ --- 122
ALMON, Hezekiah 60+ 61+ 88+ Holston
/Holstun 60 61
ALSON, John 131
AMBLER, James 38 Susan 38
AMITE CO, MISSISSIPPI 88
ANDERSON, Eliza 20 Elizabeth 130
George 97 Jacob 120 John 123 Rachel 20
Robert 83 Thomas (official) 2 14 30 50 62
71 77 90 97 100 118 122 128 (personal) 2
50 133 William 117+ 130
ANDREWS, Jane 6 Samuel 6 William 95
ANTONY, John 19
ARDAGH, Patrick 26 27+
ARDIS, Abraham 9+ Eliza 114 Isaac 87
John 87 88 Matthias 71 127 Patcy 88
ARLEDGE, Ann 5 6 John 5 6 43 45 67
ARMSTRONG, Moses 109 110
ARRINGTON, Burrel/Burrell 68 69
ASBELL/AZBELL, Abigail 98 Elisha 6
7+ Jarvis 6 7+ John 26 98
ASHLEY/ASHLY, Charles 104 Robert 76
ASHTON, Joseph 29
ATCHISON, Edmund 103
ATKINS, Robert 114
ATKINSON, D 88 Dawson 114 John 106+
Noney 106+
AUGUSTA, GA 1 3 11 13 41 55 61 69+
70 71 78 79+ 102 112
AUGUSTA ROAD 11 41 47 48 51 63 68
71 73 77 88 89 116 117 124
AUTRY, Robert 48
B---, Clainey 5 James 35 56
BACON, Edmund 1 2 31 34 42 54 69 96
Eliza 69 Thomas 70
BAGGETT, Elias 67
BAILEY, Jesse 20 Margaret 74 Martin 71
Shadrack 57 William 74
BAINS, William 89

BAKER, Nathan 100 branch 133
BALENTINE, Hugh 89 112+ 113+ 121
BALEY, Jesse 20 branch 4
BALL, Elizabeth 30
BALLANTINE, Hugh 25
BALLENTINE, Hugh 57
BANKNIGHT, Daniel 54
BANKS, Charles 62 63 115 Sarah 63 115
--- 78
BAPTIST CHURCH 77
BARENTINE, Wilson 133
BARETT, John 64
BARKLEY COUNTY 106
BARKSDALE, Daniel 2 8   Susannah 2
--- 21
BARNES, Henry 55 122 John 87 Loyd
(official) 119 (personal) 89 122 Reason 47
84 101 William 100
BARNS, Henry 41 99 100
BARNETT, Lloyd 33   Creek 34
BARNWELL DISTRICT 8 9 19 27 32+
37+ 53 57 67 69 76 81 94 106
BARONTINE/BARONTON, Wilson 103
BARR, Henry 20
BARRENTINE, Charles 78 80 James 81
BARRETT, Elizabeth 64 John 91 Matthew
64 69 70 Thomas 12
BARRON, Highden 90
BARRONTON, Charles 9 28 33 45
Wilson 54
BARTEE, John (official) 41 63 64
(personal) 56
BARTLETT, --- 51
BARTON, Benjamin 6 Mary 78
Willoughby 78
BATCHELOR, Thomas 88
BATES, Sarah 132 Widow 116 William
47 57
BAUGH, Daniel 46 John 5
BAUKNIGHT, Daniel 54 55+
BAUNETHEAU, Gabriel (official) 22 34
BAWDEN, --- 104
BEACH CREEK 89
BEACH ISLAND 47 87 114 127
BEACH ISLAND ROAD 109 111
BEACKLEY, Walter 79
BEAL, Isaac 107   --- 1

BEALS, John 55
BEAMES/BEAMS, James 15 68 108
Rebecca 68
BEAN, Alexander 51
BEARLEY, Separt 19
BEAVERDAM BRANCH 131
BEAVERDA, CREEL 3+ 5 6 11 12+ 15
17 21 27 31+ 33-35 47+ 48 56 59 62 65
67-70 72 74 77 79 81 85+ 91+ 93 96+ 101
111 123
BECH CREEK 35
BECK, Simon 85 Solomon 104
BECKHAM, Reuben 71 --- 40
BECKUM, Thomas 64
BEDINGFIELD CREEK 104
BEE TREE BRANCH 70
BEDDINGFIELDS CREEK 78
BEECH ISLAND 22 58
BELCHER, E (official) 23 57 73
(personal) 30 Edmund 83 125 Mary 125
Susannah 125 Washington 125
BELL, Isaac 106 James (official) 28 49 50
56 80 122 Joel 121 John 9 88 Mary 18
Samuel 58 Spencer 54 Stephen 18+ ---35
BELLMOUNT PLANTATION 106
BENDER, George 55
BENIGHT/BENNIGHT, James 82
BENNER, --- 76
BENNOCK, Peter 61
BENSON, Enoch 82 John 82
BERRY, Agness 100 John 77 100 Nancy 4
Samuel 4 Willy 95
BEST, John 95
BETTIS, Elijah 30 Elisha 85 Francis 17 21
35 66 85 Jesse 18 20 21 44 95 101 105
John 17 85 96 Mary 85 Mathew/Matthew
(official) 17 35 125 Moody 35 Stephen 30
85+ 96 109 110
BEUNER, --- 76
BICKER, Allen 81
BIG BRANCH 39
BIG CREEK 4+ 21 28 35 49+ 50+ 75 102
103+ 106 117 121 128 131 132
BIG HORSE CREEK 30 69
BIG MOUNTAIN CREEK 35
BILBO, James 47
BIRD, D 99 Daniel 9 15 20 23 47 84 105

106 Eborn 99 Elijah 9 Jane 84 John 99 Mary 3 Nancey 3 Nancy 99 Sarah 99
BIRD CREEK 19 37 65 66 92 105 115+ 116 125+ 133
BISHOP/BISHIP, Boling 130 Elizabeth 3 88 Esaias 80 88+ Ezekiel 2 3 89 John 130 Judas 80 Rebecca 130 Thomas 2 3+ 9
BITTLE, Andrew 22
BLACK, John 76 Joseph (official) 24 67 Mark 41 121+ Thomas 87
BLACKBORN, Elias 69 Lee 70 Mary 69 William 68 69
BLACKBOURN, Lee 113
BLACKBURN, Elias 3+ 20 23 John 44 Lee 3+ 46 Margaret 23 William 3+ 23
BLACKLEY, William 59 --- 125
BLACKWELL, Randolph 132
BLADEN, John 122 Mary 121+ William 122
BLADON, John 121 Thomas 49
BLAIR, Christopher 29 36 Gabriel 36 Rebecca 36
BLAKELEY, Sarah 70
BLAKEY, --- 124
BLALOCK, Ann 35 Buckner 2 9 35 57 89 109+ Harden 24 James 17 John (official) 32 38 (personal) 3 9 19 128 Middleton 112 Millenton 67 Richard 32 69 94 107 108+ Sarah 38 Wade 94 Waide 107 108 William 103
BLAND, Ann 80 115 P 22
BLAYLOCK, John 35 Mrs 35 --- 85
BLEDSOE, Bartlett 41 42 William 112
BLEKBURN, E (official) 10
BLOCKER, A 18 Abner 93 103 129 B 123+ 124+ Barkley 3 59 73 Bartlet 8 Eliza 123+ 124+ James 84 Jesse (official) 3 5 9 23 31 33 34 36 38 43 45 48 51 59 65 68 72 82 89 92 96 103-106 112 113 129 132 134 (personal) 45 123+ 124+ John (official) 22 23 66 72 79 87 97 111 (personal) 3 47 49 75 76 82 93+ 103 113 123+ 124+ 129 Mary 68 93 103 129
BLOW, Benjamin 9 25 Michael 3
BOATNER, Elias 128
BOBO, Burrell (official) 56 Lacy 56
BODDY, Allen 98 Sarah 98

BODIE, Allen 98 John 107 Sarah 98 --- 22
BODY, John 107 Nathan 107+
BOG/BOGGY BRANCH 16+ 57+ 58 102
BOLGAR, John 7
BOLGER, John 33 35+ 36+ 44 49+ 50+ 89 97
BOLLES, Job 1
BOLTON, John 69 Joseph 56
BOND, George 122 J 12 John 122
BONHAM, James 87 Sophia 24 112 113
BOON, --- 9
BOOTH, Adam 55 James 55 56 Richard 55
BORROM, Hidon 90
BORROUM, William 90
BOSTICK, Tolaver 44 45 Washington 5 24 25 80 William 20 38+ Willis 20 44 79 --- 14
BOSWELL, William 41
BOUKNIGHT, Daniel 120
BOURROM, William 90
BOWDON, Lewis 74
BOWERS, Aurelia 57 Benjamin 22 57 76 David 5 55 76 Elizabeth 84 George 57 Julia 57 Mary 57 76 Phileman 47 Philemon 76
BOWIE, William 56+
BOYD, Abraham 18 19 Henry 80 126 John 26 29+ 36 48 68 80 97 120 126 Mrs. 93 Robert 120 Susannah 47 Walter 47 93
BOZEMAN, Dan 122 Edward 16 H 122 132 Philemon 122 Susannah 122
BRADBERRY, Thomas 3
BRADFORD, Robert 70
BRASELL, Jesse 109
BRASSELL, Jesse 86 William 124
BRATCHER, John 14 Thomas 72
BRAZIER, John 111 William 3 13 14 101 111 134
BRAZIL, Jesse 109
BREAZEALE, Enoch 11
BREIGHTAUPT, Christian (official) 115
BREITHAUPT, C 13 Christian (official) 47 67 101 (personal) 47 51 56 81 111 --- 51
BREMAR, John 38
BRENAN, Bridges 90 Eugene 5 10 22 31

137

73 89 93
BRESHY FORK 71
BREUNAN, Margaret 43
BREWER, James 100
BREWERS BRANCH 48 65 100
BREWERS SPRING BRANCH 117
BRICES CREEK 3
BRIDGE CREEK 32 69 110
BRIGGS, Henry 40 John 39
BRIGHTAUPT, Christian (official) 115
BRITOP, Christian (official) 100
BROADWATER, James 93 94+ 126
BROOKS, Esau 14 James 117 Robert 65
Samuel 114 Smith 75 Thomas 76 Whitfield
(official) 15 60 75 77 87 (personal) 14 127
William 44 104 Zachariah 102 103
Zacheriah 35
BROOM, Thomas 9
BROUGHTON, Andrew 20
BROWN, Charles 70 George 6 Joel 28
John 66 Jon 117 Thomas 53+ 54 Whitfield
49 William 53 54 --- 81
BRUCE, Hannah 81 James 81 Martha 81
82 Moses 81 Right 81 Wright 81 --- 35
BRUNETT, Thomas 55
BRUNSON, Daniel 17 91 Joseph 17
William 17
BRUX, Thomas 5
BUCK, John 111 creek 94
BUCKELEW, John 56
BUCKHALTER, Christian 26 75 Henry
32 James 47 John 31+ 47 105 Mrs 74 75
BUCKHALTERS CREEK 47 51
BUCKLER, Garret 109
BUFFINGTON, --- 37 132
BUGG, --- 1
BULGER, John 87
BULL, Gov Wm (official) 53 60 79 103
109 110+
BULL BRANCH 85 96 109
BULL SLUICE 101 102 126
BULLOCK, Daniel 5 7 9 31+ 82 131
David 7 31+ Hannah 7 31 Jane 131 John
77 131 Martha 82 Rachel 82 Richard 58
60 Thomas 31 82 Zachariah 131
BULOW, Joachim 106
BUNANTON, James 20

BUNCH, David 119 126 Doctor 118
BUNTING, B 14 118 Isaac 44
BURDEL, William 27
BURGER, Samuel (official) 45
BURGESS, James 127 John 76 William 61
BURGHER, Allen 123
BURKE, --- 62
BURKE "BORK" CO, GA 32 86
BURKHALTER, John 56
BURNELL, Crad^k 127
BURNETT, Hesekiah 100 Thomas 25
William 25 74 creek 128
BURNS, Sally 112 --- 77
BURNSELL, Daniel 111
BURNSIDE, William (official) 45 47 104
BURRELS CREEK 68
BURRESS/BURRISS, John 19 37 115+
125+ 133 Martin 79 125
BURT, Amelia 101 Armsted 120
Augustine 101 Caroline 101 Catharine 82
101 Eugene 101 Edward 82 Francis 82 90
101 Harewood 101 Herod 80 Mary 101
Moody 101 Phillip 5 25 Susannah 39 101
William 101 Willis 44
BURTON, Allen 29 85 125 Benjamin 125
Beverly 73 John 72 Nathaniel 92 Richard
29 96 Robert 43 William 14 118
BUSEY, Redocks 39
BUSH, Betsy 130 Bibby 88+ Frederick 85
Heron 28 Herrin 105 106 Isaac 54 64 65
80+ J (official) 98 111 John (official) 6 17
61 88 98 (personal) 2 3 17+ 32+ 89
Prescott 32 57 Richard 16 17 58 mill 89
BUSHES MILL CREEK 9 28 58
BUSSEY, C (official) 97 113 121 127
Charles (official) 40 48 49 59 63 65 71 79
86 89 99-102 111 115 117 125 126 (personal) 49 119 Demsey 24 Emberson 128 J
71+ 79 111 Jeremiah 48 Martha 80 Micajah 111 Wade 80 Widow 49 Zadock 39
--- 49
BUSSY, Wade 48 --- 123
BUTLER, Abner 112 Alley 113 Andrew 9
75 Behethland 133 Elizabeth 100 Fanny
12+ General 103 George 14 18 49 60 97+
127 132 J 30 121 James (official) 22 49 67
(personal) 18 72 73 103 121 132 John

138

(official) 121 (personal) 57 64 112+ 113+
132 Mrs 132 Pierce 61 Sampson 4 36 38+
44 93 108 Seth 112 132 Stanmore (official)
72 (personal) 95 Thomas 12+ 13 53 113
119 William 30 95 100 103 113 122 132
Winefred 113 Winnifred 113 --- 20
BUZBE, Mary 68
BUZBEE, Benjamin 68 Miles 68
BUZZARD CREEK 86
CAILER/CAILES, Charles 77
CAIN BREAK BRANCH 94
CALDWELL, John 128 William 71 --- 19
CALLIHAM, John 12
CALWELL, John 118
CAMBELTOWN 11
CAMBRIDGE RD 15+ 72 77 92 95 103
CAMERON, John 123+ 124 Samuel 123+
CAMP BRANCH 81
CAMPBELL, David 9 Edward 1 Elizabeth
82 Harriet 1 John 45 Macartan 1 Maria 1
Martha 1 Robert 75 Sarah 1 Stephenson
105+ 106 Widow 123 --- 95
CAMPBELLTON ROAD 11
CANE BREAK BRANCH 56 93+
CANE PATCH BRANCH 39
CANFIELD, John 40+
CANNON, Daniel 116 Henry 83 Levi 29
30 William 86 87
CANOE CREEK PLANTATION 1
CANTELOW, Lemuel 16+ 19 28
CAPEHART, George 76 Henry 62 112
John 83
CAPSES TRACT 86
CAPTS, Ephraim 104
CARGILL, Thomas 30
CARLER, Charles 77
CARMICHAL, Abram 44
CARNES, Henry 82 Peter 19 21
CARNS, Peter 18
CARPENTER, Dennis 81 86 87 --- 12
CARROM, --- 14
CARSON, Hugh 17 58 James 38 41 49+
50+ 63 121+ 122 126 Jehew 133 Margaret
/Marget 121 122 Nancy 49 50+ 58 Robert
(official) 70 Sarah 49 50+ 58 Simpson 50
Stephen 133 William 16 17+ --- 92
CART, John 51

CARTER, Elizabeth 56 John 77 106
Patience 80 Phebe 80 Robert 33 Samuel 8
Silas 26 Thomas 81 97
CARTLEDGE, John 76 97 Samuel 42
Sarah 97
CASON, Triplet 115
CATE, Elizabeth 124 125 Huldah 126
Joshua 125 Polly 125 Robert 124 125 126
CATES, Elizabeth 124 Huldah 124 Robert
122 124 Thomas 95+ Widow 91 Wiley 124
William 122 123 124+
CATFISH CREEK 42
CAUGHMAN, West 55
CAUNOUS, --- 26
CEDAR BRANCH 37
CEDAR CREEK 4 18 19 21 22 33 44 133
CEDER CREEK 21
CHANS, John 89
CHAPELL, --- 103
CHAPMAN, Eligah/Elijah 91 Elizabeth 91
Jiles 91 John 35 58 75 83 87 Thomas 82
CHAPPELL, Thomas 1 82
CHAPS BRANCH 111
CHARLESTON 22 26 34 38+ 45 51 55 66
98+ 126
CHARLESTON ROAD 25 32 41 50 61 89
113
CHATHAM COUNTY, GA 1
CHAVERS/CHAVERSES CR 41 112+
CHAVIS CREEK 80 81
CHEATHAM, Delaveign 17 Fanny 111
John (official) 5 7 31 47 76 85 91
(personal) 47 81 90 111 Peter 111
CHENEY, James 4 John 133
CHEROKEE PONDS 2 11
CHESTERFIELD DISTRICT 95
CHEVES CREEK 55 56+
CHICKESAW LANDS 79
CHILDERS, --- 81
CHILES, Garland 73 Thomas (official) 58
77 (personal) 44 45 127
CHINCAPIN CREEK 116
CHIPLEY, William 117+
CHIPMAN, Edwin 54 65 Henry (official)
54 65
CHRISTIAN, Edward 4 44 Elizabeth 52
Gideon 4 33 77 Jesse 128 John 52 Martha

44 Ransom 28 Stephen 52 Thomas 48 52+
62 63 66
CLAGG, Elizabeth 60 John 60
CLAKELER, Elijah 114
CLARK, Cattrin 129 James 45 57 94 103
Jesse 14 Lewis 3+ 6 9+ 25 39+ 84 129
William 14
CLARKE, Catrin 129 John 127 Lewis 129
CLAY, --- 1
CLEAR WATERS CREEK 130
CLEGG, Jonathan 5 69
CLEMENT, Francis 68 Stephen 108
CLEVELAND, Elizabeth 4 James 4 103
John 4 Rice 4
CLOSE, William 35
CLOUD, James 108 John 79 Noah 79
Ransom 127 Reuben 115 William (official)
2 --- 108
CLOUDS CREEK 12+ 13+ 26+ 27 29 30
53 55 62+ 63 90+ 91+ 95+ 98+ 99+ 106
107+ 116 118+ 119 120+ 122 124+ 125
126 127 131 132 134
COALING FIELD 61
COATE/COATES, Henry (official) 53 54
91 102 103 James 9 45 48 89 90 John 128
M 37 Marmaduke 91
COBB, Thomas 23
COBBS, James 108 Jane 108 Jenny 108
John 188 Widow 101
COCHRAN, Chesly 99+ Robert 65
COCK COUNTY, TN 83
COCKEROFT, Jaen/Jennie/Jenny 125
Mary 125 Ogden 125 Susanah 125
Thomas 125 William 89
COCKRAM, --- 11 53
COCKRAN, Charles 133 Littleberry 133
Robert 53 133
COCKROFF, Ogdell 16
COCKROFT, Thomas 73 --- 46
COGBURN, Eliza 63 Elizan 47 Jesse 47
63
COLBORN, Elizabeth 19 Harman 19
William 19
COLBURN, John 119
COLEMAN, Edna 90 118 Edwd 63
George 37 James 14 44 45 71 118 John
97+ Richard 50+ 117+ Thomas 14 90 118

128 131 Thornton 131 William 41 63 ---54
COLIER, Edmund/Edward (official) 89
125
COLLETON COUNTY 26
COLLIER, Edward (official) 78 (personal)
1 39 James 5 Joseph 25 71 Lucy 39 Louisa
39
COLLINGTON COUNTY 129
COLLINS, Dennis 5 7 Lewis 85 101
COLLUM, Catarena 74 John 74 Margaret
61 Solomon 61
COLUMBIA 24+ 38 74 75 96
COLUMBIA COUNTY, GA 19 43+ 48 66
67 80 121
COLUMBIA ROAD 11 34 36 88 95
COLVIN, D 104 Daniel 45 103 David 22
COLWELL, John (official) 128
COMMING, Levi 122
CONGAREE 116+
CONNER, Catlett (official) 45 64 71 72
80 129 (personal) 73 Lucy 128
CONNICK/CONNIK, --- 98 99
CONOLLY, William 32
CONOVER, Eliza 22 34
COOK, Amanda 42 Caroline 42 Dyer 123
Ephraim 93 95 96 John 42 Joseph 59+
Martha 42 Martin 7 Prudence 42 West 11
22 42 --- 3
COOKSEY, Caleb 99
COON, Adam 107
COONCE, Christian 116
COOPER, Ann 118 C 14 Campbell 89
Charles 5 25 90 Reuben 57 89 William 36
118
CORDER, Jenny 63 Morgan 12 13 53 63
CORLEY, Abner 74 124 Adkin 62 Allen
121 122 Benjamin 62+ Catlett 22 76 Henry
28 Michael 14 127 Nat 80 Nathaniel 62 91
Rebecca 129 Robert 62 Sasrah 18 Val
(official) 90 121 131 Valentine (official) 12
17 18 87 (personal) 18 Whinea 121 122
Zacheus 17 18+ ---n (official) 56
CORMACK, Alexander 31+
CORNER LOT TRACT 11
COSPER, Harman 37 66
COSSERAT, George 38+
COTNEY, Kezia 131 Margaret 131

Stephen 14 33 William 131
COTTEN, Haley 88
COTTON, Charity 7 Deadema/Dedemia
120 Delana 7 James 7 John 77 120
Patience 7 Patsey 7 Thomas 120 Wrotha 7
COTTON PATCH PLANTATION 1
COUCH, Edward 61 John 47 84 112 Sarah
112 William 28
COUGHORN, John 45
COURSER, John 24
COURSEY, Chs 39 James 41 John 7 36+
45 William (official) 83 91 114 (personal)
6 36 38 39 44 59 79 86 133
COVINGTON, E 49 Jane 11 John 102
Mrs 101 Richard 11 49 65 70 71+ 79 117
Susannah 70 William 101 102
COWTHER, Isaac 11
COX, Arthur 67 Bailey/Baily/Baley 104
123 Christopher 85 104+ 123 Eliza 67
Gabriel 104 123 George 67 Henry 104
James 67 86 Jane 123 Jesse 67 John 104
Mary 104 Michell 104 Sarah 67 Talliver
118 William 29 36
COXON, Levi 70
CRABTREE, Ezekiel 33
CRAFTON, J 121 Joseph 2 121 Lucy 2
Samuel 81 121
CRANE, Wilson 31
CRAWFORD, David (official) 40 Robert
68 William 81
CREEK BRANCH 48
CRESWELL, Elihu 30 --- 1
CRONER, John 16
CRONEY, John 58
CROOKED BRANCH 75 run 41
CROSS, George 41 John 88
CROUCH, Isaac 30+
CUFFEETOWN CREEK 2 6 8 10+ 21 23
25 28 62 69 70 83+ 84 123+ 124 125
CUFFYTOWN CREEK 105
CULBREATH, Hazel 131 John 131 Joseph
131 William 131
CULPEPER, Benjamin 16 Joice 16
CUMBASS/CUMBESS, --- 12 27
CUNNINGHAM, John 97 Joseph 37 42 78
Martha 97 Sarah 78
CURBO, Joseph 5

CURRY, Benajah 64 Cader 64 John 64
Lewis 64 Susannah 64+
CUTTER, Benjamin 37
CYPER CREEK 32 38 92
DABBS, Jonathan 9
DAGNAL, John 81
DAILEY, Elizabeth 102 John 102 Owen
21 102 103 Sarah 103
DAILY, David 21
DALEY/DALY, John 75 103
DANIEL/DANIELS, James 123 Jesse 72
Stephen 70 William 22
DARBY, Benjamin 35 48 52 62 96 James
51 Olive 48
DARK BRANCH 32
DAVICE, Thomas 91
DAVIS, Arthur 128 Benjamin 24 Bud 19
John 129 Samuel 18 Terry 27 Tolaver 133
Warren 101 William 127 --- 62 103 111
DAVISE, John 91
DAWSON, James 90 John 38+ Jonas 90
Jonathan 51 72 Joseph 70 Lemuel 90
DAY, Daniel 63 Elizabeth 71 115
Frederick 112 Henry 70 85 James 63 70
71+ 77 79 100 115 John 112 Mary 70
Peter 78 Polly 63 Sanders 111 Silas 85
William 86
DAYES, James 101
DEAN, William 95
DEAS/DEES, Charles 73 Daniel 60 Esther
73 Joel 60+ 61 88+ Mary 88 Nancy 88
Squire 73 Tabitha 88
DEAVENPORT, D 60
DEEN, Samuel 13 74 134 Sarah 119
Thomas 13 74 119 120   Creek 3 9
DELAIG---, --- 1
DELAUGHTER, Frances 49 George 99
100 J 111 James 49
DELAVIGNE, Casimir 111 Emile 111
DELOACH, Thomas 57 80+ William 12
---30
DEMING, Mary 21 Simeon 21
DENNIS, --- 48
DESHAZO, John 92 Robert 118+ 119
William 119
DEVALL, Samuel 45 89 Sarah 89
DEVORE, Caty 64 Jonathan 59 126 130

Luke 64 Mathew 92
DEVOUR, Jonathan 113 Luke 113
DICKS, Elizabeth 5 J 5 John 37 Jonathan 5
9 54 114+ Thomas 37 William 37
DILLARD, Arthur 102 Nicholas 4 Phillip
60 77
DKINSON, John 122
DLOACH, Saml 127 William 13 124+
126+ 127+
DOBEY, David 64 66 Patsey 64 William
20 branch 27
DOGAN, Joseph 80
DOGGINS, Sarah 4
DOLTON, John 6
DON, James 32 88
DONALDSON/DONALSON, David 36
Gasper/Gosper 36 132
DOOLITTLE, Agnes 81 Ephraim 81 Polly
40 Samuel 40+
DORLTON, John 39
DORN, Peter 69
DORRAS, Widow 83
DORRIS, Elizabeth 82 William 84
DORTON, John 39
DOUBLE BRANCH 26 120 122
douglas, James 27+ 43 John 27+ 43 Polly
27 Sally 27 Solomon 27
DOVER, John 30
DOWNEY, John 42 Sally 42
DOZIER, A 44 Abram 20 Catey 60 James
28 45 John 60 Richard 117+ Thomas
(official) 6 9 16 24 28 33 39 60 68 89
(personal) 117+ William 24
DRAKE, Harvey 94+ 103 Henry 30
DRAYTON, William 84 86
DRINKWATER, Josiah 108 Lucy 81 108
Sarah 108
DRUMBLADES PARISH, Scot 13 15
DRY FORK 81
DRY CREEK 27 46 47 51 57 81 98 99
101 108 113 124 132+
DUCK BRANCH 32
DUFFEY/DUFFIE, Hugh 17 58
DULEYS ROAD 97
DUN, William 53+ creek 3 9
DUNCAN, William 96
DUNHAM, Richard 134

DUNKIN, Peter 120 Samuel 119 120
Selah/Seley 120
DUNN, William 66+
DURHAM, Rachael 132 William 119
DURKIN, --- 90
DURKINS, Nelson 134
EARLE, George 83
EARNEST, Jacob 61 76 101 Nancy 101
EASTER, John 20
EASTLAND, William 102 103
EATON, Joseph 123
EDDINS, Abram 80 Benjamin 8 Elizabeth
15 John 20 41 Joseph 3 15 Mary 96
Widow 35 96
EDGEFIELD ACADEMY 34
EDGEFIELD COURTHOUSE 8 15 21 34
69 103
EDGEFIELD ROAD 19 28 31 62
EDGEFIELD VILLAGE 3 13 14+ 52 72
73 87 102 108 133
EDISTO 45
EDISTO RIVER 9 35 48 52 58 80 88+ 94
109+ 110+ 116 SOUTH 3+ 7 9 16+ 17+
25 57+ 60+ 61+ 82 109+ 110 111
EDMONDS, A 71 Samuel 83
EDMUNDS, A (official) 8 16 24 26 29 39
47 74 80 83 114 Alexander 24 Sally 39
(official) --- 2
EDSON, James 95
EDWARDS, Solomon 53
EFURT, Adam 116
EIDSON, James 98 124 John 89 98+ 99
124
ELAM, John 47+ 48
ELDERS, John 15
ELIM PLANTATION 11 66+
ELLIOT, Allen 117 Thomas 105
ELLIOTT, William 20
ELLIS, Mary 69 road 65
ELLISON, M 101 Robert 78 W 14
William 3 13 15 42 78+ 87 --- 75
ELSTRE, John 115
ENGLAND 13
ENGLISH, William 73
EPHRAIM BRANCH 14 35
ESKRIDGE, Austin 91
ETHERAGE, Edmund 90

ETHEREDGE, Edmund 91 Gilfird/Gilford 62
ETHERIDGE, Aron 128+ 129 131 Henry 91 William 62
ETHRIDGE, Lewis 4 19 Solomon 36 ---62
EVANS, Batt 73 92 Benjamin 89 Cadwell 23 50+ 73 92 126 Easter 115 Elizabeth 130 Robert 73 92 Thomas 121 William 51 131
EZARD, Mason 88
f.m.c. Anderson 97 Andrew 97 March 2 Marmaduke 92
f.w.c Dina 92 Fan/Fanny 112 Mary 97 Mary Scott 115 Susannah 97
FAIR, Lucilla 79 Thomas 32
FAIRCHILD, John (official) 26 109 129 Thomas (official) 116
FAIRCLOTH, Barbary 95 Benjamin 95
FAIRFIELD DISTRICT 20
FALKNER, Nathan 42 Russell 60 --- 4
FALL CREEK 72 98 99
FALLOW, Henry 25 120
FANNY f.w.c. 112 113
FANNIN, Joseph (official) 117
FARCHILD, J 27
FARGUSON, William 65
FARRAR, Chaney 68
FARRIER, Thomas 92
FARROW, Cheney 108 John 8 Waters 108
FAUST, J (official) 24
FEARS, Absalom 1
FEASTER, John 12 127
FEDERICK, Lewis 16
FEDRICK, Lewis 16 Stephen 6 28 57
FELL, Charles (official) 26 51 Elizabeth 47 W 13 William 47 51 --- 81
FENZER, Dan¹ 79
FERGUSON, Charles 103 Morning/ Mourning 74 William (official) 117 (personal) 74 102 103+ 106
FERRELL, Ephraim 51 66
FIMBER, John 120
FINDLAY/FINDLEY/FINDLY, Charles 26 68+ 97 Polley 86 Richard 68+ 97
FINNEY, John 90 128
FIVE NOTCHED ROAD 11 93 105 113 126

FLAT ROCK BRANCH 96
FLETCHER, Edward 111 Ezekiel 111 Widow 49 William 111
FLICK, Hannah 26
FLINN, William 26 --- 75
FLUKER, George 12 91 Hardy 12 91 Isabel/Isabella 98+ Sophia 91 William 91 98+ 107+ --- 62
FOLKNER, Russel 60
FOOSHE, David 109+ Nathaniel 109 110 111 --- 110+
FORBES, Nathaniel 15 Robert 15 William 15
FOREMAN, Isaac 57
FOREST, James 6+ Jesse 27
FORGASON, James 95
FORGUSON, William 65
FORREST, James 9 Jesse 89 William 56
FORSYTH, William 7 --- 1
FORT, Drury 113
FORT MOORE BLUFF 51
FORTNER, Keziah 57 William 131
FOSHE, David 110
FOSHEE, Nathaniel 109 Sary 109 --- 110
FOSTER, Joel 107
FOUTS/FOUTZ, Martin 12 107
FOWL CREEK 72
FOX, John 55 56+ 81 Jonathan 57 113 Nicholas 31 116 William 113
FOXES CREEK 63
FOY, William 113
FRANCIS, --- 105
FRANKLIN, Berry 68 Charles 44 Littleberry 68 109
FRANKLIN COUNTY, TN 88
FRASER, Reuben 102
FRAZER, Daniel 11 79 102 Philip 102 Reuben 101 Robert 97
FRAZIER, Benjamin 9 23 35 43+ 62 67 86 90 93 96 109 Daniel 71+ 102 James 70 Jesse 8 John (official) 96 (personal) 31+ 36 77 William 70
FREDERICK, Mary 96 Polly 130 Stephen 96+ 129 130
FREDRICK, Stephen 28 57
FREEMAN, Garrett (official) 11 45 48 H 51 Hamlin 36 Isaac (official) 110 James

76+ 104 John 74 Samuel 48 Thomas 48
Wiley 48 --- 123
FRISH, Michael 32
FULLER, Joseph 106+ 114 Thomas 67
FUNDERBURGH, Anthony 53
FUNDERBURK, Peter 119
FURGURSON, Abraham/Abram 24 27
Frances 27
FURGUSON, William (official) 133
(personal) 102
FURYS ROAD 1
GABLE, Jacob 83
GAINY SPRING BRANCH 9
GALLAHER, Samuel 83
GALLMAN, Benjamin 84 112 Casper 116
Conrod 77 Daniel 116 Gasper 95 Gosper
18 101 Harman 116 Jemima 116 Lydia
116 Sally 49 Sarah 49
GALPHIN, George 55 Thomas 22 mills 76
GANTE, John (official) 91
GANTT, Richard 13 19 47 51 81 Sarah 81
Thomas 81
GANYS SPRING BRANCH 9 25
GARDENER, Thomas 13
GARDNER, Leven 75 Levingston 70
Levington 63 71 Robert 71 101 102 Sarah
63 75 --- 21 74
GARNER, Age 41 Luke 90
GARRETT, Henry 104 Jainusary 12 John
33 104 Mrs 34 Robert 119 William 86 104
111 118 --- 101
GAULMAN, Gasper 67 --- 36
GENTRY, Elizabeth 51 John 50+ 51 Levi
18 Runnels 50
GENTY, Runnels 117
GEORGE, John 65 W 4
GEORGETOWN DISTRICT 82
GEORGIA 1 3 5 6 11 13 19 32 43 46+ 48
50 55 56+ 61 66 67 69+ 70 71 79-81 86-
88 93 94 99 102 112 120 121 123+ 124+
GETER, --- 54
GETZEN, George 26 41
GIBSON, Amey 55 Benjamin 55 Catharine
55 John 55 113 Patrick 65 82 Samuel 55
GILCHRIST, Arther 44
GILES, A 23 Andrew 24 branch 19
GILL, David 17 21 Jolly 95

GILLAM/GILLIAM, Isome 87 Robert 6
21 128 129 Samuel 83 branch 123
GIPSEN, Sarah 130
GIST, Jeremiah 26
GLACKLER, John 112
GLANTON, Elizabeth 92 126 John 84
Jonathan 38 57 73 92 126 130 L 92
GLASCOCK, Eliza 14 19 John 14 18+ 19
21 31 86 108 111 120
GLAUSIER/GLAUZIER, John 68 Widow
105
GLEN/GLENN, James 53+ John 53
Margaret 53
GLOVER, David 33 126 Elizabeth 9 126
John 5 9 84 114 Wade 114 Wiley 122
William 33 41 72
GOFF, John 53 99+ branch 53+
GOGGINS, Daniel 109 William 109
GOLMAN, James 59
GOLPHIN, Thomas 5
GOMILLION, Andrew 20 89 John 93
GOMILLON, Andrew 16
GONSLY, James 105
GOODE, Freeman 71 72 Mackerness 5
71+ Permelia 39 William 38
GOODMAN, Daniel 17 132
GOODWIN, Charles 15 78 R 95 Wiley 42
GORDIN, Moony 106
GORDON, Mary 114
GORLEY, Ariaus 5
GORMAN, John 14
GOUDY, James 105
GOWAN, Robert 21
GRAHAM, John 82 --- 132
GRAMLING, Andrew 56
GRANVILLE COUNTY 34 38+ 64
GRAVES, George 86 Polley/Polly 86 --- 1
GRAY, Archibald 60 J 84 James 38 42 44
John 54 67 133 134 Widow 123 William 4
123 Grays point tract 57
GREAT BRITAIN 61
GREAT CANEBREAK CREEK 24
GREEN, Clement 41 69 Dicy 99 J 117+
Jacob 33+ Lucy 2 Samuel 94 Thomas 26
40 90 Wm 117
GREEN COUNTY, GA 46 50 87
GREENVILLE DISTRICT 83

GREGORY, Jonathan 73
GRICE, Barnabas 115 Deborah 80+ 84
John 80+ 84
GRIFFIN, Adino 61 62 David 61 James 5
58 Joseph 14 128 L 61 Larkin 62 71
Nicholas 37 125 Parthenia 128 Snowdon
120 William 102
GRIFFIS, Francis 97 Judith 97 L 37
Melinda 97 Nicholas 125
GRIFFITH, Henry 55 James 55 John 24
Joseph 55 William 55
GRIGSBY, --- 14
GRISOME, Ambrose 12
GROCE, Jared 6 21 44+ 45
GROVES, George 119
GRUBBS, Mary 70 71 Polly 63
GRUBS, William 92
GRUMBLE/GRUMBLES, Benjamin 48
49 65 Keziah 49 John 97
GUARDNER, ---sdell 63
GUBS, Philip 116
GUFFIN, J 118
GUIGNARD, James 75
GUITON, Jacob 5 54
GUNNELS, Avery/Avory 36Eliza 22
Sarah 22 23 Stanmore 22   creek 20 39+
83 85 114 133
GUNTER, James 117
GURGANUS, David 15 33 68 Rebecca 33
68 William 52
GWYN, Rhoda 36
HA--- pond 114
HA---, Revd Samuel 46
HACKNEY, Joseph 42 Polly 42
HADDOCKS, Moses 28
HAGENS, William (official) 3 15 29 33 44
48 66 75 76 84 133 (personal) 4 10 133
HAGOOD, Halley 38 Partin 12 Richard 58
Sarah 38+ Susan 38 William 60
HAHNBAUM, Elizabeth 8+
HAIR, Peter 94
HALF MILE BRANCH 11
HALFWAY SWAMP 18 71 92 100   creek
31 32 61 71 100
HALL, Thomas 63 William 63 75 115
HALLBACK, --- 46
HALLEY, Henry 25 William 25

HAMILTON, Delphy 86 John 58 60 74
Mathew/Matthew 115 Robert 14 118
William 115
HAMMOND, Charles (official) 20 26 36
37 40 46 49 68 70 74 75 78 79 81 112 114
119 132 (personal) 19 20 71 F 117 Isaac
75 James 78 John 65+ 71 117 Joshua 33
Leroy 20 63 65 100 115 118 126 Lewis 84
Samuel 16 118 Sarah 65 117 118
HAMMONS, Capt 20
HAMPTON, Edward 118 Elizabeth 118
Man 94 Richard 69
HANCOCK, --- 65
HANDLEY CREEK 14
HANEY, Rasha/Rasher 132
HARD LABOR CREEK 25 30 37
HARD LABOUR CREEK 10 85
HARDEN, H 84 Henry 2 11 66 67 112
Martha 2 Sarah 71 79 William 2 11 66+
67 75
HARDWICK, John 82 Widow 82
HARDY, Betcy 51 Clarissa 100 Covington
59 77 Daniel 40 59 99 Freeman 64 Jenney
51 Jermey 51 Jesse 51 John 40 77 78 99
100 Julian 51 Keziah 64 Kit 51 Lewis 131
Mary 40 Polly 51 Richard 37 125+ Robert
40 Thomas 37 William 131
HARDYS MEETING HOUSE 77
HARGROVE, Briton 14 Ealy/Elay 34 John
127 Temple 14 33 William 115
HARKINS, James 130
HARLEN/HARLIN, Jacob 36 43 45 John
43 Michael 36 45
HARLING, Jacob 7 36+
HARRIS, Charles 1 George 30 Hardy 99
125 Hezekiah 3 James 5 129 John 20 21 36
45 Joshua 2 130 Moses 103+ 133 Rachel
20 Thomas 63   --- 120
HARRISON, Benjamin 44 101 E 134
Edmd 102 Edmund 108+ James 109+ 110+
123 John 118+ Louisa 37 125 Robert 25
66 131 Sterling 37 125+ Tho 101 William
63
HARRY, Benjamin 75 76 Dorcas 76
Hannah 75 76
HART, Duke 12 119 Haartwell 119 James
24 37 113 John 72 Samuel 46   --- 22

145

HARTLEY, Daniel 130 Frederick 19
Michael 130
HATCHER, Benjamin 66 J (official) 45
70 118 (personal) 4 73 Jeremiah (official) 8
42 44 62 69 95 102 114 117 118
(personal) 28 109 Mary 66   ponds 86
tract 42
HAUPT, Woolen 123
HAUTTON, M 69
HAW BRANCH 98 99
HAW POND PLANTATION 106
HAWORTH, Jane 38+
HAYS, Dines 129
HEARD, John (official) 76 (personal) 9 51
HEARN, John 58
HEM---, --- 112
HEMPHILL, --- 1
HENDERSON, John 129 Obediah 49
Richard 63 Shade 11 Thomas 63
HENLEYS CREEK 44 118
HENSON, --- 98
HERN---, --- 112
HERN, Daniel 58
HERNDON, Abram 86 John 56 Nancy 86
HERNTON, Nancy 86
HERON, Andrew 74 122+ 123 Frances 23
24 Thomas 23 24
HERRIN, James 71 John 70 107 Peter 70
Susan 71 Thomas 23 William 16 70
HERRING, Isaac 100 James 71
HERRONDON, John 56
HEWIT, Jacob 102 103
HIBBLER, Edmund 23 Jacob 73
HIBLER, Edmund 92 Jacob 92 Thomas 92
HICKS, Armsted 110 Elizabeth 9 Jemima
9 John 9 Sarah 9
HIGGINS FERRY 69
HIGHTOWER B 81 Mrs 11
HILL, Anna 30 Anne 67 Barsheba 36 Ba-
sheba 37 Denet 100 Joel 30 131 John 59
Rhydon 32 Solomon 110 Theophilus 9
Travis 67 William 19 67 75 100 110   ---
112
HINES, Mary 103
HITT, Henry 78 John 78 Peter 78+
Susanna 78 Tillman 100
HIX, Armsted 110 Asa 5 106+ Jemmima 9

Joseph 9
HOFFER, John 42
HOGAN, Nancy 87 Ridgeway 106
William 106
HOGE, Stephen 67
HOGH, John 50 Joseph 46 50 51
HOLLAND, Edwin 66 Harfrey/Harphrey
61+ Henry 109+ 110+ 111 John 130
William 109
HOLLEMAN, Edmund 70 75
HOLLINGSWORTH, Barsheba 93 94
James 83+ John (official) 17 36 47 76 81
93 94 101 111 126 (personal) 3 33 72 76
HOLLINGWORTH, John (official) 44 53
(personal) 32 65
HOLLOW CREEK 37 76 106
HOLLOWA, John 118 122 Margaret 113
William 113 130
HOLLOWAY, Asa 6 Douglass 77 J 59
Jesse 58 59 69 John 92 Jordan (official) 9
36 44 45 50 58 74 84 90 (personal) 32 59
89 90 105 Jourdan 69 74 Lewellwyn 74
Louis 20 Ransom 69 105   --- 46 123
HOLMES, Anderson 32 Barbara 57
Edward 6 59 79+ 84 86 91 113 133
Federick 88 Frederick 88 Hardaman 48
Hardyman 47 48 Jeremiah 91 Jesse 32
John 77 Jonas 44 79 81 86 Lewis (official)
3 16 23 28 32 46 48 57-59 68 82 86 88 89
96 99 109-111 124 125 130 (personal) 32
William 32 36 79 Wyatt 47 59
HOLSENBACK, J 115
HOLSONBACK, Abraham 20 Jacob 59
Jane 20 John 59+
HOLSTEN, William 47
HOLSTON, Moses 127 Willliam 35 120
125
HOM---, Jonas 36
HOMES, Amos 91 Edward 39+ 91 Reubin
32 Wyett 91   --- 54
HOPEWELL TRACT 11
HORLBECK, Henry 26 Margaret 26
HORN/HORNE, Josiah 23 72
HORNES CREEK 19 40 48 52 62
HORNS CREEK 21 39+ 40 46 47 67 75
84 86 92+ 94 95 101 131
HORSE CREEK 1 5 25 114 118 130

146

HORSEPEN CREEK 74
HOUGH, Joseph 90
HOWARD, Richard 91 99 William 116
HOWELL, Joseph 56
HOWERTON, Joel 71 William 101 102 ---
65
HOWL, William 75
HUCKLEBERRY POND 116
HUDSON, Alsey 43 44 Ann 24 Isaac 24+
56 James 24+ 56 82 Nancy 24
HUFF, Douglas 84 115
HUFFMAN, Jacob 60
HUGHES, John 16
HUGHS, Benjamin 114 John 101
HUIET, Jacob 75
HUMPHREYS, William 80
HUMPHRIES, Margaret 92 Rachel 92
Robert 92 William 92 113
HUNT, Thomas 38+
HUNTER, A (official) 24 (personal) 23
Alexander 54 James (official) 54 112 114
118 (personal) 51 ---mes 106
HURRICANE BRANCH 49
HURST, Silas 122
HURT/HURTT, William (official) 12 13
19 55 74 98 107 114 116 118 119 120 122
123
HUSKEY, James 33 34
HUTCHENSON, Adam 13
HUTCHINSON, Adam 62
HUTCHISON, Adams 61
IKENER, Philip 84 85
IKNER, Philip/Phillip 47 48 112
INDIAN CREEK 17 18 131
INGRAM, John 41
INLOW, John 41
INNES, David 15
ISLAND ROAD 110
IVY ISLAND 61+
IZARD, B 103
JACK BRANCH 127
JACKSON, Aaron 113 David 83 Ebenezer
1 Walter 108 William 55 56+ ---nes 55
Moses 44
JACOBS, Moses 44
JAMES, Widow 35
JAY, Christian 68 Jesse 68

JEFFCOAT, --- 35
JEFFERSON COUNTY, GA 6
JEFFERSON COUNTY, MS 104 129
JEFFERSON SREET 3 14 87 102 108+
JENINGS, Henry 92
JENKINS, Alexander 9 25 Ann 43+ Esther
43 James 43+ 67 John 43+ 66 Jonas 39 62
Martha 43 Sampson 66 67 Samuel 43+ 67
Sarah 43
JENNING, Jesse 131 Robert 123
JENNINGS, Elizabeth 29 Henry 115+ 116
Jeremiah 29 116 Jesse 80 John 80 Thomas
29 116 William 123
JERVEY, James 41
JESTER, Levi 8 28 72 Polly 59 Rozannah
28 Thomas 59
JETER, John 6 13 14 38+ 49 62 63 67 72
87 94 95 107 W (official) 61 93 95
(personal) 29 William (official) 18 93
(personal) 101 133
JILLSON, Alex 68
JINKINS, Alexander 82
JINN BRANCH 68
JOHNS, Elizabeth 118 James 132 Obediah
118 119 Robert 112 William 132
JOHNSON, Arnold 29 Burrel 85 Daniel
115 Edward 29 30 116+ Francis 66 George
9 Haley/Haly 68 85 93 103 129 Jesse 30
120 122 John 47 73 100 115 Judge 81
Major 82 Mary 47 57 113 Ned 30 Philip
122 Richard 21 81 101 Samuel 115 Sarah
51 Stephen 24 Theophilus 44 William 51
67 68 75 100
JOHNSTON, Arnold 36 Edward 30
Howell 29 Jacob 29 30 Jesse 29 122 John
55+ Keziah 126 Richard 56 90 Widow 90
William 41
JONES, Abiah 93 Charles 22 45 47 103
104 Clainy[Clairy?] 5 Clary 72 Edward 67
Ephraim 93 George 1 Godfrey 32 Henry
110+ Hicks 77 James 5 54 57 76 John 5
40+ 54 Mary 54 93 Mathew 88 Mathias/
Matthias 35 57 58+ 69 72 88+ 98+ 129
130 Nancey 45 47 Nancy 104 Noble 1
Obadiah (official) 41 Perrin 47 Quintina 77
Richard 78 88 Sarah 1 98 120 Sion 5
Susannah 54 Theophiulus 110 Thomas 53

147

133 W 98 Widow 96 William 53 54 61 98
103 104 120 Wright 13 --- 60+ 61 72 90
JONES COUNTY, GA 124
JOPP, Andrew 15
JORDAN, William 83
JORDIN, John 127 Polly Ann 127
JUDGE, Thomas 100 102
JURRELL, Benjamin 65
KAIRDEN, William 82
KATE, Betty 126 Huldah 124 126 Libby
126 Robert 124 126+ 127 Sibby 127
William 124 127
KEADLE, George 51
KEDDINGFIELD TRACT 42
KEEL, John 92
KEELING, Edmund 68+
KEILING, Edmund 4
KELLEY, Esther 80 Martin 81 Salley 58
Thomas 81 William 16+ 17 58
KELLY, Sally 58 William 16 57+
KELTISON, Michael 82
KEMP, Richard 127 Starling 21 Wiley 124
127
KENEDAS, --- 33
KENNEDY, John 9 Richard 104
KENNEY, John 93+ 94 Rachel 93 94
KENP, Wiley [see Kemp]
KENTUCKY 10+ 37 61
KERBEE, James 35
KERBLAY, Jeane 78 79
KEY, Gabriel 99 Henry 53 70 74 75 83
99+ 125+ 126 James 115 John 82 92 115+
116 125 Joshua 39 40 119 Martha 39 111
Robert 36 Samuel 99 Tandy 40+ 99+
Thomas (official) 21 26 39 41 (personal)
24 William 40 99
KILCREASE/KILLCREASE, Abraham/
Abram 59 68 James 114 John 20 26 29+
37 68+ Mary 37 114 Miner 81 Obediah 6
59 Thomas 36 86 William 53
KILLGORE, Josiah 38
KILLOCH, Lemuel 1 Maria 1
KIMBER, John 120
KIMBRELL, John 23
KINARD, Christiana 114 John 114
KING, Amelia 35 Avarilla 28 Henry 4 28
75 James 120 Mary 28 128

KINSLOW, John 26
KIRBY, James 103
KIRKLAND, Aaron 61 Benj 109 Elizabeth
57 Isaac (official) 85 (personal) 21 35 56
85+ 96 Moses 72 90 Reuben 16 Zechariah
85 --- 116
KIRKSEY, John 5
KITSON, George 26 Sally 26
KITTING, Francis 123
KORER & LINDSEY 132
KUNN, Valentine 41
LABORD, Peter 108
LABORDE, P 52 Peter 72 73 108
LABOURD, Peter 102 118
LAGRONE, David 91
LAIN, John 70
LAKE, Joseph 127
LAKEY, Thomas 58
LAMAR, Edmund 24 Eliza 127 James 118
Lydia 51 Mack 51 Philip 106 Phillip 5 51
54 Rebecah 51 Robert 127 Thomas 1 87
106 ferry 42
LAMBARD, Uriah 55
LAMKIN, George 2 3 65 James 65 Peter
(official) 3 13 25 30 35 58 61 85 123 130
Susannah 2 3 65 road 119
LANCASTER, ENGLAND 13
LANDERM, Absalom 32
LANDRUM, Abner 14 15+ 34 35 54 94+
95 96 103 Amos 23 85 96+ John 94 117+
Reuben 93 112
LANG, L 126 Robert (official) 3 66 71-73
77 78 88 95 102 114 (personal) 16 26 39+
--- 106
LANGDON, John 107
LANGLEY, Isum 55+ Josiah 8 123
LANSDON, John 107
LARAMAN/LARIMAN/LARIMON,
Barbara 50 Hixey 56 William 56
LARK, A 130 Andrew 113 Elizabeth 23
John (official) 43 72 81 82 89 92 99 113
122 (personal) 32 37 113 124 125 130 ---
123
LASER, James 20
LASSETER CREEK 121
LASURE, Murtle 132
LAURENCE DISTRICT 22 103 104

148

LAURENS DISTRICT 82
LAWEDS CREEK 20
LEAVENWORTH, Meline 112 Melines 118
LEE, John 95 111 114 132 F 134 Mary 95 Reuben 111 ferry 70
LEEK, John 109
LEIGH, Walter 78
LEMAR, William 61
LESESNE, Ann 34 Hannah 22 34+ Isaac 22 23 34+ 54+ 65 Mary 34
LESSENDRUM, SCOTLAND 13
LESSESNE, Isaac 20
LEVINGSTON, Toliver 5
LETCHER, Agness 37 125+ Mrs 37 Willa 125+
LEVENWORTH, Melines 51
LEVINGSTON, Tal° 44 William 38
LEWIS, Ann 112 Charlotte 24 John 4 5 82 101 Latisia/Lettina 5 Richard 15 95 William 27
LEXINGTON DISTGRICT 9 55 114 119 122
LICK branch 85 creek 26 70 114 fork 40+
LIGHTFOOT, Benskin 73 Philip 104
LIMBECKER, Charles 46+ Christian 77 Jonathan 46+ 77 132
LINCH, Milly 10 Thomas 53
LINDSAY, Benjamin 67 William 67
LINDSEY, Benjamin 44 Edward 26 Elizabeth 44 --- 132
LINDY, Nehemiah 26
LINEAR, Betsy 64 Lewis 64 Patsey 64 Robert 64 Silas 64
LIPSCOMB, John 87 121 Nathan (official) 21 44 58 62
LITTLE, William 128
LITTLE BULL BRANCH 68
LITTLE CREEK 4
LITTLE MOUNTAIN CREEK 35 36 44
LITTLE ROCKEY CREEK 72
LITTLE SALUDA RIVER 4 16-18 24+ 27+ 28+ 43 46 50 57 62+ 68 74+ 75 80 89-91+ 95 96 98-100 102 103 106 116 117+-120 122 124+ 128 129+ 131+
LITTLE SALUDY RIVER 103
LITTLE STEPHENS CREEK 15 23 107

LITTLE STEPHENS MTG HOUSE 15
LITTLE STEVENS CREEK 33+ 42 105+ 106 112
LITTLE TURKEY CREEK 43+
LITTLEFIELD, Absalum 122
LIVERPOOL, England 13
LOACH, Samuel 113 William 119 120+
LOANHEAD, SCOTLAND 15
LOCKHART, Samuel 45
LOCKWOOD, Joshua 17
LOFTEN/LOFTIN, John 75 93
LOFTON, John 33 75 103 Robert 75 ---19
LOG CREEK 3 20 36 54 93
LOGAN, Catharine 54 64 65 George 65 John 54 64 65 William 103 116 129 ---34
LOGIN, John 20
LOMAX, William 45
LONG, Jacob 114 116 James 20
LONG BRANCH 109 110+ 111
LONG CAIN ROAD 31+ 89 93
LONG CANE branch 76 road 5 35 36 42
LONG MEADOWS BRANCH 95
LONG POND 40
LONGMIRE, George 51 Charlotte 64 Hannah 70 John 64 69 70 Matilda 64 William 104
LONGSTREET, James 111 112 William 51
LORICK, Jacob 91
LORT, Arthur 95
LOTT, Emsley 85 creek 130
LOVELACE, D 90 John (official) 80 (personal) 73
LOVELESS, Aaron 79 112 Benjamin 16 D 90 David 48 John (official) 3 7 9 17 25 28 57 58 60 61 63 73 85 88 91 115 127 William 7
LOW PLACE 121
LOW/LOWE, Anthony 30 130 131 Elizabeth 53 Francis 53 H (official) 14 Henry 13 48 John 19 126 Nicholas 47 Rebecca 130
LOWERY/LOWRY, Conrad 104 Conrod 23 34 105 106 George 34 105 106 Jacob 105+ 106 Robert 22 76 Sarah 22
LOYDS CREEK 70 74 75 126
LUCAS, Solomon 86 87

149

LUNDAY, Hezekiah 39+ Nehemiah 26
LUNENBURGH COUNTY, VA 12 52
LYON, Elijah 1 Jincey 64 John (official) 2
3 10 25 29 30 37 42 46 54 59 62 64 65 66
70 79 83 85 115 116 125 126 130 131
(personal) 69 70 74 83 92 128 Mary 56
MACHIN, Edward 70
MACKAY, Alexander 7
MACKBEES CREEK 7
MACKEY, John 106 --- 55 107
MADISON CO, MS TERR. 1 11 41
MADISON STREET 3 102
MAGNESS, George 19
MAIRHEAD, James 88
MALLET, Abraham 76 Joicy/Joycy 76
MANN, Elizabeth 132 Gilbert 132 Joel 50
Watts 114 132 William 46 50
MANUMISSIONS 2 92 97
MARBARY, Thomas 55 56+
MARBERRY, Reuben 92
MARIS, Simon 45
MARKES, Andrew 34
MARKS, --- 23
MARLER, William 35
MARLOW, William 55
MARQUIS, Dahl 40
MARSH, Martha 104 Samuel 49 50 70 72
77 94+ 104 111 Robert 131 Thomas 110
MARSHALL, Allen 83 br 77 cr 67 132
MARSHAND, Samuel 75
MARSTON, B 45
MARTIN, Abram 65 Absalom 19 Ben-
jamin 19 40+ Charles 42 David 129 Ed-
mund 19 28 29 Elizabeth 26 Enoch 121
George 19 83 Henry 16 19+ 66 Israel 12
13+ J 103 Jacob 67 James 16+ 26 32 63 70
126 John 37 50 69 Joshua 91 106 Lewis
40+ 99+ Marshal/Marshall 28 29 Matt
(official) 53 (personal) 114 Moab 19 105
Nancy 67 Prudence 42 Reeves 5 Robert 29
Sally 19 Sarah 49 Simon 118 Temple 105
Thomas 19 105 William 16 40 --- 37 128+
MARTIN BRANCH 127
MARTINTOWN 40 road 16+ 19 21 26 71
100
MARYLAND 18 19 22
MASON, John 73 75

MASSEY, Thomas 13
MATHESON, Duncan 75
MATHEWS, Daniel 91 Drury 107 122
Lewis 80 Sugar 72 William 63 107
MATHEWS ROAD 107
MATHIS, Abram 51 Henry 112 Mark 5
6+
MATTHEWS, Drury 127 James 58 Mark
6 Sugar 71 131 road 14 33
MAUL, James 101
MAULDEN, Caleb 27 43 James 45 83
MAULDIN, Judith 44
MAULL, James 16
MAY, Charles 33 James 77 86 John 33
Peter 78 William 69 --- 50
MAYES, Mathew 114
MAYS, Abney 18+ Mathew 100 Matthew
22 77 Samuel (official) 28 (personal) 109
117 Stephen 18 22 William 18 61 84
MAYSON, Archey 5 30 71 Ch (official)
92 Charles 46 73 James 30 John 5 24 25
73 Ramsay 25 Willis 46
MAZYCK, Benjamin 10 Daniel 59 77
Peter 26
MAZ---, William 77
McADAM, John 13
McCAIN, John 36
McCALL, Jos 66
McCARRY, John 5 31+
McCART, James 131
McCARTES, Widow 116
McCARTEY, Amos 57+ James 122
Michael 123 126 Philip 122 123 126
McCARTIE, Dennis 127
McCARTY, Dennis 12 Edward 123 Phillip
62 William 13
McCLENDON, Allen 8 67 Ezekiel 8 10 48
52 65 88 117 Henry 109 Jesse 67 Joel 8
William 3 9+ 25 70
McCOOLE, John 11
McCOXON, Levi 70
McCOYS ferry 78 road 78
McCRACKEN, James 73
McCRELESS, Surles 113
McDANIEL, Anguish 15 68 Angus 3 Anna
33 Edward 48 81 John 20 21 75 Levi 39+
47 48 81 83 84 85 Mary 21 Thomas 15

William 20
McDANIELL, William 69
McDOWALL, Patrick 75
McDOWEL, William 51
McDUFFIE, George 11
McEACKIN, A 109
McGINNIS, Hannah 93
McGITTON, Andrew 95
McHAN, Mark 44
McHANN, M 109
McKEE, Daniel 128 Lucy 128
McKELLER, John 124
\McKEY, Archd 88
McKIE, Daniel 8
McKINNE, Benjamin 35 Joseph 35 --- 1
McKINNEY, William 78
McKINNIE, Roger 123
McKINZE, Charles 64
McMANUS, John 15
McMILIAN, Elizabeth 127
McMILLIAN, Abner 11 12 77 78 127
McMILLION, Abner 11
McPATRICK, --- 76
McWATHEE, Doc 119
McWHORTER, A 78 Alexander 73 D 48
Dr 63
MEAD, --- 1
MEADOWS, Richard 86
MEALER, Elizabeth 118
MEALING, Joseph 26 46
MECLENDEL, Henry 89
MEDLOCK, Benjamin 46 117+ Moses
124 Samuel 7 46 124 Stephen 20 21 23 ---
80
MEE, George 127
MEEK, John 121 122
MEGEE, --- 107
MEGEHE, David 55
MEGINIS, Mrs 90
MELTON, Benjamin 56 Matthew 23
MERCHANT, Messer 128 Sarah 34 ---
128 129
MERIDITH, James 15
MERIT, William 112
MERIWEATHER, Thomas (official) 24
(personal) 8
MERIWETHER, Thomas 2 119 121

MERRING, John 57
MERRIT, William 112
MESSER, John 116 Joseph 106 107
Samuel 116+ William 116 pond 120
MESSERSMITH, John 23 34
MEYER, Jonathan 37
MEYERS, David 37 James 69
MICHAEL, --- 55
MICHEL, Abraham 98
MICHELL, William 107
MIDDLE CREEK 59+ 64 76 103
MIDDLEBROOKS, William (official) 124
MIDDLETON, Adness 86 Arthur 58
Henry 72 Hugh 86 John (official) 120
(personal) 86 119 Polly 86 Widow 86
MILES, Aquila 39+ Aquilla 71 82
Augustus 40 Lewis (official) 34 35 56 75
(personal) 39 Sally 39 --- 80
MILL branch 118 creek 3 9 56 82
MILLER, Capt 88 George 81 James 57 59
113 John 21 Polley/Polly 67 Zachariah 98
107+ --- 14 107
MILLS, Ambrose 57 Barbary 117 John
108 117 Morgan 50 117 William 117
MILLWEE, James 64
MILTON, William 88
MIMS, Briton 46 David 72 Drury 19 46
72 Eliza 4 72 John 33 46 72 Livingston 22
M (official) 1 2 5 6 8 11 14 15 17 18 22-
24 29 30 32 33 36-38 42 44 46 47 49-52
54 56 59 60 63 66-70 72 73 75 77-79 82
84 86-88 94-97 99 102 104 105 107-109
111 114-116 118 120 127 128 132 133
(personal) 62 133 134 Matthew (official) 4
14 19 21 22 44 68 69 80 81 84 93 96 108
123 124 (personal) 3 4 44 68 72   --- 47
MINE CREEK 16 22 24 27 28 43 70 81
113
MINER, Stuard 50
MINOR, Alias/Elias 29 Nicholas 29+
Stewart 46
MINTER, Bethuley 32 Ebenezer 111
James 111 113 John 111 Mackeness/
Mackerness 111 Mackness 99 Macness 79
Martha 111 Permelia 111 Rebecca 111
William 79 111 115 116
MISSISSIPPI TERRITORY 1 11 33 41 70

151

74 88 STATE 104 129
MISSORS BRANCH 95
MITCHELL, Abraham 54 55 Abram 107
Anderson 116 Fon--- 55 Forrest 107
Hinchey 13 14 15 108 116 Jeremiah 15
Jesse 74 John 45 Martha 93 Polly 55
Samuel 33 Sion 107 Starling/Sterling 67 93
Thomas 66 William 55 107
MIXSON, John 67
MOBLEY, Anson 68 Jeremiah 20 80 John
28 68 Lewis 80 129
MOBLY, --- 46
MOCK, John 133
MOHEAD, James 88
MONDAY, David 56
MONING, John 57
MONK, Isaac 109 110 111 John 61+ 109+
110+ 111 Joahua 30 61 109+ 110+ 111+
Sarah 110+ 111 Sary 61 109 mill 110
MONROE STREET 72 73
MONROUGH CO, MS TERR 70 74
MONTAGUE, Charles (official) 111 129
MONTGOMERY, Benjamin 73
MOO---, --- 118
MOORE, A 87 Arvin 9 James 5 25 Davis
133 John 38+ 39+ 46 73 84 100 115 126
Jonathan 44 45 79 80 Rebeccah/Rebeckah
59 William 2 40 42 67 97+ 132 133
MOORES CREEK 53 63 120+ 127
MOORS CREEK 74 124
MORGAN, Eli 33 Evan 40 John 16 70 75
83 Nias 123 William 32 40 80 81 --- 54
100
MORING, John 58
MORIS, Joseph 92
MORKLEY, --- 115
MORNING, John 102 William 102
MORRING, John 57
MORRIS, Ezekiel 31 James 1 103 John 41
Jordan 92 Joseph 30 32 71 92 122 Thomas
(official) 19 (personal) 19 William 1 11 82
105 --- 9 72 103
MORTAN, W 19
MORTON, John 10 Thomas 2 65
MOSELEY/MOSELY, Absalom 69 Daniel
4 Hugh 83 James 39+ John 8 28 --- 53+
MOSES, --- 76

MOSLEY, Absalom 69 George 105+ 106
133 Hugh 105 John 123 Nancy 133
Thomas 115
MOSS, Hugh 133 --- 53 branch 107
MOULTRIE, Gov William (official) 16 17
26 28 39+ 61+ 44 55 58 87 109 111 112
116 127 128
MOULTREY, Gov Wm 110
MOUNT VINTAGE 81
MOUNT WILLING 87
MOUNTAIN CREEK 7 14 36+ 44 45 59
60+ 68 74
MUCKLE, William 127
MUD CREEK 57
MUIRHEAD, James 60 61 Mary 60
MULTREE, Gov Wm (official) 107
MUNDAY, --- 78
MURPHEY, John 33 115
MURRAH, Thomas 16 19 40
MURRAY, Andrew 57 David 67 James 57
58+
MURRELL, Benjamin 54 65 John 80
MUSGROVE, J 126
MUSTER GROUND BRANCH 131
MYERS, James 30
MYRICK, Lyttelton/Lyttleton 44 45
NAGEL, Augustus 3 26 36 62 63 70 87
102
NAIL, Casper 127
NANCE, F 128 Frederick 128
NAPPER, Absalom 32 69 94 Elizabeth 32
NATCHEZ, MS 129
NEAL, Hugh 7
NEALE, Charles 7
NEGEL, John 72
NELSON, James 85 W 85
NEW MARKET ROAD 75 108
NEWBERRY DISTRICT 37 44 53+ 58 71
91 126 127
NEWBURY DISTRICT 128+
NEWMAN, Patty 119 Reuben 29 Richard
79
NEWPORT, Robert 24 27 68
NEWSOM, Anselm 68
NIBBS, William (official) 4 (personal) 73
NICHOLS, Jefferson 36
NICHOLSON, David 9 33 89 Davis 89

Elizabeth 72 J 23 James 45 Joseph 34
Josiah 23 72 Latisha 72 Mrs 8 Right 59
Shemuel 23 34 41 42 72 104 105+
Theophilus 23 Urbane 2 49 50+ William
51 Wright 34 51
NINETY SIX CREEK 5 14 25 44 45 60
71 90 118 128
NINETY SIX DISTRICT 26 38+ 42 55
NIX, Charles 12+ 16 36 37 42 92 115+
133 Martin 12+ Mary 115
NIXON, Alexander 76+ 116 Elizabeth 76
H 104 Hugh 22 76+ 104+ Robert 78
Thomas 76+ W 45 64 103 William 76+
NOBLE, --- 51 63
NOBLES, Elizabeth 59 John 84 Joseph
132 133 Josiah 116+ Lewis 47 66 81 100
Zephanah 44   --- 71+ 75 79
NORDAN, Thomas 34
NORRED, Millican 24 128 Samuel 24 56
NORRIS, Nathan (official) 21 26 30 48 63
92 99 107 114 124 126 127 132 (personal)
118 119+ 122 William 48
NORTON, Thomas 34 William 96
NORWOOD, Beaufort 69
NOTT, Abram 73
NOWLAND, Dennis 52
NUETONS OLD PLACE 28
NUNN, G 37 George 22 Joseph 22 37
Phillip 37 William 22
NUSOM, Anselm 97 William 97
OAK & HICKORY TRACT 37
OBICKLEY, Waller 80
ODEN, Hezekiah 20 Thomas 20 24
Dildatha 16 89 James 35 Martha 7 8+ 17+
25 Mary 124 Moses 35 Richard 123 124
William 35 Willis 42
ODON, Alexander 121
ODUM, Martha 25 William 91
OENBEY, W 64
OGILVIE, James 24 Thomas 32
OHARA, Cynthia 108 James 27 108
OHARRA, James 24
OHARROW, Cynthia 108 James 27 108
OLD FIELD FISHERY 101 102
OLD/OLDS, Ann 102 William (official) 20
(personal) 11 49 102
OLIPHANT, William 5 31

OLIVER, Dionysius (official) 35
(personal) 2 11 Thomas 69 118
ONEALE, Charles (official) 2 8 13 58 72
120 (personal) 21 98+ 99 102 Mary 8 99
ONEALL, Charles 98+ 102 103 106
ORANGEBURGH DISTRICT 37 60 61
88+ 112 116 117
OSBORN, Brittain 27
OSBORNE, David 28
OUTS, Martin 41
OUTZ, David 111
OWEN, Jonathan 118
PACE, Drury 26   br 79 ferry 42 road 68
PADGET, Job 134 Mark 63 120+ Samuel
119 120+
PADJETT, Mark 120
PAINE, Jesse 60 William 131
PALMER, Dabney 36 Elisha 24 Elizabeth
46 Hezekiah 46 Martha 29 Wilson 29
PALMORE, Clarisy 84 Nancy 11
PANTELOW, --- 19
PANTHER BRANCH 49+ 121
PANTON, Ann 9 101 James 9+ 71 76 100
102
PARDUE, Elizabeth 52 Fields 108 Joel 4
Sarah 52 108+
PARK/PARKE, Rachael/Rachel 128
PARKER, Daniel 95 Elizabeth 11 65 66+
67 95 George 2 10 11 22 65 66+ 67 71
Isaac 10 11 65 66+ 67 James 95 William
85   --- 51
PARKINS, Charles 87
PARKMAN, Charles 33 Charlesey 33
Daniel 33 46 David 68 Henry 7 32 33 35
36+ 44 130 Izebel 33 John 33 Lucretia 33
Lydia 32 33 Massa 36 Serana 32 33
PARMER, Dabney 74 William 85
PARSONS, James 18 19 21+
PARTAIN, William 33
PARTIN, Ch 27 James 86
PARTRICK, George 97+
PATES, Margaret 10+ Reuben 10+
PATRICK, Lewellen 58
PATTERSON, A 37 Thomas 6 West 32 88
PATTON, Thomas 113
PAULETT, John (official) 6
PAY, H 57 Henry 9

153

PAYNE, James 14 118
PEARS, --- 123
PEARSON, Abel 24 43 Joseph 62
PELOQUIN, George 38
PENDLETON DISTRICT 82 101 109+
PENN, Thomas 56 creek 46
PENNSYLVANIA 40
PEPPERS BRANCH 5
PERDUE, Jack 28 Joel 28
PERMENTER, James 32 John 32
PERRIN, Robert 69 Samuel (official) 84
(personal) 10 William 10 --- 37
PERRIS, Abner 10
PERRY, Allen 72 Andrew 35 57 78+ 130
Crawford 55 Ezekiel 35 98+ Martha 8
Mary 8 17+ 25
PERRYMAN, Mumford (official) 27 28
31 41 46 74 (personal) 24 28 113 --- 22
PERSIMMON branch 100+ creek 100
PERSIMON LICK CREEK 53+
PETERS CREEK 58
PETERSBURGH, GA 123+ 124
PETERSON, John (official) 117 131
(personal) 41+ 42 Martha 117
PETRE/PETREE, George 34+
PETTICES TRACT 76
PEWS, Widow 82
PHELPS, Aaron 73 Mary Ann 73
PHILLIPS, Ralph 20
PICKENS, Gov . A 66
PICKET, James 76
PIERCE, Abram 65 John 63 65 78 117
119 Thomas 123
PIKE, Margaret 89 William 89 creek 38 54
PINCKNEY, Charles (official) 26 27 85
96 131 Thomas (official) 12 27+ 128+
PINE HOUSE 62
PINES, Wheaton 26
PINEWOOD HOUSE 79
PINKETT, Thomas 4
PITMAN, Jesse 69
PITT, --- 34
PITTS, Jesse 26 27+ 28 122 Thomas 24
28 31 William 31
PIXLEY, Stephen 3 107 134
POINDEXTER, Thomas 55
POINT LOOKOUT 54

POLLARD, Austin 30
POND, Abraham 38 William 11
POOL, Hulday 72 John 71 72
POPE, Elijah 131 Elizabeth 90 George 129
Helen 90 Henry 27 Jacob 129 131 John
(official) 131 (personal) 12 24 26 27+ 62
68 74 113 117+ 128+ 129 131 Marget 129
Sampson (official) 18+ 27 87 90 91 128+
(personal) 24+ 43 89 90 96 97 128+ 129
Solomon 129
PORCHER, Peter 10
PORTER, Nathan 27 Polly 27
POSEY, Absalom 110+ William 110 br 52
POW, John 37
POWEL, Bartlet 116 Elkanah 90 Lewis
119 Martin 116 Milley 116 Nathaniel 26
Rhody 91 Seborn 106+ --- 89 118
POWELL, George 80 --- 54
PRESCOAT, Moses 107+
PRESCOT, Moses 26
PRESCOTT, Moses 56 107 William 32
PRESLEY, John 113 Thomas 15+ 95 103
PRICE, Ambrose 79 Christopher 104 Dan-
iel 12 104+ Nancy 131 Pamela 104 Phera-
by 104 Saml 130 131 Spear (official) 44
62 (personal) 80 91 131 Thomas (official)
12 19 29 37 40 42 45 59 64 68 76 97 104
116 (personal) 16 William 78 131
PRINCE GEORGE CO, MD 18 19 22
PRINGLE, Robert 98 99
PRIOR, John 121
PUCKETT, Russell 129
PURKINS, Charles 91 ford 28
PURSELL, John 39 William 21 46+
PURVES, John 31 38+
PURVIS, John 31
PUTNAM County, GA 46 88 124
PYNES, Wheaton 26
QUARLES, Hamblen 100 James 131 John
23 Richard 2 86 Sally 30 Samuel 25 40
104 Sarah 23 86 William 25 65
RABORN, William 7+ Susanna 7+
RABUN, John 127
RACKFORD, Adalied 31 32
RADFORD, Smith 86
RAIFORD, Philip 80 Phillip 8
RAINEY, Jesse 122

ROFF, Francis 123
ROGERS, Daniel 31 34 Elijah 130 James (official) 20 Thomas 94 Richard 114 ---77
RONGASS, John 38
ROPER, Joel 65 75
ROSE, Hugh 112
ROSS, David 63 John 71 Osmund 24 Thomas 63 64 William 13 75
ROTTIN, John 130
ROUNDTREE, Jethro 2 11
ROUNTREE, Daniel 85 Dudley 114 John 5 106
ROWAN, William 10+
ROWE, Samuel 22
ROWEL, Edward 127
ROWLS, Phillip 48
RUDULPH, Zebulon 24+ 74 96
RUMLEY, Elisha 120 Nancy 120
RUNNELS, Joseph 130 --- 91
RUSH, David 83 84
RUSHTON, Hannah 63 James 63 John 63 Joseph 63 64 Nathan 63 64 William 63 64
RUSSELL, --- 40
RUSTIN, James 43
RUSTON, Daniel 8 28 James 124 125 Rachael/Rachel 125 Thomas 123
RUT, John 95
RUTHERFORD, Joseph 55
RUTLAND, Abraham 2 3+ 9 57 82 Martha 82
RUTLEDGE, Gov (official) 12 27 John 41
RYAN, Benjamin 17 49 50 75 86 104 105 115 John 20 23 95 108 Lacon 75 115 --67
SADDLER, Isaac 50 --- 50
SADLER, Isaac 28 William 28
SALE, John 46
SALMON, Hezekiah 22
SALTER, John 89
SAMFORD, Asa 18+ Jesse 17
SAMUEL, Beaverly/Beverly 108 120 133 John 133 Lucy 133 Maria 133 Robert 133 Walker 133 William (official) 25 (personal) 47 65 66+ ---ert 56
SANDERS, James 10 25 60 126 John 130
SANDY, James 60
SANSUM, Murtle 25
SANTEE RIVER 106

SATCHER, Amos 91 98 99 113 123 130
SAVAGE, Frances 23 Robert 101 102 Samuel 23 62 75 --- 71
SAVANNAH, GA 5 13
SAWYER, Anel 48 Ansel 92 119 Benjamin 12 Elkanah (official) 26 91 98 (personal) 118+ 119+ 127 George 92 John 119+ Lewis 122 124 Marium 119 Ralph 26
SAXON, William 106
SCARBOROUGH, Sarah 16
SCEIBLES, William 51
SCOTLAND 13 15 61
SCOTT, Col 42 Franklin 45 ira 17 25+ 61 James 39 44 77 Jenny 115 John 95 Mary 115 R 33 Robert 34 78 105 Samuel 44 120
SCOTT COUNTY, KENTUCKY 10
SCOTTS BIG SURVEY 42
SCRUGGS, Matt 53
SCURRY, Ralf 131 Thomas 106
SEARLES, John 42 Covington 32
SEGLER, Nicholas 107
SEIBLES, Martha 112 William 112
SEIGH---, --- 40
SETTLE, E (official) 19 37+ 83 Edward 2 3 11 83 115 116 130 Martha 116
SETTLES, Francis 2 11 pond 11
SHACKELFORD, James 25
SHANNON, William 22 45 104
SHARPTON, Jeff 121 Jeptha 120 Mary 39+
SHAW, Christopher 2 Hobson/Holson 104 129 Saxon/Saxton 104 129 Thomas 25 112 113+ 121 Thompson 104 129 William 71 73 creek 35 48 52 62 80 85+ 94 96+ 108 115
SHEETS BRANCH 9
SHEIRER, John 13
SHEPHERD, Sarah/Sary 128 William 128
SHIBBLEY, J 70
SHIVELY, Jacob 70 John 84
SHOCKLEY, --- 31
SHOEMAKER, John 23
SHORES, Willis 4
SHOTS, Daniel 30
SHRIRAH, Charles 26
SHULTZ, Henry 3 11 70 102
SIGLAR, Nicholas 98

156

SILVER BLUFF 76
SIMKINS, Arthur 14 24 43 67 68 87+ 102
108 114 Charles 48 Eldred (official) 4 15
28 48 72 73 (personal) 11 13 14 34 72 73
94+ 102 108+ Jesse 25 61 John 34 87
Mary 114 --- 24 34+ 49 96
SIMPSON, James 38 John 13
SIMSON, James 46 59
SINGLETON, Benjamin 124 Eliza 124
Enoch 51 81 James 124 Leroy 124 Polly
51 Samuel 124 --- 65
SIZEMORE, Henry 2 11
SKANNEL, Abel 60 Loyd 60
SKRINE, Thomas 82
SLAIT BRANCH 62
SLAPPY, Frederick 123
SLAVES: ---LEASEN 121 Aaron 74 Abel
74 Abram 24 79 Ader 99 Allen 97 Alley
124 Alsea 121 Amey 6 132 Amy 5 7 69
121 Anderson 97 116 Andrew 97 121 Ann
76 Anna 57 Arena 84 Arther 69 Atterman
49 Belfast 45 Benjamin 41 Bill 121 Bristol
45 Briton 79 Cain 74 Charitas 8 Charles
41 74 Charlotte 41 Cipis 45 Clarasa 69
Clarisy 5 6 Creasy 24 Creese 125 Cu--- 7
Darcas 74 Dave 94 99 David 49 Davy 121
Delphy 121 Diana 76 Diannah 69 Dice 35
Dick 116 Dilly 8 Dina 92 Dolly 121
Dorces 69 Dorkas 80 Draper 84 Edmond
74 Edmund 79 Eliza 94+ Emily 31 Ephr---
69 Fanny 112 113 121 132 Farmer 45
Fenah 57 Fenar 8 Flora 6 Frances 82
Gabriel 84 George 84 Gerry 17 Goodwin 7
Gower 45 Hannah 10 50 67 Harry 6 29 49
Henry 6 121 Hnchan 97 Isaac 24 Jack 24
31 121 124 Jacob 29 38 69 James 121
Jenny 57 Jerry 84 Jim 57 132 Joe 47 John
6 Jude 64 Juner 7 Juno 121 Kezziah 74
Kissey 108 Kitty 79 Leavy 69 Let 24
Lewis 74 Limerick 45 London 45 Louis
121 Louisa 31 100 Lucy 5 6 69 76 121
Lucinda 92 Lydia 29 121 Malinda 121
Mar--et 57 March 2 Maria 41 Mariah 100
Marmaduke 92 Mary 6 41 92 97 Mathew
16 Matilda 84 Matildy 82 Michiel 82 Mick
45 Milley 12 Milly 50 Molley 78 Molly 69
78 Morris 78 Muggy 8 Nan 7 Nancy 31 57
Ned 132 Nell 121 Pascal 132 Patty 57
Peter 31+ Phebe 121 Pheby 97 Phil 97
Phillis 8 31 Polladore 105 Pompey 6
Pompy 45 Queen 79 Rainy 8 Randol 97
Robert 64 69 Rose 6 30 Rozetta 69 Ruth
82 Sally 6 78 Sam 25 Sandy 45 Sarah 41
92 132 Sealy 121 Sicily 84 Silvy 49 Squire
97 Stephen 6 Sulta 41 Susan 41 Susannah
97 132 Susasa 69 Sylvia 7 Tab 38 Tobe 80
Tom 57 74 132 Tony 45 Violet 84 Wash-
ington 31 84 Will 69 97 121 William 82
Willice 7 Willis 6 Winney 29 52 97 Winny
97 Worley 6 Writter 84 Young Abram 24
SLEEPY CREEK 4 14+ 23 33 35 41 42
107 127
SLOAN/SLONE, John 110+
SMART, Joseph 70 126 Margaret 126
SMELDES, John 129
SMILEY, James 15
SMITH, Anna 121 Daniel 95+ 119 120+
Dorcas 12 13 Elijah 3 Elisha 52 Elizabeth
13 George (official) 88 130 (personal) 60
Gilbert 53 Jacob 24 47 87 89 112 121 122
126 James 58 92 104 Jeney 134 John 14
129 Jordan 12 13 Joseph 87 Lot 36 Lott 60
Luke 30 43 62 87 121 Margarett 106
Moses 51 Rachael 120 Rachel 120 Sarah
30 47 121 Sarry 52 Simon 53 Stephen 36
60 114 Wilken 134 Wilkin 13 119 William
(official) 51 (personal) 51 53 69 127 ---
31 54 120
SNEAD, Susan 66
SNEED, John 95
SORGEE, William 59
SOTCHER, Amos 27 81 82 Samuel 81
SPANN, Elizabeth 20 Henry 3 9 25 57
58+ 72 89 James 20 49 John 49
SPANN'S SPRING BRANCH 58
SPARTANBURGH co 110+ dist 56
SPEER, Robert 54 William 54
SPENCE, John 15 Robert 129
SPENCER, Hannah 96 97 Joel 62 Shep-
herd (official) 18 74 121 (personal) 38 51
54 92 96 100 Wiley 54 --- 65 73
SPIKES, William 73
SPIVEY/SPIVY Moses 8 39 Tapley 39
SPRAGENS, Thomas 2

157

SPRAGINS, Martha 121 Orsamus 87
Patcy/Patty 87 Thomas 50 William
(official) 18 (personal) 69 121
SPRING BRANCH 22 41 120
SPRINGFIELD 37
SPROTT, James 105
SPROUL, James 105
SQUIRES, Coleman 45 Eleventon 32+
STALLSWORTH, Joseph 114
STALNAKER, Samuel 36 51
ST BARTHOLOMEWS PARISH 64 65
STARK, A 122 Alexander 130 Rebecca
117 Robert 20 --- 18 75 107 road 77
STAYLEYS CREEK 80
ST STEPHENS GOOSE CREEK 10
STEDHAM, John 36
STEEL, William 28
STENT, William 26
STEPHENS, Abraham 95 Daniel 101
Epenetus 89 Expenetus 88 89 Samuel 116
STEPHENS CREEK 1-3 8+ 10-12 17 19
20 23-26 29+ 36+ 37 39 50 51+ 53 59 62
63 65+ 70-72+ 74 75 77-79 83+ 85 86+
89+ 97 99+ 100+ 102 104 107 111 112
114-117 120 121 123-126 130 131 133+
STEVENS, Ebenetus 33 Elisha 33+
STEVENS CREEK 30 34+ 37+ 40+ 41-49
53 59 66 79 92 101 105 111 113 123 130
STEVENS CR MEETING HOUSE 42
STEWART, A 75 115 Alec 119 Alexander
63 100 102 Daniel 83 Destimony 83 Dud-
ley 49 Fanny 83 James 71 Mary 83 Rebec-
cah 83 Sarah 83 Thomas 83 William 83
STIBHAM, --- 4
STILES, Jacob 114
STILL, Bartholomew 133 Benjamin 41
Cakthran 41 David 41 James 105 Jolly 95
STILL BRANCH 110+
STILL WATER BRANCH 92
STOCKLEY, --- 5
STOKES, Batt 54 E 54 Robert 32 54
Shadrack 72 Wiley/Willey 54
STONE, Charles 51 John 26 29 30 92
Jesse 104 --- 51 104
STOUKS GULLY 112
STRADER, Jeremiah 26
STRAIGHT BRANCH 37

STREETS BRANCH 2 3 9
STRINGER, Leroy 100
STROBLE, Gasper 132
STROM, William 113
STROTHER, Charlote 15 George 15 24
Solomon 12 27
STROUP, George 55 Jacob 55 --- 56
STRUM, Prosey 55 Rosey 55 Samuel 90
STUART, Alexander 115 James 79
STUBBS, Ebenezer 83
STURGES, William 65
STURZENEGGER, John (official) 5 9 22
57 69 106+ (personal) 5 51 56+
SUCK BRANCH 19
SUDDATH, Benjamin 16 Lewis 16
SULLIVAN, George 10 John 40 Mrs 46
Presley 21 --- 37
SUMERS, William (official) 44
SUMMERS, Elijah 37 James 87 Jesse 21
102 103 John 128+ Sally/Sarah 103
William 72
SUTTON, Phineas/Phinehas 46 124 Nancy
46
SWAMS HORSE[?] 38
SWEARINGEN, Federick 85+ 88
Frederick 96 117+ Henry 115 Joel 88 John
96 Moses 96 117 Thomas 79 94 110 Van
(official) 85 (personal) 79 88 William 79
SWEETWATER CREEK 78
SWIFT, Elizabeth 30 Jonathan 30 Mary 30
William 28 30 119 --- 58 creek 48
SWILLIVAN, John 17 Presley 132
Thomas 46
TALBERT, Ansel (official) 12 133 (per-
sonal) 19 125 John 22 William 48
TALLEY/TALLY, Nancey 17 Nathan 17
TANT, Thomas 23
TARANCE, John (official) 113
TARRANCE, John (official) 2 11 49 65 66
81 86 94 108
TARRANT, --- 11
TATE, Henry 30 84 122 126 Nathaniel 30
122 126
TAYLOR, Asbel 45 Chapman 111 Francis
48 114 Freeman 81 Jeremiah 118 Jesse 44
John 26 48 49 114 121 Joseph 4 49 50+
121 Josiah 47 48 81 Mary 13 15 48 121

158

Moses 23 Samuel 13 15 61 62 T 64
William 13 15 16 48 61 62 63 75 77 115
111 50
TELL, Charles 10
TENNENT, William 86
TENNESSEE 83 88 113
TERRY, Anna 32 Jincy 65 John 32 36 51
90 118 126 Stephen 47 65 101 Thomas 67
William 17 76 92
THOMAS, Arther 96 109 110 Atha 85+
Elizabeth 126 James 40 102 John 29 85+
96+ Joseph 70 75 Judy 85 Lucy 96 Mrs
115 Samuel 85 Sarah 126 Stephen
(official) 40 (personal) 40 99 W 101
William 2 29 81 119 127
THOMKINS, James (official) 78 Stephen
(official) 78
THOMPKINS, Samuel 89
THOMPSON, David 81 89 Herod 13 114
132 Wady 102
THOMSON, Joseph 107
THORN, Hightower 11 Joshua 48
THORNE, Char 20
THORNTON, Eli 21 Elizabeth 129 James
60 Joseph 83 84 Mary 83 --- 123
THREEWITS, C 22
THURMAN, John 112 Philip 112
THURMOND, John 39+ 81 83 84 85
Philip 84 Phillip 39+ Pleasant 10 William
(official) 126 133 (personal) 57 65
THURSTON, E 94 Elizabeth 14 Joshua 13
14 Martha 14
TILLERY, Richard 85
TILLMAN, Ann 77 132 Annsibell 132
Ansibell 131 David 76 93 Elizabeth 93
Frances 132 Frederick 93+ 94 131 George/
Georgi 77 131 132 Jacob 78 131 132
Lewis 93 Paschal 47 Reuben 90 Stephen
(official) 11 19 26 34 40 47 51 70 74 75
93 (personal) 18-21+ 96 101 102 108 131
132
TILMAN, Frederick 67
TIMMERMAN, Henry 69 Jacob 42
--- 41
TIRK, Thomas 4
TIPSON, --- 107
TOBLERS OLD FORD 30

TOD, Ann 56 Thomas 56
TODD, Josiah 130 Patrick (official) 122
William 65
TOLBERT, Ansel 105 Henry 73 Mary 103
TOLISON, Abraham/Abram 123
TOMKINS, Arthur 129 James (official)
105 133 (personal) 45 59+ 64 Samuel 25
45 59+ Stephen 25 --- 48
TOMLIN, Jacob 116+ James 58
TOMPKINS, Francis 92 James (official)
92 Stephen (official) 92
TOMPSON, Robert 132
TONBY, James 104
TORRENCE, --- 20
TOSSETYS/TOSSITY CREEK 58 83
TOWN CREEK 76 106+ 114
TRAVERS, Mark 46 Smallwood 46
TRAVERSE, Barratt 28
TRAVIS, Alexander 5 25 Mary 5 Polly 5
TRAYLER, John 97 George 48 John 65
117 T 48 49
TROOP, John 71 100
TROOPS, John 18
TROTER, Jeremiah 31
TROTTER, Jerry 77 N 50 Nathan 4+ 50
TROUBLESOME BRANCH 37
TUCKER, --- 73
TULLEY, Allen 119
TULLIS, Aaron 65 Moses 92 Newel 65
TURK, Thomas 4+
TURKENET, --- 1
TURKEY CR 3 9 14+ 17 20 23+ 31 32 34
36+ 38+ 40+ 43+ 46-48 50 51 53+ 54+
59+ 60 67+ 68 70 72+ 77 79 80 84 90+ 93
99+ 101 104 111-113+ 118 130 133
TURNAGE, Elisha 99+
TURNER, George 7 29 Henry 29 Richard
4 Sarah 29 William 43
TURPIN, John 64 69
TUTT, Benjamin 8 40+ 70 George 10
Lewis 10 Richard 4 8 10+ 22 33 36 42 51
54 70 95 96 102 114 118+ --- 4
UPPER SPRING BRANCH 12
USARY, John 12
UTZ, Micael 72
VA---, John 95
VANN, Isaac 29 70 74 75 J 126 James 117

VANNER, C 105 Christopher 95
VARDELL, John 116
VARNON, John 36
VAUGHAN, Anne 68
VAUGHN, James 27
VAUNER, C 50
VERDREY 1
VILLERS, --- 1
VIRGINIA (state) 12 52
WABLE, John 89
WADE, Sarah 113 tract 81
WAISTCOAT CREEK 44
WAITE, Henry 105
WALDO, Joseph 87+ 121
WALDRUM, Charles 26 70 74 75 Henry
70 75 83 Jesse 75 Mary 70 75
WALKER, Christian 129 David 10+ 21
Ezekiel 16 91 Francis 28 57+ 58 61 89
James 6 12 21 129 John 12 57+ 58 77 102
124 Joseph 3 9 16 28 57+ 77 86 Kesiah
114 Levi 82 Milley/Milly 10 Robert
(official) 7 12 31 60 78 105 130 (personal)
82 101 Samuel 35 57+ 58 67 95 Widow 16
WALL, William 79
WALLACE, George 5
WALPOLE, Agness 18 Richard 18 19 21
WALTERS, George 5
WALTON, Elizabeth 49 Moses 69 97
Thomas 69
WARD, Christopher 24 34 56 Daniel 34
Frederick 71 James 71 Jane 4 William 4
WARDLEWORTH, Samuel 6 45 --- 71
WARE, Henry 8 Nicholas 61 86
WARGUT, James 59
WARREN, Dennis 17 James 118 119+
John 12 17 Lott 77 Thomas 13 30 74 120
122
WARTERS, John 72
WASH, Augustus 108 John 53 Richard 53
William 53+ 72 133
WATERMELLON/WATERMILLION
BRANCH 50+
WATERS, Nancy 128 P 129 Phileman/
hilemon 128+ 131 Sarah 128 Wilks 128+
WATRY BRANCH 17 18+
WATLEY, Shear--- 132 Frederick 132
WATSON, Absalom 98 Amos 91 99

Arthur 57+ 72 98+ 99+ Benjamin 43
Clowey/Clowy 99 Elijah (official) 27 30 53
74 95 98 120 134 (personal) 25+ 52 91 99
125+ Elizah 126 Hezekiah 123 Huldah 95
John 53+ 124 Jonathan 89 Michael 98 99
Richmond 91 98+ 99+ Sarah/Sary 98+
Thomas 83 --- 1 47 74
WATTS, James 121 William 103
WATTSMAN POND 119
WEAKES, Easter/Easther 5 6
WEATHERFORD, Widow 39
WEATHERINGTON, Manoah 83
WEAVER, Aaron 43 Dempsey 124 Fede-
ick 83 Henry 83+ 100+ John 24 43 122
Jonathan 8 16 Martha 83 --- 18 120 122
WEAVOUR, Henry 100
WEEKS, Aaron 45 59 80 Nancey/Nancy
59
WEBB, Ann 13 Hendley/Hendly 18+
Leonard 13
WELCH, William 31
WELSH, Absalom 82 Winey 90
WEST, Jacob 91 John 90 Joseph 62 90+
91+ Thomas 62 William 90
WEST CREEK 116 118 119+
WESTS FOARD [FORD] 62
WETHERFORD, Widow 39
WHATLEY, Abner 14 52 80 Edmund 104
Eliza 14 Frederick 46+ Lewis 41 Nancey/
Nancy 41 Shearly 20 Sherley 29 46 Shur-
ley 46 William 111 Willis 77 Wilson 29 46
WHEELER, John 21 Susannah 21 --- 129
WHITE, Anthony 59+ Balentine 127
Blumer 62 Daniel 37 39 Elizabeth 62
Frederick 43+ James 41 47+ Jonathan 62
Nathan 77 103 Robert 78 Samuel 40 41
Stephen 62 Valentine 74 75 Vallentine 70
William 4 112 --- 84
WHITE LICK BRANCH 133
WHITEHEAD, James 60+ 61 88 --- 109
WHITLEY, Ann 77 Elizabeth 18 31 77
John 77 Lewis 31 77 100 Stephen 18
WHITLOCK, Winfrey 95
WHITNER, B (official) 20 25 44
(personal) 127
WHITTLE, James 12 13 Micajah 63
WIDEMAN, John 82

WIGFALL, Arthur 41 Eliza 41 James 41
Levi 41 Lewis 41
WIGGONS, James 55
WIGHTT, John 18 19 22 Jonathan 18 19
22
WILBERN, Richard 53
WILBORN, Pamela 79 Richard 79
Thomas 70
WILBURN, Champin 111
WILKINSON, James 84
WILKINSON COUNTY, GA 80
WILKINSON COUNTY, MS 33
WILL, Martin 75
WILLEY, --- 56
WILLIAMS, Abigail 97 Ann 10+ Cath-
arine 10 Charles 1 11 49 David 10+ 26 37
80 126 Davis (official) 60 74 106 (person-
al) 45 97 105 E 9 Eliza 60 Elizabeth 10+
Gabriel 10+ H (official) 89 James 60
Jefferson 35 60 Jeremiah (official) 118 119
Jesse 107 John 10+ 26 37 60 71 98 107+
120 Joseph 7 58 77 95 Marcus 60 Paul 10
37 Polenah 130 Rebecca 60 Richard
(official) 98 130 Roger 21 70 Rolan 81
Sally 10 Samuel 74 Stephen (official) 117
(personal) 48 114 Thomas 30+ 120 121
122 William 38 65 107 Willoughby 93 94
Winnyford 80 --- 5 114
WILLIAMSON, Charles 6 88 Eliza 14
Frederick 117 Mrs 13
WILLIS, Keziah 8 Robert 21 90
WILLISON, Rebecca 79 William 33
WILLS, Jones 2 83 Matthew 4
WILSON, Alexander 130 George 16 17
Henry 61 James 61 71 101 130 Jean 130
Jeremiah 4 Joab 4 Littleberry 61 Mary Ann
101 Russell (official) 116 122 Simpson 30
Thomas 61 William 16 28 --- 14 90
WIMBERLEY, John 82 89
WIMBERLY, Mrs 9 William 28
WINE CREEK 36 40+
WINFREY, Thomas 127
WINN, Benjamin 9 Thomas 20 29 54 96
WINSTANLY, Thomas 34
WINSTON, William (official) 41
WISE, Henry 108+ John 94 William 54
WISEMAN, Daniel 14

WITT, Martin 7 95 98 Michel 95
WOFFORD, Anna 56 Benjamin 56
WOLF/WOLFE, James 37 92
WOODFORD COUNTY, KY 10 37
WOODROFF, Wilson 51
WOODROOF, Mary 81
WOODS, Joseph 76
WOOLEY, Basel 107 Ezekiel 119 Minor
26 Rezin 107 Zachery 114
WOOLF, James 15
WOOLFOLK, John 18-22 Margaret 22
WOOLLEY, Basil 107
WOOTAN, John 31 61+ 69 Martha 31
Mary 31 --- 110
WOOTEN, John 6
WORTHINGTON, Elijah 87+
WRIGHT, Betsy 108 Elizabeth 9 James 6+
8 45 59
WYBERGH, Elizabeth 73
WYNN, Elizabeth 96 Green 124 Thomas
95 96+ --- 93
YARBROUGH, Gilson 97 100 133
Richard 55
YEATEN, John 55
YORK DISTRICT 31
YORKVILLE 31
YOUNG, Abram 44
YOUNGBLOOD, Abner 4 Amy 35 Henry
129 Lewis 33 Seaborn 83 Thomas 22 35 -
-- 34 70
ZACHERY, William 48
ZEIGLAR, Nicholas 98
ZINN, Jacob 2 9+ 51 88 114+ Mary 114
ZUBLY, John 55

Other books by Carol Wells:

Abstracts of Giles County, Tennessee: County Court Minutes, 1813-1816 and Circuit Court Minutes, 1810-1816

CD: Tennessee, Volume 1

Davidson County, Tennessee County Court Minutes, Volume 1, 1783-1792

Davidson County, Tennessee County Court Minutes, Volume 2, 1792-1799

Davidson County, Tennessee County Court Minutes, Volume 3, 1799-1803

Dickson County, Tennessee County and Circuit Court Minutes, 1816-1828 and Witness Docket

Edgefield County, South Carolina Probate Records, Boxes Four through Six Packages 107-218

Edgefield County, South Carolina Probate Records, Boxes One through Three Packages 1-106

Edgefield County, South Carolina: Deed Books 13, 14, 15

Edgefield County, South Carolina: Deed Books 16, 17, 18

Edgefield County, South Carolina: Deed Books 19, 20, 21, and 22

Edgefield County, South Carolina: Deed Books 23, 24, 25, and 26

Edgefield County, South Carolina: Deed Books 27, 28, and 29

Edgefield County, South Carolina: Deed Books 30 and 31

Edgefield County, South Carolina: Deed Books 32 and 33

Edgefield County, South Carolina: Deed Books 34 and 35

Edgefield County, South Carolina: Deed Books 36, 37 and 38

Edgefield County, South Carolina: Deed Books 39 and 40

Genealogical Abstracts of Edgefield, South Carolina Equity Court Records

Natchez Postscripts, 1781-1798

Rhea County, Tennessee Tax Lists, 1832-1834, and County Court Minutes Volume D: 1829-1834

Robertson County, Tennessee Court Minutes, 1796-1807

Sumner County, Tennessee Court Minutes, 1787-1805 and 1808-1810

Williamson County, Tennessee County Court Minutes, July 1812-October 1815

Williamson County, Tennessee County Court Minutes, May 1806-April 1812

www.ingramcontent.com/pod-product-compliance
Lightning Source LLC
Chambersburg PA
CBHW071441090426
42737CB00011B/1743